Contributions to Economics

The series *Contributions to Economics* provides an outlet for innovative research in all areas of economics. Books published in the series are primarily monographs and multiple author works that present new research results on a clearly defined topic, but contributed volumes and conference proceedings are also considered. All books are published in print and ebook and disseminated and promoted globally. The series and the volumes published in it are indexed by Scopus and ISI (selected volumes).

Gilmar Masiero

Brazilian Socio-Economic Dynamics

Contexts and Contemporary Realities

Springer

Gilmar Masiero
São Paulo, Brazil

ISSN 1431-1933 ISSN 2197-7178 (electronic)
Contributions to Economics
ISBN 978-3-031-87684-4 ISBN 978-3-031-87685-1 (eBook)
https://doi.org/10.1007/978-3-031-87685-1

This Springer imprint is published by the registered company Springer Nature Switzerland AG
The registered company address is: Gewerbestrasse 11, 6330 Cham, Switzerland

Foreword

Organizations influence a country's economic development and serve as the framework for economic exchange within and between nations. As students and development researchers, we have long comprehended the necessity of understanding these organizations in the context of the politics, culture, and values of the societies from which they evolved. For this reason, the book *Brazilian Socio-Economic Dynamics: Contexts and Contemporary Realities* is a much-appreciated contribution.

The book aims to enhance our understanding of several "themes" that have been instrumental in shaping South America's largest economy, emphasizing the historical and socio-economic dynamics of their emergence. Many insightful perspectives emerge when we examine Brazilian development through a multidisciplinary lens. The examples presented constitute vivid and detailed cases that assist in understanding the immense challenges confronting Brazilian society and provide insight into why the nation's struggles have yielded significant accomplishments in some areas while dramatically failing in others.

Brazil is emerging from the devastating fallout caused by the coronavirus disease 2019 (Covid-19) pandemic. Recent findings show significant regressions in Amazon Forest and environmental protections. A continuing political upheaval and crisis persist, particularly in a society marked by inequality. In light of this, it is essential now more than ever, to understand how Brazil reached this point and apply this knowledge when considering the crossroads at which the nation finds itself. Fortunately, we have this thoughtfully curated and skillfully written book to guide us.

FFCLH-USP
São Paulo, Brazil

Lorena G. Barberia

Preface

My understanding of Brazil has been honed over many decades and through countless conversations with both nationals and foreigners. Over time, I have come to appreciate that the vast size and diversity of Brazil pose a significant challenge for many. Existing theories on development, despite their value, frequently do not fully encapsulate the unique milieu of a country as large as Brazil. This recognition has driven the latter part of my academic career and culminated in the creation of six chapters on *Brazilian Socio-Economic Dynamics: Contexts, and Contemporary Realities*.

My academic life has been characterized by a profound curiosity about social and political phenomena, especially the development trajectories of East Asian countries such as Japan, South Korea, and China. This curiosity brought me to Japan, where my colleagues demonstrated an eagerness to understand South Korea's economic vitality. This interest subsequently led me to South Korea, where I discovered a similar fascination with China's economic transformations. During my numerous visits to China, I came to realize the limitations of current political economy textbooks in thoroughly understanding the complexities of large, dynamic societies.

After years of inquiry and assimilating a blend of Eastern and Western knowledge, I encourage readers to persist in their research and reflection on Brazil's socio-economic dynamism. Brazil has taken considerable strides in enhancing the well-being of its populace. While its progress might not be as swift as East Asia's, Brazil's unique attributes warrant attention for us to understand and contribute significantly to its development.

In the book, I have crafted a multidisciplinary narrative centering around themes that warrant the attention of students, scholars, and corporate executives interested in Brazil's diverse contexts (Part I) and contemporary realities (Part II). The overarching intent is to bring forth an overview of Brazil's socio-economic dynamism. Using a descriptive approach, I illuminate and align various social and economic historical features with contemporary themes, thereby making Brazil more accessible to a foreign audience.

São Paulo, Brazil
June 15, 2024

Gilmar Masiero

Competing Interests The author has no competing interests to declare that are relevant to the content of this manuscript.

Introduction

In our modern, scientifically organized world, it is challenging to find a theoretical background that can fully explain the development of large countries like Brazil. The context is dynamic, with 'reality' changing more frequently than academic theories. This is the underlying motive for us embarking on the writing of this book: *Brazilian Socio-Economic Dynamics: Contexts and Contemporary Realities*. We warmly invite you to delve into the complexities of Brazil's socio-economic dynamics.

Our work is driven by a profound understanding of the needs of non-Portuguese-speaking students and professionals interested in comprehending Brazil and its developmental challenges. This book, an interdisciplinary endeavor, is thoughtfully divided into two parts. The first part, emphasizing socio-economic dynamism, provides a foundational understanding of Brazil's unique characteristics. The second section addresses the contemporary realities, exploring current issues and developments that shape the country's present and future. We believe this structure, coupled with your active participation, will guide you through your learning journey, ensuring a comprehensive understanding of Brazil's dynamics.

The first part of our book takes you on an engaging journey through Brazil's socio-economic characteristics. We aim to illuminate the country's diversity and contrasting regions. Chapter 1 explores the Brazilian regions and the diversity of characteristics across their vast and varied areas, illustrating how Brazil's large size and population are not easily comprehended. Chapter 2 examines the Brazilian socio-economic context, emphasizing population statistics and wealth inequalities, while considering the country's peculiarities. We hope this comprehensive understanding—designed to leave you feeling well-informed and enlightened—will offer a deep insight into Brazil's socio-economic dynamics.

Chapter 3 explores Brazil's sustainable development hurdles, concentrating on Sustainable Development Goals (SDGs), poverty alleviation, and strategies for rebooting industrialization efforts. It also outlines a crucial Brazilian endeavor, the Amazon Fund, intended to conserve and sustainably develop the country's Northern region. Furthermore, it investigates the nation's efforts to hinder deforestation and foster ecological restoration in the Amazon, including the relatively uncharted Blue

Amazon, for which Brazil has sought recognition from the United Nations. These significant subjects will grant you a more profound comprehension of Brazil's dynamics and the country's dedication to sustainable development.

The second part of the book focuses on contemporary themes in Brazil. Three chapters outline the country's development challenges on a micro level. Chapter 4 introduces a selection of Brazil's historically influential entrepreneurs. It also examines institutions that provide support for research, development, and innovation (RD&I) as well as the distinct Brazilian "S System", which enhances workers' learning and leisure activities. Furthermore, this chapter illuminates the progressive banking sector, noting the market concentration typically controlled by four to six large banks.

Chapter 5 focuses on Brazil's expanding international presence, spotlighting leading Brazilian multinational corporations and foreign multinationals functioning within the nation. Chapter 6 speaks to the contemporary challenges encountered by Brazilian businesses. While not deeply exploring every issue, this chapter provides an overview of significant "big issues" that dramatically influence Brazil's vibrant political, social, and economic backdrop. With these discussions, readers will acquire a better understanding of the complexities and the ever-evolving nature of Brazil's business environment.

The fluid reality of Brazil's socio-economic landscape is depicted in this book, aiming to furnish a nuanced comprehension of a constantly evolving nation. By incorporating a thoughtful structure and detailed explorations in each chapter, our objective is to equip non-Portuguese-speaking individuals, be they students or professionals, with the tools required to comprehend and engage with Brazil's distinctive development trajectory. As readers navigate the interdisciplinary insights and contemporary analyses presented in this study, we aim to cultivate a profound appreciation and critical understanding of the elements shaping Brazil's socio-economic dynamics. Consequently, a well-rounded perspective on its present and future challenges is encouraged.

We are confident that our comprehensive approach will keep you well-informed and prepared to engage with Brazil's socio-economic dynamics. These dynamics are rapidly evolving; this manuscript was prepared amidst the Covid-19 pandemic and later revised in the first half of 2024. Standard artificial intelligence tools were employed for translations and editing. Only in the recently developed Chap. 6 are modern generative AI tools potentially employed by some students, who significantly contributed to the production of this chapter and the copyediting of the entire book. We extend our gratitude and dedicate this book to these students, along with their past and future colleagues, all interested in the Brazilian socio-economic dynamics.

Book Description

This book offers an in-depth exploration of Brazil's structural issues and provides suggestions for handling them. It is divided into two parts. The first part lays a foundation in Brazilian socio-economic dynamics, tackling regional diversity, economic disparities, educational access, and the country's agribusiness global commodity supplies. The second part addressed the contemporary realities in the business and management sector, such as entrepreneurship, small businesses, and incubators, the country's financial system, its global footprint, and its current and future challenges. The book also emphasizes the need for academic literature to support discussions on Brazilian issues. Although this book primarily presents original research for academics, it can also be used as supplementary reading in instructional contexts.

Contents

About the Author

Gilmar Masiero is a Professor in the Business Department of the School of Business, Economics, and Accounting at the University of São Paulo. His main areas of interest include strategies and decision-making processes, international trade and investment, and economic development in a globalized world. He conducted postdoctoral research at Harvard University's David Rockefeller Center for Latin American Studies and the Center for International Relations Studies at the University of Campinas, known as UNICAMP. Moreover, he was a visiting researcher at the Korean Institute for International Economic Policy (KIEP) in Seoul, the Núcleo de Pesquisas em Relações Internacionais (NUPRI) at the University of São Paulo, the Center for Iberian and Latin American Studies (CILAS) at the University of California, San Diego, and the Institute of Developing Economies (IDE) in Tokyo. Throughout his career, Professor Masiero has authored numerous academic papers, book chapters, and books. He has also actively participated in business-related associations.

Part I
Brazilian Socio-economic Dynamics

Chapter 1
Contrasting Regions and the Diversity of the Country

1.1 Introduction

As we begin this chapter, filled with elementary school-level facts and information (most of which can be sourced from https://www.ibge.gov.br/ and is liberally used throughout the chapter), it is a good point to acknowledge the immense responsibility that Brazil, one of the world's most significant nations, shoulders. Brazil is nestled between the Atlantic Ocean and ten other South American nations. Its climatic diversity nurtures various biomes, including the Amazon, the Atlantic Forest, the Cerrado, the Caatinga, the Pampa, and the Pantanal.

Over half of all living organisms find sanctuary in the Amazon Forest, a jewel that covers 49% of Brazil and encompasses the world's largest tropical rainforest. A comprehensive study by the Chico Mendes Institute for Biodiversity Conservation (ICMBio), conducted by 1300 scientists from more than 200 institutions, revealed that 1173 Brazilian fauna species are at risk of extinction. This stark reality accentuates our urgent need to collaborate on initiatives that protect Brazil's unique wildlife and vegetation.

Brazil's borders were more than just lines on a map until the sixteenth century. They served as tangible evidence of the Treaty of Tordesillas, a pivotal historical document that divided South America between Portugal and Spain. This division led to the formation of 13 significant hereditary captaincies that shaped the colonial era of Brazil. These captaincies were governed by nobility tied to the Crown. Traces of this historic land and power consolidation can still be seen in modern Brazil, where a mere 0.8% of households own 42% of the nation's rural land, averaging 6185 ha. In the latter half of the twentieth century, technologies from the Green Revolution were introduced to rural areas, stirring a transformation in Brazil's agricultural sector. These advancements brought farming methods to a new level, boosting farm productivity and food production across the country.

G. Masiero, *Brazilian Socio-Economic Dynamics*, Contributions to Economics,
https://doi.org/10.1007/978-3-031-87685-1_1

In the countryside, not everyone is adopting new technologies. There are still many places in the country where new frontiers for agricultural development are established using antiquated techniques. Forests are being burned, and cattle are raised in open spaces, particularly in the North. Despite being the most substantial region in the country, it has one of the world's lowest population densities, with five people per square kilometer. The situation is exacerbated by the fact that most people reside in certain urban regions, such as Manaus, the capital city of the Amazon State.

The city's growth relied predominantly on rubber extraction, the second most exported product in the nineteenth century following coffee. The Amazon River, boasting the largest water volume globally, bisects the region from the highlands of Peru to Pará before discharging into the Atlantic Ocean. In the 1960s, the Brazilian federal government established the Superintendency of Development for the Amazon (Sudam) and the Superintendency of the Manaus Free Zone (Suframa) to provide economic stimulus to Northern Brazil and settle this vast territory. Despite five decades of diverse initiatives, the region remains inadequately integrated into national and international markets.

A contrasting scenario is observable in Brazil's extreme south, largely attributed to the efforts of European immigrants. In the late 1800s, nearly 11 million Europeans immigrated to Latin America. A majority of these immigrants, primarily of Polish, German, Italian, and Spanish descent, settled in Brazil's south. They are credited with triggering the region's industrialization in various ways. Nevertheless, some did assimilate and incorporated local customs into their everyday lives.

For example, the traditional Gauchos living in Rio Grande do Sul do not abandon their characteristic attire, which includes *bombacha*, scarf, and shawl, nor their custom of consuming churrasco and chimarrão. Owing to the famous *Oktoberfest*, a renowned German celebration, Blumenau in Santa Catarina is referred to as the "capital of beer." In the culture of Paraná, the third state of the South region, one can find strong influences from the Poles, Ukrainians, and Dutch. Brazil's Itaipu Hydropower facility, considered the largest in the world, is situated in this state.

The consumption of Itaipu's electrical energy is concentrated in the Southeast regions. The relocation of the nation's capital from Salvador to Rio de Janeiro, coupled with the expansion of coffee production, marked the start of the Southeast region's economic vitality. Although it is the most developed and industrialized, the Southeast region's share of the GDP has been decreasing as other areas have gained more significance.

The Southeast region, where most Brazilians reside, is a kaleidoscope of racial and cultural displays, particularly during Carnival. Every nation has its customs, and almost 50 of them celebrate Carnival. Nonetheless, millions of people have flocked to Brazil for its Samba-themed parades, blocks of live music, and choreographed dancing. This region has the highest population density, has the highest level of development, and is the most industrialized area in the country.

The biomes of the Cerrado and Pantanal are situated in the Center-West, another significant region of Brazil. This region was often visited by Spanish Jesuit priests before the arrival of Portuguese colonists in pursuit of gold. Mato Grosso, Mato Grosso do Sul, and Goiás are the sole three states that make up the Center-West region, representing 19% of the country's total area. This region is notable for its large plateau zone and the Pantanal—the world's largest floodplain—home to diverse and unique flora and fauna. The Central Plateau area shelters various environmental preservation parks like Chapada dos Veadeiros National Park, simultaneously accommodating extensive agro-industrial activity. Land ownership disputes between farmers and indigenous peoples are a significant issue in this region.

One of the greatest contrasts in the world is evident in the Northeast region of Brazil, combining stunning beaches with destitute rural landscapes. This region encompasses nine states with a developed coast and an impoverished, arid populace living in the area known as the *sertão*. Substantial funds have been invested in modern irrigation and water distribution infrastructure in this region. However, a significant portion of these funds has been misappropriated, primarily by established political figures in the region.

Most rivers are minor and irregular, with no rainfall providing water to the *sertão* for 8 months of the year. The São Francisco River, however, remains notable and perennial throughout the year. The drought polygon, stretching over 1,108,000 km^2, encompasses 1348 municipalities. It is larger than the combined territory of France and Germany (547,000 km^2 + 348,000 km^2). This region is home to some of the least developed populations in the country, including those who are illiterate.

1.2 The Territory and the Fauna and Flora Diversity of Brazil

Brazil is one of the largest countries in the world, surpassed only by Russia, Canada, the USA, and China. It is located on the American continent, sharing borders with several South American countries: French Guyana, Suriname, Guyana, Venezuela, Colombia, Peru, Bolivia, Paraguay, Argentina, and Uruguay. From north to south on the east, the country borders the Atlantic Ocean. The Equator and the Tropic of Capricorn intersect its territory, resulting in its majority being typified by a tropical climate.

Brazil is divided into five regions: North, Northeast, Midwest, Southeast, and South, and has a centralized federal government composed of three branches: the judiciary, the legislature, and the executive. The 26 states, each with its capital serving as the state government headquarters, form the most extensive political-administrative hierarchy in the country. These states are further divided into numerous municipalities and districts. Given the large size of the country's territory, there is significant climatic diversity, although generally, the climate is warm.

The country boasts three climates: equatorial, tropical, and temperate. The equatorial climate covers a significant portion of the territory, predominantly the Amazon Rainforest region, where rainfall is near-daily and the heat is intense. The tropical climate also presents heat but with less consistent rainfall and variations depending on the area. The southern region of Brazil, the coldest part of the country, experiences a temperate climate where winter temperatures can plunge below zero degree Celsius.

Owing to its diverse climate, Brazil is home to an array of biomes. A biome is essentially a community of flora and fauna characterized by vegetation groups nearby. It is identifiable on a regional scale by similar geological and climate conditions. The biomes in Brazil include the Amazon, the Atlantic Forest, the Cerrado, the Caatinga, the Pampa, and the Pantanal. Historically, these biomes have been subjected to the same landscape formation processes, resulting in a wide variety of flora and fauna.

The animals inhabiting these biomes were cataloged by ICB Bio. The Amazon Forest is deemed the most significant biological reserve on the planet, reputed for its remarkable diversity. It is home to at least half of all living species: 311 mammals, 163 amphibians, 550 reptiles, 1000 birds, and 3000 fish (ICB Bio, 2014). The Amazon biome encompasses approximately 49% of Brazilian territory. This region boasts the world's largest tropical rainforest, equivalent to 1/3 of global humid tropical forest reserves, and it is teeming with a plethora of flora and fauna species. Also, it accommodates 20% of the world's water resources and vast mineral reserves.

The Atlantic Forest, home to water resources that supply 70% of Brazil's population, occupies approximately 13% of the country's territory. Situated in the coastal region, it is where over 50% of Brazilians reside. However, it is also the most endangered biome; only 27% of its original forest remains preserved. As of 2014, data from ICB Bio reveals that it contains 18,713 species of flora, while its fauna comprises 270 mammal species, 456 amphibians, 311 reptiles, 934 birds, and 350 fish.

Boasting the richest and largest biodiversity globally, the Cerrado is the Brazilian Savannah, home to 252 mammals, 113 amphibians, 187 reptiles, 850 birds, 1000 unique fish species, and a flora assortment of 12,683 species (ICB Bio, 2014). This biome is situated in the Central Plateau and makes up approximately 24% of Brazil's territory. Until the 1950s, the Cerrado landscape remained almost unchanged. However, since the 1960s—when the Federal Capital was shifted from Rio de Janeiro to Brasília and a new road network was introduced to this region—the natural vegetation has gradually been displaced by cattle raising and agriculture.

The Caatinga biome occupies ten percent of Brazil's territory. Even though it is situated in a semiarid climate area, it boasts a rich variety of landscapes, notable biological diversity, and species unique to this biome, hosting 148 types of mammals, 49 amphibians, 107 reptiles, 510 birds, and 240 fish and a flora comprising 5311 different species (ICB Bio, 2014). The vegetation within this biome is often altered by the substitution of native plant species for pasture and agricultural purposes. Deforestation and burning are standard practices in preparing the land for agriculture and cattle raising in this and other biomes. Beyond the obvious destruction it causes to vegetation, this practice contrarily affects the preservation of wildlife, water quality, and the balance of climate and soil.

The Pampa biome covers less than 2% of the national territory. It is known for its rainy climate, lacking a dry season, but experiences negative temperatures in the winter. This climate significantly influences the diverse fauna and flora species, including 74 mammals, 50 amphibians, 97 reptiles, 120 birds, 18 fish, and 1623 different species of flora (ICB Bio, 2014). Human activity has resulted in a uniform vegetation landscape, typically used as natural pastureland, or appropriated for agricultural activities, chiefly rice cultivation, in the Pampa region.

The Pantanal, the smallest biome, occupies less than 2% of the national territory. However, it is the most extensive continuous floodplain on the planet and its formation and differentiation from other biomes is primarily due to this factor. Almost all of Brazil's fauna call the Pantanal home, with 132 different mammal species, 35 amphibian species, 85 reptile species, 463 bird species, 263 fish species, and 1197 species of flora (ICB Bio, 2014). Despite being subject to economically significant activities such as cattle raising and tourism, the Pantanal biome remains the most well-preserved.

The Brazilian relief primarily consists of plateaus, plains, and depressions. The plateaus are relatively flat, with older terrains situated at higher altitudes. Noteworthy plateaus include the Brazilian Central, the Southern Minas Gerais, the Eastern Amazon, and the Parnaíba and Paraná Basin plateaus. The plains are primarily flat areas, formed from the deposition of sediments originating from higher regions. The depressions, on the other hand, form part of the existing relief at lower altitudes. A case in point is the Amazon depression.

Brazil holds the largest freshwater reserve on the planet. However, water distribution across Brazilian territory is uneven; 80% of its surface water is found in the Amazon Hydrographic Region. The Brazilian water system is segmented into 12 hydrographic regions, each encompassing one or more hydrographic basins. A watershed, marked by water dividers commonly formed by mountains and plateaus, represents a geographical unit. If it does not infiltrate the soil, rainfall within the watershed area runs off the surface towards the main river.

In Brazilian territory, there is an enormous variety of plants. According to ICMBio (2014), there are over 46,000 known species of plants, which are itemized as follows: approximately 4754 algae, 33,108 angiosperms, 1568 bryophytes, 5719 fungi, 30 gymnosperms, and 1346 ferns and lycophytes. However, more than 2300 plant species are threatened with extinction. As per the Institute's data, the country possesses the most extensive biodiversity in the world, including more than 120,000 species of invertebrates and approximately 8930 vertebrate species.

To Further Research and Reflect

- Describe some features of the size of the territory, climate, and administrative structure of your country and contrast them with those of Brazil.
- As a world environmentalist militant, what would you do to reduce the risk of fauna extinction in your country and Brazil? Consider the pros and cons of protecting the fauna and the flora.

1.3 Five Large and Contrasting Regions of Brazil

Brazil boasts the fifth-largest territory globally. The Brazilian population is largely concentrated in its biggest cities, largely situated in the coastal region. Due to Brazil's settlement pattern, the earliest urban centers emerged on the coast. Before the sixteenth century, Brazil's borders were formed based on the boundaries outlined in the Treaty of Tordesillas. Signed in 1494 by Portugal and Spain, the treaty divided South America between the two colonial powers of the era.

The historical heritage often explains Brazil's remarkable land concentration. Although there is substantial debate about land concentration, a topic of historic significance in Brazilian policy discussions, there has been little progress. The Brazilian countryside, influenced by export-oriented monocultures and historical factors, is heavily concentrated in the hands of a few landowners. Albuquerque et al. (2013) delineate the Brazilian landholding structure in Table 1.1, which indicates that 42.5% of the area is concentrated in 0.8% of properties, each averaging about 6185 ha.

In 1970, the Instituto Brasileiro de Geografia e Estatística (IBGE), divided Brazil into five regions. These regions, named North, Northeast, Center-West, Southeast, and South, were determined based on natural, social, cultural, and economic criteria. In 1988, an administrative division occurred in Goiás, resulting in the creation of the State of Tocantins in the North region. Da Silva (2019) points out that despite significant social progress, Brazil's quest for modernization has led to the destruction of its biomes, conflicts over land concentration, insufficient urban rights for the poorest, and low household income for millions of Brazilians.

Brazil encompasses five regions, each containing a total of 26 states and 1 Federal District. The largest regions in terms of total land area, the North and Northeast regions, account for several states. The North region, which spans seven states (Amazonas, Pará, Tocantins, Amapá, Roraima, Acre, and Rondônia), corresponds to around 45% of the Brazilian territory. With an area of approximately 3,850,000 km^2, this region is larger than Argentina and Chile combined. Meanwhile,

Table 1.1 Brazilian landholding structure in 2009

	Properties		Total area		
Total area (ha)	N° properties	%	Hectares	%	Area average (ha)
10	1,744,540	33.7	8,215,337	1.4	4.7
From 10 to 25	1,316,237	25.4	21,345,232	3.7	16.2
From 25 to 50	814,138	15.7	28,563,707	5.0	35.1
From 50 to 100	578,783	11.2	4,096,597	7.0	69.3
From 100 to 500	563,346	10.9	116,156,530	20.3	206.2
From 500 to 1000	85,305	1.5	59,299,370	10.4	695.1
From 1000 to 2000	40,046	0.8	55,269,002	9.7	1380
More than 2000	39,250	0.8	242,795,145	42.5	6185
Total	5,181,645	100.0	571,740,920	100.0	110

Source: Albuquerque et al. (2013)

the Northeast region spans nine states (Maranhão, Piauí, Ceará, Rio Grande do Norte, Paraíba, Pernambuco, Alagoas, Sergipe, and Bahia), occupying close to 18% of the territory, or 1,544,000 km^2.

The Center-West region comprises three states: Mato Grosso, Mato Grosso do Sul, and Goiás, which collectively account for about 19% of the country's territory, including a small area allocated to the Federal District. This district is home to Brasília, which serves as both its capital and the capital of the country. The Southeast region, on the other hand, consists of four states: Minas Gerais, Rio de Janeiro, Espírito Santo, and São Paulo, and represents roughly one-tenth of the national territory. The South region encompasses three states: Paraná, Santa Catarina, and Rio Grande do Sul. In relation to the population, economy, and natural resources, Fig. 1.1 illustrates the distinct characteristics of each region.

Since 1964, Brazil has been conducting a census of rural properties and a census of the nation's population. The rural property census collects data on location, soil fertility, climate, and the types of crops cultivated. Small farms account for about 70% of all food consumed in the country and primarily rely on family labor. Meanwhile, rural enterprises and large properties produce raw materials—including oranges, soy, sugarcane, milk, and meat—which are destined for industrial food processing for both human and animal consumption.

To a greater or lesser extent, all these rural properties were significantly affected by the so-called Green Revolution, one of the most profound transformations the world underwent after World War II. This innovation, responsible for enhancing agricultural productivity and boosting food production from the 1960s to the 1970s, was characterized primarily by technological breakthroughs that penetrated the primary sector of the economy (agriculture and livestock), bolstering its production. These advancements were enhanced by thorough technical knowledge, with scientists dedicated to fortifying agricultural production in Brazil and worldwide.

To Further Research and Reflect

- Contrast the land distribution of Brazil with the one in your country and discuss the advantages and disadvantages of organizing the primary sector's economic activity based on small and large properties.
- How would you manage fire to clear lands for cattle rearing and various agro-industrial activities across large areas, like the Brazilian Pantanal and the Amazon?

1.4 The Largest and Little-Known Area of the World: The North of Brazil

Despite being the largest region in the country, with a demographic density of five inhabitants per square kilometer, it is among the least inhabited areas worldwide. The capitals of the states in the North house the majority of its 18 million residents. In the seventeenth century, the colonial government established a military fort at the Amazon River's mouth to ensure the region's occupation, leading to the creation of the city of Belém.

North Region	
	• Population: The region has 18.2 million inhabitants, and the demographic density is 4.72 inhabitants per km^2. • Economy: The region is based on primary activities such as mineral and vegetal extraction, agriculture, and cattle raising. • Natural aspects: This region has the world's largest tropical forest, the Amazon Forest, and the world's largest hydrographic basin, the Amazon River. It has a predominantly humid equatorial climate, with a well-defined rainfall regime and high air humidity.
Northeast Region	
	• Population: Northeast Brazil has almost 60 million inhabitants, the second-most populous region in Brazil. The demographic density is approximately 32 inhabitants per km^2. • Economy: Tourism is one of the most prevalent activities in the northeastern economy. The region also develops extractive and agricultural undertakings. • Natural aspects: It includes the Caatinga biomes, Atlantic Forest, and transition zones with the Cerrado. The prevailing climate is semiarid, but some areas have humid, equatorial, and tropical weather. A significant part of this region suffers from a lack of rainfall, and extreme drought is one of the obstacles to its development.
Center-west Region	
	• Population: The region is home to a little over 16 million people, and the demographic density is approximately ten inhabitants per km^2. • Economy: The economy is based on agriculture and cattle raising. There is also an intense mineral extraction practice and the largest niobium reserve in the world. Tourism is also representative because nature lovers seek many places, such as Chapada dos Veadeiros, Chapada dos Guimarães, and the Pantanal. • Natural aspects: The region includes the Central Plateau and aquifers like the Guarani. Its prevailing climate is tropical, with two well-defined seasons: dry winter and rainy summer. The Cerrado and Pantanal biomes predominate in the area.

Fig. 1.1 Features of Brazilian regions. Source: IBGE (2024).

The intense extraction of rubber in the nineteenth century was integral to the establishment of the city of Manaus. Driven by the demand for this resource during the Second Industrial Revolution and the process of vulcanization, this raw material

Southeast Region	
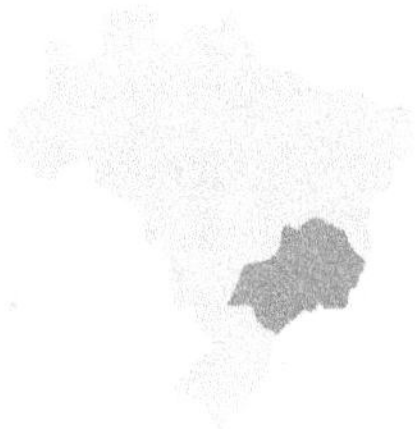	• Population: Southeastern Brazil has around 90 million inhabitants. It has the highest demographic density in the country, with approximately 92 inhabitants per km^2. • Economy: It has the largest share of GDP, corresponding to more than 50% of national GDP. The economy is based on the industrial, financial, and commercial sectors, emphasizing the automobile, steel, and oil industries. Tourism is also an important income source. • Natural aspects: This region consists primarily of plateaus. Its climate is tropical, and it covers the Atlantic Forest biome. There are also strips of Cerrado and Caatinga.
South Region	
	• Population: Southern Brazil has 29 million inhabitants. The demographic density is 47 inhabitants per km^2, and it has the best social indicators. • Economy: It is based on vegetal extraction, carried out in the Araucaria Forest region, and on agriculture, with swine breeding and grape production. This region has the second-largest national GDP. • Natural aspects: Due to its location below the tropical zone, the region presents well-defined seasons. Winters have low temperatures, with the occurrence of frosts. Rain is distributed evenly throughout the year.

Source: IBGE (2024).

Fig. 1.1 (continued)

became pivotal to the Brazilian economy. In the early twentieth century, it was the country's second most exported product, trailing only coffee.

The extraction of latex was a key factor that instigated the settlement in the North of Brazil. Rubber wealth was amassed by a small group of oligarchs based in Manaus, the capital city of the State of Amazonas. Nonetheless, the process of extracting latex from rubber trees attracted a high number of workers, predominantly from the Northeast, who migrated to the Amazon in pursuit of higher wages. Vast portions of Northern Brazil were populated by these migrants, hoping for rapid wealth through the extractive activities of minerals and the exploitation of the Amazon Forest's fauna and flora. This phenomenon, albeit with less intensity, remains prevalent today.

The North of the country is the only region in Brazil traversed by the Equator. Much of this region has an equatorial climate, with some exceptions in areas of Tocantins, Pará, and Roraima. Hot and rainy, this climate is distinguished by two clearly defined phases: a dry winter and a wet summer. The average temperature remains consistent, between 25 and 27 °C. Three factors contribute to this region being the rainiest in the country: the proximity to the Equator, the vast and dense Amazon jungle, and the numerous extensive rivers. Due to the high temperatures and lush forest, evaporation intensifies, forming clouds during the day that precipitate into rain by late afternoon.

Much of the northern region possesses low altitudes in terms of relief, except for the border regions with Guyana and Venezuela. In these regions, plateaus can reach heights of up to 3000 m, as seen with Pico da Neblina, the country's highest point, located on the border with Venezuela. There are also depressions and lower surfaces within the neighboring areas, including the North-Amazon and South-Amazon depressions. These depressions do not exceed altitudes of 300 m. Generally flat, the Amazon River represents a significant volume of water both within the region and globally. This river originates from the Peruvian mountains, flowing towards Pará before reaching the Atlantic Ocean.

When the Negro River meets the Solimões River to form the Amazon, it creates a magnificent landscape due to the contrast of the waters. The Amazon River has tributaries with extensions of more than 1000 km, such as the Madeira, Juruá, Tapajós, and the Jari rivers. The region also features a basin formed by the Tocantins and Araguaia rivers, which cross the states of Tocantins and Pará, flowing into the Atlantic Ocean. During the Amazon River's flooding season and the high tide of the Atlantic Ocean, a well-known phenomenon called "pororoca" occurs. This phenomenon, resulting from the encounter of these waters, attracts tourists worldwide as it is unique to this region and globally.

The vast Amazon Forest underscores the diversity of the North region's vegetation. The region's intense rainfall supports notable biodiversity, with dense, perpetually green foliage. As the largest forest in the world, it houses the most substantial terrestrial biodiversity globally. The forest is filled with species that have adapted to the humid climate and large trees nearby. Furthermore, it is abundant in raw materials such as wood, piassava, and medicinal plants.

Unfortunately, jungle deforestation is one of the most significant global issues, generating great concern among both Brazilians and foreigners. If not managed properly, minor alterations in the Amazon biome can lead to the desertification of the area. The population of the northern region did not grow significantly until the 1970s when ores were discovered, mines were established, and deforestation was accelerated by farmers engaged in agricultural activities and cattle raising. These factors triggered a mass migration to the region, resulting in Brazil's second-highest population growth rate. This rate is only surpassed by migration to the Center-West region, which has attracted a large number of migrants seeking opportunities in the dynamic agribusiness sector.

The North region has approximately 20 million residents. At the start of the current century, the Amazonas state, the largest in the area, held the nation's lowest population density at 2.23 inhabitants per km^2. In the 1960s, some governmental organizations, such as the Superintendency of Development for the Amazon (Sudam) and the Superintendency of the Manaus Free Zone (Suframa), were established for economic stimuli in Northern Brazil. The latter corresponds to a significant industrial hub, conceived in 1967 and situated in Manaus. It houses many large multinational companies, contributing to significant industrial growth and job creation. The production in this zone primarily aims to supply the Brazilian domestic market.

According to Suframa (2021), an autarchy associated with the Ministry of Economy that has been in existence for five decades, more than 600 industries operate in the area, generating over 500,000 direct and indirect jobs. The most prominent industrial production sectors include electronics (cellphones, televisions), two-wheeler vehicles (motorcycles), and chemicals (production of raw materials for soft drinks). Alongside this industrial development, economic activities such as agriculture, cattle raising, and vegetable and mineral extraction coexist in this region.

Black pepper production commenced with the Japanese in agriculture during the last century. The cultivation of jute, a type of tree planted alongside rivers, from which plant fiber is extracted to produce carpets and ropes, became a significant industry. Particularly in the North region, the production of threads is greatest, with jute and mallow being pivotal plants in this process. Cattle breeding has also expanded extensively, emphasizing raising cattle and buffalo. Buffalo farming particularly thrives in the flooded regions of Pará.

Vegetable and mineral harvesting represent essential sources of income for the local population. The harvesting of wood is intensive in the states of Pará and Amazonas. Many local trees in the North region produce palm hearts, açaí, and other vegetables. While rubber extraction remains a part of the area's extractive activities, it is comparatively less important than agriculture and cattle raising. The Amazon rainforest's biodiversity attracts the pharmaceutical industry, which is on the hunt for medicinal plants and natural products for the beauty industry.

Mineral exploration, initiated in 1950 as a federal government strategy for settling the region, continues to be a crucial economic activity. The North region is rich in various minerals, with substantial productions of manganese in Amapá, cassiterite in Rondônia, iron, bauxite, and nickel in Pará, and gold, which is prevalent in several states, including the Amazon and Pará, particularly in Serra dos Carajás and Serra Pelada. Many operations of Vale, the world's largest mineral company, are situated in these regions.

To Further Research and Reflect

- Given the extensive territory of the North of Brazil and the need to develop the country's largest area, design some ideas to raise awareness on why efforts should be made to protect and preserve the largest tropical rainforest.
- The Amazon rainforest covers a vast part of Brazil. Can you think of arguments favoring having an international body responsible for preserving the forest and developing the region considering supranational interests?

1.5 Europeans Outside Europe?: The South Region

The southern region of Brazil has a strong European influence, evident in its colonization and settlement processes, which is one of its defining characteristics. Its architecture, cuisine, population, and climate show European features. It is the only region in Brazil that lies entirely below the Tropic of Capricorn. During the nineteenth and twentieth centuries, numerous Europeans settled in the area, giving the regional colonization processes a distinctive character compared to other regions in Brazil. The climate, which was more akin to that of Europe, was another significant factor that attracted Europeans to the Southern region.

Non-Portuguese European immigrants came to Brazil to replace slave labor. Many started working as wage earners, usually for entrepreneurs who were either immigrants themselves or already established in the country. The South occupies a comparatively modest part of Brazil's territory, bordered by the Atlantic Ocean, Uruguay, Argentina, and Paraguay. Three states belong to this region: Rio Grande do Sul, Santa Catarina, and Paraná.

According to Schwartz and Starling (2019), approximately 22% of the 50 million European immigrants—around 11 million—who departed Europe in the late nineteenth century, arrived in Latin America. This significant portion of migrants of Italian, German, Spanish, and Polish descent primarily settled in the southern regions of Brazil. European peasants, impoverished and seeking a better life, abandoned their home continent for the "new world"—a land of unexplored opportunities in the southern states of Brazil.

Data from IBGE indicates that the region extends over approximately 564,000 km^2, which represents 7% of Brazil's territory. With an estimated population of 30 million people, the demographic density is 54 inhabitants per km^2. The region's Human Development Index (HDI) is among the highest in the country at 0.756, roughly equivalent to the central-western area but lower than the Southeast. This region contributes to 16% of the national gross domestic product. The closer the HDI index is to one, the better, as exemplified by Switzerland, which had the world's highest HDI at 0.967 in 2022.

More than 85% of the population in southern Brazil resides in urban areas, primarily in the metropolitan regions of the state capitals. This is due to the concentration of essential services and job opportunities in these areas. The birth rate has experienced a significant decline in recent years. For instance, in Paraná, the student population in elementary schools was over 1.6 million in 2009, but by 2019, this number had reduced to 1.4 million, indicating a drop in the school-age demographic. The region boasts the best infant mortality, education, and health indicators.

Different colonization processes have resulted in heterogeneous social and economic development throughout Brazil's history and geographic territories. Given its distance from the Empire's capital—Salvador—the South of Brazil did not pique the Portuguese crown's interest during the early colonial period. In the sixteenth century, a series of occupations began in the present-day state of Santa Catarina, with the village of São Francisco do Sul being particularly noteworthy. At the end of that century, in 1693, the capital of Paraná, Curitiba, was established.

Initially, the whole region was inhabited by the indigenous population. The Jesuits were the first foreigners to settle in the southernmost areas, promoting cattle breeding and establishing the "Seven Peoples of the Missions"—predominantly indigenous settlements set up by Spanish Jesuits in the region of present-day Rio Grande do Sul. This region has consistently been a subject of territorial dispute between Portugal and Spain.

During the nineteenth century, amid the Brazilian Empire period, immigration was encouraged as a means to replace a labor force primarily composed of enslaved people from various African locales. The majority of these immigrants hailed from European regions and, despite their diverse economic, cultural, and political origins, largely committed themselves to agriculture and animal husbandry for survival. German migrants began to arrive in Brazil during the 1820s—the years of Brazilian independence. Although these communities were scattered across three states in the region, they predominantly settled in Santa Catarina. Today, Blumenau, founded in 1850 (preceded by the founding of the capital, Florianópolis, in 1673), is recognized as one of the cities most similar to its German counterparts outside of Germany itself. The city has earned the moniker "capital of beer" due to its famous Oktoberfest celebrations, where Brazilian residents honor German cultural traditions.

Italian immigrants arrived in the region in the 1870s and continued to settle for several subsequent decades. They established communities in the present-day cities of Caxias do Sul, Bento Gonçalves, and other areas in the mountainous region of Rio Grande do Sul, the capital of which, Porto Alegre, was founded in 1772. In various locations, settlements of German immigrants emerged, giving rise to cities such as Gramado and Canela. These cities contrast significantly in linguistic, culinary, and architectural aspects with their relatively nearby neighbors, which were predominantly occupied by Italians. During the same period, many immigrants described as "Polish" (which included Poles, Germans, Austrians, and Russians, as country designations were not as distinct as they are today) settled in the region. They are primarily established in the northern parts of Santa Catarina and Paraná. The extensive intermingling of immigrants from Europe transformed the area into a diverse cultural mosaic, featuring varied habits, customs, and culinary traditions.

Natural beauty is the main attraction for tourists in the South. The coast, rich in beaches, offers a milder climate than other parts of the country. The Itaipu Plant, the largest hydroelectric power plant in the Americas, is situated near the Iguazu Falls on the Paraná River. This plant was constructed in partnership with neighboring Paraguay, a country where Brazil experienced its most notable war conflict in imperial times. Housing more than 270 waterfalls, the Iguazu Falls serve as one of the region's major tourist attractions.

Until the end of the Colonial Period, a vast Araucaria forest spread across the southern region, but it was devastated by road construction and the lumber industry. Remnants of this forest are still visible in the higher parts of the plateaus in Paraná and Santa Catarina. The tropical rainforest, known as the Mata Atlântica, is found all along the Brazilian coast, including a large area known as the Serra do Mar bordering the coastline. However, it is at risk of extinction due to the expansion of agriculture. Additionally, large fields called the Campanha Gaúcha or Pampa—grasslands akin to prairies—also sprawl across the region.

The Rio Grande do Sul is the most industrialized state in the region. However, its traditional inhabitants—the *gauchos*—still don traditional clothing, including the *bombacha*, scarf, and shawl, and maintain the habit of drinking mate tea and eating barbeque. Most gaucho dances are of Portuguese origin, with Spanish dances, such as the Tirana, also being prevalent. The Portuguese-originated feast, Nossa Senhora dos Navegantes, is held in Porto Alegre on the Guaíba River, where hundreds of boats and thousands of devout followers participate in the river procession. Some cities in the South celebrate their ancestors' traditions through typical festivals, such as the Festa da Uva (Grape Festival) in Caxias do Sul, a significant region for grape and wine production in Brazil.

This prosperous state is also a significant agro-industrial and livestock producer. Its neighboring state, Santa Catarina, bases its economy on agriculture, civil construction, fishing, cattle breeding, and tourism. The main products produced by the state include rice, corn, soybeans, and wheat. The technology sector has a notable presence in the capital, Florianópolis, while in the countryside, crops such as oats, bananas, onions, barley, beans, tobacco, apples, soybeans, and grapes are produced. Santa Catarina is the country's largest pork producer and exports mainly to Europe, specifically Russia.

The southern region ranks second among Brazil's largest industrial parks, contributing approximately 20% of the country's total commercial volume. Most of these industries, particularly textile and food production, are distributed throughout the region. Wine, a tradition started by Italian immigrants, accounts for 85% of the country's total production. Intensive livestock farming, especially pig and poultry, also plays a significant role in the economy.

Brazil experienced numerous separatist movements from Portugal during its colonial period. However, there have been initiatives aimed at separating states or regions from the Federative Republic. The movements currently ongoing include the Independence of the Northeast Region, the proposed state of the Republic of the Peoples of the Amazon, the Republic of Pernambuco, the Republic of São Paulo, and the Republic of Espírito Santo, and the Independence of the South Region of Brazil, advocated by the "O Sul É o Meu País"—The South is my Country movement. So far, none of these movements have gained significant momentum.

To Further Research and Reflect

- Describe the historical presence of immigrants in your country. Which groups contributed more to its development?
- Find at least one cultural characteristic from the South of Brazil and contrast it with a similar one from your country.

1.6 The Southeast Region: A Developed Country?

The country's most affluent region, the Southeast, includes the states of São Paulo, Minas Gerais, Rio de Janeiro, and Espírito Santo. Large urban conglomerations are concentrated in these states' capitals, namely, São Paulo, Belo Horizonte, Rio de Janeiro, and Vitória, as well as their neighboring municipalities. These metropolitan regions represent home to 90% of the region's population, leaving only 10% in rural areas. Over the past century, the region has attracted migrants from rural areas, mostly from other Brazilian states, who have settled here in search of improved living conditions.

The rapid occupation of the Brazilian Southeast was largely driven by the discovery of gold and other precious stones, including diamonds, in the region in the late seventeenth century. Initially, these minerals were found in Minas Gerais, leading to the establishment of several settlements that eventually evolved into cities. For instance, Mariana, founded in 1696, was the first city and capital of Minas Gerais. Nearby cities such as Ouro Preto, Tiradentes, and Diamantina were primarily settled due to extensive mining and export activities. All these cities feature Baroque architecture and numerous churches, demonstrating the influence and power of the Catholic religion during the colonial period.

Interest in precious stones attracted numerous migrants in the eighteenth century, stimulating the slave trade, predominantly from Africa. This was because enslaving the local indigenous people was no longer profitable. Coupled with the decline in sugar production in the Northeast, these factors prompted the Portuguese government in 1763 to shift the capital from Salvador to Rio de Janeiro. Hence, the hub of the colonial economy became the Southeast region. After exploiting "white gold," another form of "black gold"—coffee—began to be harvested intensively during the nineteenth century. Initially, this crop was introduced in Rio de Janeiro, but production eventually expanded to other southeastern states, particularly São Paulo, where the soil yielded better returns.

Although São Paulo was established in 1554, the region experienced little economic dynamism until the early nineteenth century. According to Schwarcz and Starling (2019) one of its co-founders, the Spanish Jesuit priest José de Anchieta, authored *The Grammar of the Tupi-Guarani Language*, a book deemed mandatory reading for almost every literate citizen in the colony. By the turn of the sixteenth century, a push towards the territory's interior had commenced, spurred by the search for gold and enslavable Indians. This movement, which originated in São Paulo and reached the Minas Gerais region in the latter part of the seventeenth century, was led by a group known as the Bandeirantes. These explorers were driven by the prospect of profit derived from hunting the indigenous population and mining gold and other precious minerals.

The solid internal and external opposition to slavery, coupled with the exhaustion of mineral exploitation in Minas Gerais, led to the abolition of slavery in Brazil in 1888. The monarchy transitioned to a republican system in 1889. Since then, there has been increased emphasis on coffee production and salaried labor. A significant proportion of this labor force consisted of European immigrants. The accumulation of capital from coffee production and export sales prompted the emergence of industrial activities in the country, particularly in São Paulo. The Southeast region remained the driving force of economic development throughout the twentieth century and continues to be so today.

The climate in the Southeast is consistent with the tropics, with high temperatures prevalent in most states. The altitude significantly influences differences in rainfall distribution and climate. Coastal cities, which receive more moisture from the ocean, generally have higher rainfall rates compared to areas at higher altitudes.

Cities situated at higher altitudes, like Campos do Jordão in São Paulo state (over 1600 m above sea level), exhibit lower temperatures. Moving further north, the climate becomes semiarid, characterized by high temperatures and sporadic, scarce rainfall.

Serra do Mar, Mantiqueira, and Canastra are found in the Southeast region. These encompass plateaus and a vital hydrographic basin—Paraná and São Francisco. The Paraná Basin is situated in the states of Minas Gerais and São Paulo, hosting significant rivers that contribute to water supply and electricity generation, notably via the Furnas power plant in Minas Gerais. The São Francisco river basin, flowing in a south-north direction, originates in the Serra da Canastra and is critical for the water supply to the metropolitan region of Minas Gerais' capital.

Four types of vegetation are predominant: the Caatinga, the Cerrado, tropical forest (Mata Atlântica), and coastal vegetation (Manguezais). The Caatinga is dominant north of Minas Gerais due to the semiarid climate. Its landscape is similar to that of the Northeast region, especially in the Jequitinhonha Valley. The Cerrado, with typical vegetation for tropical climates, is present in São Paulo and Minas Gerais. Its foliage is characterized by small to medium twisted branches with deep roots that search for water underground during the dry season. The Atlantic Forest, which boasts extraordinary biodiversity, can be found across all four states. However, it has been heavily deforested for commercial and urban purposes.

Industrialization and urbanization have significantly contributed to deforestation in the region. Large areas have been occupied for the construction of cities, railroads, and industrial parks. Today, the territory boasts substantial industrial parks, predominantly in São Paulo and its encompassing metropolitan region (ABC Paulista: the industrial cities of Santo André, São Bernardo do Campo, and São Caetano), and the oil industry in Rio de Janeiro. The economic strength of the Southeast is historically enrooted, beginning with gold extraction and then transitioning to prosperous growth during the coffee cultivation era. More recently, the region continues to be a hub where numerous national industries and companies from other countries consolidated in the mid-twentieth century.

The region's minerals and energy resources catalyzed the expansion of industries, given their essential and fundamental role in industrialization. At the close of the 1940s and 1950s, Brazil's industrial base emerged in the Southeast region, with large, publicly owned enterprises such as Companhia Siderúrgica Nacional (CSN), Vale do Rio Doce, and Petrobras leading the pack. This implementation of foundational industries fostered growth across various industrial segments.

The Metropolitan Southeast, comprising the São Paulo-Rio de Janeiro axis, serves as the country's primary economic hub. Its comprehensive, diversified industrial park encompasses nearly every sector of industry. The Belo Horizonte region also features an extensive industrial pole, bolstered by crucial mineral reserves found in the Iron Quadrangle. The country's largest oil reserves, including most of what is known as the "pre-salt layer," are situated in the Southeast and constitute another significant growth vector in the economy.

In recent years, the Southeast's participation in the Brazilian economy, particularly in agriculture and industry, has decreased due to frequent national and international crises and an emerging decentralization of industrial activity to other regions. The secondary sector has experienced a process known as industrial deconcentration, characterized by the migration of production units to varied areas of the country. Conversely, commerce, finance, and services in general, have grown in economic significance. The region is home to the leading research centers and universities, notably the largest one, the University of São Paulo (USP).

Economic development in the Southeast has given rise to new problems and challenges that remain unresolved. Slums and environmental issues are the byproducts of unplanned urbanization; these include the destruction of riparian forests, soil erosion, as well as water, air, and visual pollution. These challenges are far from resolution. Rural areas in the Southeast have experienced drastic changes due to rapid urbanization, which has impacted agricultural ecosystems and native forests. The volatility of labor relations has also extended into these rural areas, particularly affecting temporary workers, also known as "floaters" (*boias-frias*).

The region is also renowned for its cultural manifestations, housing one of the world's most famous festivals in Rio de Janeiro and São Paulo: the Carnival. Celebrations in these two cities attract massive crowds and feature the spectacular parades of samba schools, drawing attendees from across the country and beyond. The Southeast's cuisine is diverse, heavily influenced by the indigenous people, enslaved populations, and the influx of various European and Asian immigrant cultures. Notable dishes include moqueca capixaba from Espírito Santo; pão de queijo, feijão tropeiro, and pork served with cabbage, okra, corn, or cassava, popular in Minas Gerais; feijoada, fried aipim, bolinho de bacalhau, and picadinho in Rio de Janeiro; and virado à paulista, cuscuz paulista, farofa, and pizza in São Paulo.

To Further Research and Reflect

- In the past, the development of the Southeast region was primarily supported by coffee production. Nowadays, this region has become the industrial engine of the country. How can Brazil implement strategies to industrialize other areas of the country in the same way it has achieved in the Southeast region?
- Carnival is the largest festival in the world. Explore its origins and main features, and contrast this celebratory event with other significant parties worldwide.

1.7 A New Agribusiness Frontier: The Center-West

The Center-West region, an exclusive agribusiness frontier, exhibits an intriguing blend of vast territory and sparse population density. It encompasses three states: Goiás, Mato Grosso, Mato Grosso do Sul, and the Federal District. Spanning 1.6 million km^2, which amounts to 19% of the national territory, the region is sparsely populated. Home to 16.3 million residents, it flaunts one of the lowest demographic densities in the country, at just 12 inhabitants per km^2. The majority of the population dwells in the state capitals, namely, Goiânia, Cuiabá, Campo Grande, and the most populous, Brasília. This unique amalgamation of expansive land and low population density lays the groundwork for a prosperous agribusiness sector, presenting copious opportunities for growth and expansion.

Understanding the historical context is crucial to grasping the potential of the Center-West region. Due to the Treaty of Tordesillas, which split the South American territory in half from north to south, only Spanish Jesuits traversed this central region of Brazil as part of their missionary activities for two centuries. Later, in the seventeenth century, the Bandeirantes sought gold in the area but did not settle. It was only at the dawn of the eighteenth century that some settlements were established, and cattle breeding became an economic activity. The construction of the Estrada de Ferro Noroeste do Brasil (Bauru-Corumbá Railroad) in 1905 was a game-changer for the region's integration, which truly began in the twentieth century, particularly in the 1960s, with the relocation of the national capital from Rio de Janeiro to Brasília.

The Center-West region's agribusiness growth has been significantly influenced by migration. Roughly 30% of the resident population consists of migrants from other regions. Emigrants from Minas Gerais, Maranhão, Bahia, and São Paulo have significantly populated large parts of Goiás, while migrants from the Northeast, Minas Gerais, and São Paulo primarily established Brasília. Mato Grosso and Mato Grosso do Sul were primarily occupied by Brazilians from the South. The expansion of the agricultural frontier and infrastructure investments have provided further impetus to migratory flows to the region. The government, in the 1970s, incentivized companies and individuals to relocate to the area, thereby fueling its agribusiness potential.

The construction of the Belém-Brasília, Brasília-Rio Branco, Cuiabá-Porto Velho, and Cuiabá-Santarém highways, which were conceptualized and built between the 1960s and 1970s, facilitated the expansion of numerous farmers and ranchers' activities such as soy cultivation and cattle rearing. In recent years, the Center-West has emerged as the country's largest soybean-producing area, which has, in turn, played a key role in Brazil becoming the world's second-largest producer of this crop. Besides soy, significant activities in the region include cotton and corn farming and extensive cattle breeding.

Central and southern plateaus, along with the Pantanal plain, characterize the region. The former has altitudes varying from 600 to 1000 m. This area is dominated by a mix of crystalline and sedimentary rocks and is notable for its moderate mountain ranges and plateaus. Chapada dos Veadeiros, a National Park established in 1961 and declared a Natural World Heritage Site by UNESCO in 2001, stands as a premier example. According to the park's managing authority, ICMBio (2021), Chapada dos Veadeiros showcases "diverse plant formations; numerous springs and watercourses; rocks over a billion years old, in conjunction with landscapes of rare beauty, marked by varying characteristics throughout the year." These attributes serve as the park's primary attractions.

The second plateau features a less rugged terrain and possesses more fertile soils. "Terra roxa" soils, derived from the sedimentation of basalt, a volcanic rock originating from the region's distant geological past, dominate in some areas. The Plateau of the Pantanal, which encompasses the western portion of the region, is considered the most expansive floodable plain worldwide and boasts a considerable diversity of flora and fauna. The climate in the Center-West region, primarily covering most of Goiás and the Mato Grosso territory, is predominantly humid tropical with two well-defined seasons throughout the year: a dry winter and a sweltering, rainy summer. The average temperatures hover around 22 °C (71 °F) but can reach up to 40 °C (104 °F). With the weather being predominantly dry throughout the year, a considerable variance exists between the day's lowest and highest recorded temperatures.

The Center-West region is the most economically dynamic and fastest-growing in contemporary Brazil. The region's primary activities consist of livestock farming, agriculture, and a burgeoning industrial sector. Cattle raising is dominant, contributing to 36% of the national production, equating to roughly 70 million cattle. This cattle raising activity primarily occurs in large landholdings. The meat production derived from these ventures supplies both the domestic and international consumer markets. The second major activity is pig raising, primarily practiced in the southern parts of Goiás and Mato Grosso do Sul.

Agriculture in certain states benefits from the quality of the "terra roxa" soil, which is standard in some areas of Mato Grosso. However, the majority of the region has soils with poor fertility, which led to agricultural challenges until the last century. In the 1970s, the Brazilian Agricultural Research Corporation (Embrapa) developed several techniques to boost food production adapted to local conditions. One of these methods involves using limestone to balance the Cerrado's soil acidity and develop soybean seeds suitable for this biome.

Recently, the Center-West region has begun to emerge as a source of industrial dynamism, primarily in Goiás and the southern part of Mato Grosso do Sul. This is due to their geographical proximity to the large consumer centers of the Southeast region. Several industries have been established in the Center-West to process a portion of the locally produced raw material and leverage the benefits of promoting industrial development. These industrial activities include soybean crushing and processing, animal feed production, meat processing (beef, pork, and chicken), and dairy.

The region's diverse culture encompasses indigenous peoples, migrant Paulistas, and Gauchos, as well as individuals from neighboring countries such as Bolivia and Paraguay. The area is characterized by typical cultural manifestations, such as the Cavalhada of Goiás, the Cururu in Mato Grosso and Mato Grosso do Sul, and cuisine like rice with pequi, sopa paraguaia, arroz carreteiro, and arroz boliviano. In Goiás, the Cavalhada, an open-air theatrical presentation in Pirenópolis where men on horseback reenact a medieval fight between Christians and Moors, is especially noteworthy.

Mato Grosso showcases its unique cultural manifestation, the cururu. This indigenous-originated dance pays tribute to city patron saints in the state's interior. Only men participate in this event, dancing in circles to the sounds of the cocho guitar and reco-reco. Other cultural events include the Feast of São Benedito, Siriri, Rasqueado Cuiabano, and Viola-de-Cocho. The culinary highlights consist of bolinho de arroz, mojica de pintado, and farofa de banana. The cultural rituals in

Mato Grosso do Sul are quite similar to those in Mato Grosso, with dances like cururu, siriri, and guarânia being quite popular.

To Further Research and Reflect

- Based on your country's agricultural experience, recommend at least three actions that the farmers of the Center-West region could implement to obtain higher prices in the sales of their products in world markets.
- Discuss what the country should do to transfer the Center-West region's agricultural labor productivity to the other areas.

1.8 The Northeast: A Dry Land with Solid Political Power Concentration

The Northeast region of Brazil comprises nine states: Maranhão, Piauí, Ceará, Rio Grande do Norte, Paraíba, Pernambuco, Alagoas, Sergipe, and Bahia. Although the region has a relatively high population in comparison to other areas, many inhabitants reside in large urban centers along the coastal areas, while some regions remain sparsely populated. The cities that serve as the capitals of these states are São Luís, Teresina, Fortaleza, Natal, João Pessoa, Recife, Maceió, Aracaju, and Salvador, each brimming with a significant portion of the state's population.

The economy of the Northeast region is diverse, reflecting its population. The Zona da Mata, the most industrialized and developed region of the Northeast, situated in the coastal areas, is a hub for mineral extraction and agricultural production for export. In the countryside, economic activities revolve around manioc cultivation and cattle and goat farming. The latter is also prevalent in the sertão, a region known for its semiarid climate and long periods of drought. This economic diversity is a testament to the resilience and adaptability of the population in the Northeast.

The Northeast region, with its unique geographical features, faces a significant challenge—drought. This issue can be traced back to three main factors: natural variables (physical and climate), historical events (legacy of colonization), and political factors (associated with the so-called drought industry). The region, situated at equatorial latitudes, experiences high temperatures due to the increased incidence of sunlight. Its inter-plateau relief, characterized by depressions between plateaus, impedes the circulation of humid air masses, leading to insufficient rainfall. Unlike the Amazon region, the Northeast lacks large rivers that promote evaporation and consequent precipitation. Many of the rivers are fleeting or seasonal, drying up during particular periods, with the São Francisco River as a notable exception, serving as the primary water resource in the region.

Aside from the natural climatic factors that contribute to the aridity of the northeastern region, the so-called drought industry also plays a role in the region's developmental challenges. Significant resources have been funneled into implementing advanced irrigation and water distribution projects in the area. However, a large portion of these funds has been misappropriated, typically by traditional regional political power-holders. According to Bursztyn (1984), politicians make promises of improvement to the population and provide basic necessities in exchange for votes. Upon being elected, these individuals prioritize serving the interests of the region's more economically powerful landowners.

The majority of rivers in the region, like the Canindé and Poti which run through the semiarid area, are intermittent, meaning they disappear during the dry season. The São Francisco River, the most prominent, remains perennial all year round. It originates in Minas Gerais and passes through Bahia, Sergipe, Alagoas, and Pernambuco. As a significant water source for human consumption and agro-industrial activities, it also provides the majority of energy for the region's hydroelectric plants, such as Paulo Afonso and Sobradinho. Since 2007, the federal government has been working on a large-scale project to divert the waters of the São Francisco River to restore the water supply to the northeastern sertão.

Owing to the hot climate and varied terrain, the vegetation in the region is remarkably diverse. The coastal strip, where Brazilwood was historically extracted from the Atlantic Forest that spans the entire Brazilian coast, now hosts intense fruit cultivation and remnants of the once vast forest. Previously, sugarcane was also grown in this area. The coastal mangrove ecosystems, known as manguezais, provide a habitat for crabs that are used in the cuisine of northeastern tourist destinations.

The Cerrado in the interior of Bahia, Maranhão, and Piauí, characterized by scattered small and medium-sized trees, clearly differentiates the rainy summer and dry winter periods. Additionally, in parts of these last two states, carnauba and babassu palm species can be found. These species provide the raw material for the local population's soap, margarine, fuel, and food industries. A vital metallurgical complex also exists, which arose in connection with the Carajás Project and the construction of the Carajás railroad. This railroad connects Pará to the port of Ponta da Madeira in São Luís do Maranhão.

In the interior of other states, predominantly in the northeastern sertão, the landscape is dominated by the Caatinga—a vegetation type characterized by its twisted forms, thick thorn-laden bark, and deep water-capturing roots. The region is also marked by a drought polygon that spans 1,108,000 km^2 and encompasses 1348 municipalities. Within this region, the primary enterprise is extensive goat farming, occasionally supplemented by cattle farming. Interestingly, the Northeast accounts for 90% of all goats reared in Brazil. Cotton production is also apparent in Paraíba, in Ceará, and, most significantly, in Piauí, the region's largest producer.

In the late eighteenth and early nineteenth centuries, Brazil, amid the decline of gold extraction and prior to the expansion of coffee production, was a significant producer and exporter of cotton. This raw material is deeply associated with the labor-intensive textile industry, historically one of the first to stimulate various industrial economies worldwide. Due to its proximity to Europe, the Portuguese colonized the Northeast coastal strip in the mid-sixteenth century. Initially, these colonies were concentrated on the extraction of Brazilwood, which was subsequently supplanted by sugarcane cultivation, and handled by enslaved indigenous and African workers. The sugar economy was the central focus of Gilberto Freyre's

1933 book, *The Masters and the Slaves* (Casa-Grande & Senzala): *A Study in the Development of Brazilian Civilization* (1987).

Freyre vividly describes how the *senhores de engenho* (landowners with expansive sugarcane plantations) resided in large mansions, while groups of enslaved individuals were housed in *senzalas*. Every individual owed respect and obedience to the lord of the mill, significantly shaping the patriarchal society known today, where a singular family head sets the rules and demands adherence. Moreover, many of the colonial era's *engenho* lords directly influenced, or through family representatives, the established political powers of the region. Descendants who inherited the wealth of the colonial period continue to dominate the region's political and economic power structures.

The majority of this region's population resides in sizable cities within the coastal capitals, making tourism a core part of these respective states' economic activities. As for commercial and extractive sectors, sea salt production contributes significantly to Rio Grande do Norte's income. However, there are states with more diversified economies, such as Bahia. This state garners a portion of its revenue from industrial pursuits, including those undertaken at the Camaçari industrial center located on the coast, as well as cocoa production inland. Notably, Bahia spearheads over 60% of Brazil's cocoa production.

The state of Bahia, particularly its capital, Salvador, the first capital of Brazil, is known for its rich cultural traditions, notably its Carnival. This festivity is also vigorously celebrated in Olinda and Recife in Pernambuco. Significant too are the June festivities in Caruaru in Pernambuco and Campina Grande in Paraíba. The Bumba Meu Boi festivities are a traditional feature in all northeastern states. Capoeira, introduced by enslaved Africans, is viewed as both fight and dance and is quite prevalent in Bahia and Pernambuco. The berimbau, a musical instrument, comprises a bow, a cut gourd, a caxixi (a basket with seeds), a stick, and dobrão (a coin).

Many cultural and religious manifestations of African origin are prevalent in the Northeast region, such as Bahian candomblé, known as xangô in Pernambuco. During the Feast of Iemanjá—the queen of the sea—all candomblés from Bahia lay flowers and gifts, mainly mirrors, combs, jewelry, and perfumes, to pay homage to their queen. In Bahia, the Lavagem do Bonfim, associated with the African Orixá, is significant; pilgrims travel to the Santuário do Senhor do Bonfim and other temples and churches to wash their staircases with water and flowers.

Each state boasts its unique cultural peculiarities, often characterized by frequent handicraft activities such as weaving hammocks, making lace, sieves, leather products, ceramics, and woodwork. A unique way of promoting local culture in the region is via Cordel literature. This consists of small books containing stories, written in prose or verse, on various subjects such as challenges, religious tales, rites, or ceremonies. The cuisine is diverse and includes dishes like carne de sol, buchada de bode, sarapatel, acarajé, vatapá, cururu, feijão verde, canjica, tapioca, and a variety of fish and fruits, including ciriguela, umbu, buriti, cajá, and macaúba.

To Further Research and Reflect

- The production of sugarcane was greatly stimulated in the Northeast during colonial times. Considering the economic opportunities today, what are the core activities that should be developed in the region?
- What policies would help reduce the political control of the so-called drought industry and landed elites that persist in the region?

References

Albuquerque, M. A. M., Vitiello, M. A., Bigotto, J. F. (2013). Geografia: sociedade e cotidiano: volume 2 - Fundamentos - manual do professor. 3. ed. ed. v. 2. EscalaEducacional. 304 p.

Bursztyn, M. (1984). *O Poder dos Donos: Planejamento e Clientelismo no Nordeste*. Editora Vozes. 177p.

Da Silva, C. A. F. (2019). *A Modernização Distrópica do Território Brasileiro*. Consequência. 552 p.

Freyre, G. (1987). *The masters and the slaves (Casa-Grande & Senzala): A study in the development of Brazilian civilization*. University of California Press. 2nd edition. 622 p.

IBGE. (2024). *Dashboard of indicators*. Available at: https://www.ibge.gov.br/en/indicators.html.

ICMBio. (2014). *Espécies Ameaçadas*. Available at: https://www.icmbio.gov.br/cepsul/especies-ameacadas.html.

ICMBio. (2021). *Parque Nacional da Chapada dos Veadeiros*. Available at: https://www.icmbio.gov.br/parnachapadadosveadeiros/.

Schwarcz, L. M., & Starling, H. M. M. (2019). *Brazil: A biography*. Penguin Books. 816 p.

Suframa—Superintendência da Zona Franca de Manaus. (2021). *Histórico*. Available at: https://www.gov.br/suframa/pt-br/zfm/o-que-e-o-projeto-zfm.

Chapter 2
The Brazilian Socioeconomic Context

2.1 Introduction

Portuguese, a language of rich cultural heritage, is the official language of Portugal, Brazil, and seven other countries that are members of the Community of Portuguese Language Countries. This linguistic bond unifies these nations and fosters a profound sense of shared identity. Brazil, populated with several large metropolitan cities like São Paulo (with a population of 21 million surpassing many European capitals), testifies to the vibrancy and diversity of the Portuguese-speaking world. As the fifth-largest country worldwide by total area and seventh-largest by population, Brazil depends on its institutions for reliable data on its economic and social variables.

Key data sources: Much like the Census Bureau in the USA and e-Stat in Japan, Brazil has a crucial agency named Instituto Brasileiro de Geografia e Estatística (IBGE). These establishments are pivotal for understanding a nation's socioeconomic background. For instance, data from the IBGE reveals that women outnumber men in Brazil and that women's average life expectancy is 80 years compared to men's 73 years. In 1940, the average life expectancy at birth in Brazil was 45 years. This number has since progressed, reaching 76 years in 2018. Approximately, 43% of Brazilians identify as white, 47% as brown, 9% as black, and 1% as yellow or indigenous.

While Brazil's geographical size and diverse population are impressive—with states such as Bahia and Minas Gerais surpassing the area of France and Spain—its socioeconomic context paints a different picture. The Amazon, a natural marvel that is larger than the next two biggest rainforests (the Congo Basin and Indonesia) combined, is in stark contrast with high wealth inequality and low levels of education. These comparisons not only underscore Brazil's vastness and rich biodiversity but also highlight its socioeconomic issues such as wealth disparities and a lack of

G. Masiero, *Brazilian Socio-Economic Dynamics*, Contributions to Economics,
https://doi.org/10.1007/978-3-031-87685-1_2

emphasis on education. Providing healthcare and education can be particularly challenging for extensive countries like Brazil.

Wealth inequality is a prevalent aspect of Brazil's current economic development model. The Southern Cone—Brazil, Argentina, Uruguay, and Chile—is among the world's most unequal regions. In the 1970s, during Brazil's dictatorship, its gross domestic product (GDP) averaged 11% during the so-called "economic miracle" period of 1968–1974. However, wealth concentration persists. A striking example is that Brazilians with a complete college education earn an average monthly income nearly six times higher than those workers without formal schooling.

The income of white individuals is 30% higher than the national average, which is approximately US $400, while the revenues of brown and black individuals are about 26% lower than this average. The highest-income formal workers in Brazil earn 34 times the monthly income of the bottom 50% who make less than US $150. Despite these inequalities, the lowest earnings are in the workforce, particularly in agribusiness activities. In rural areas, Brazil faces challenges in eradicating working conditions similar to those of enslaved people.

Agribusiness encompasses the relationships between agriculture, industry, and commerce. In 2020, agribusiness constituted more than 26% of the Brazilian GDP. However, soybean production and cattle raising account for one-quarter of the agricultural sector, indicating that production and exports are highly concentrated. Despite being one of the primary pillars of the Brazilian economy, concerns about agribusiness' social and ecological impacts persist. Even though Brazil is one of the world's largest food producers, substantial wealth disparities result in a significant portion of its population living in poverty.

2.2 Overview of Brazil in Numbers and Facts

The phases of Brazilian economic growth and development are key to understanding the current economic situation. As Maddison (2000) outlines, these are (1) the colony (1500–1822), (2) the empire (1822–1889), (3) the oligarchic republic (1889–1929), (4) the developmental era (1929–1980), and (5) the adjustment or the "maladjustment" era, which began in 1980 and persists as the present economic phase.

The colonial phase began with the arrival of Portuguese ships on Brazil's coast and extended until Independence. It was marked by slow growth; however, this was also the case in other parts of the world during the same period. Political transitions were relatively smooth, as the Portuguese prince became an emperor without any struggle. Territorial expansion was straightforward, as the Treaty of Tordesillas (1494) peacefully divided Latin America between Spain and Portugal, 48 degrees west of the Greenwich meridian. There was a certain amount of struggle to prevent the territory from fragmenting into several countries shortly after, as happened with the rest of Latin America.

However, several centuries later, the Treaty of Madrid induced a significant shift in South American territorial rights, particularly for Portugal. This new treaty awarded Portugal with territorial rights three times larger than those in 1500, marking a crucial turning point in Brazil's history. This treaty remodeled Brazil's geopolitical landscape, triggering notable events such as the Dutch occupation in the Northeast of Brazil from 1630 to 1654, and the French and Spanish incursions in the Southeast.

During the empire phase, which spanned from Independence (1822) to the proclamation of the Republic (1889), Brazil underwent a significant transformation. The population dramatically increased from 4.5 million in 1820 to 14 million by 1889. Despite this, GDP per capita growth only marginally outpaced the global average; it was merely a seventh of the US rate. However, it is necessary to acknowledge that the Brazilian economy, supported by its plentiful natural resources and the employment of slavery as a labor force, managed to maintain itself. This period was marked by a substantial increase in population, the exploitation of natural resources, and the contentious use of slavery, all contributing to Brazil's economic growth.

Brazil has operated as a federal presidential republic and has implemented seven constitutions to guide its social and economic development since the Republic Declaration in 1889. The government of Brazil has been led by various entities, spanning the colonial period (1500–1822), the empire period (1822–1889), and the era of oligarchs (1889–1932). Since the 1930s, Brazil's political landscape has alternated between dictatorships and democratic governments. The third and most enduring period of democracy in Brazil has been unbroken since 1984, after emerging from 20 years of dictatorship.

During the oligarchic phase, Brazil's southern region underwent significant changes. Economic growth remained restrained, yet it was four times higher than in the previous phase, and immigration helped boost population levels. The construction of railroads facilitated closer ties to the global economy. In this period, many governments implemented programs to attract immigrants, with the goal of replacing the intensively used slave labor force. Meanwhile, Brazil grappled with the collapse of the world economy, leading to a breakdown of its exports.

Through the administration of Getúlio Vargas, characterized by interventionism and autocracy, power shifted from the states to the central government within a federal republic. From 1929 to 1980, in an era characterized by state-controlled development, Brazil grappled with issues such as managed economy, defaulting on external debts, manipulation of exchange rates, and restrictive foreign trade policies. This period witnessed the establishment of numerous state-owned enterprises. Despite the slow pace of political progress during this time, Brazil saw higher economic growth than the rest of the world in the 1930s and 1940s, mirroring trends observed across most of Latin America.

The successes of this period solidified a policy amalgam that would persist in the following decades. At the time, Western Europe was going through reconstruction, aided by the massive Marshall Plan funding, a situation quite distinct from that in Latin America. Economic policies during the Kubitschek administration and the military regime had far more in common with Vargas' economic policies than with the neoliberal policies enacted under the early republic. Throughout the five decades of the developmental era, the country managed to reduce its underdeveloped economic levels, though income concentration intensified.

After World War II, political institutions became more sophisticated, and inflation was a generally tolerated phenomenon, with a complementary wide-scale indexation of prices. The 1980s brought a significant slowdown to the world economy, with a high impact on Brazil. Following the oil price shocks of the 1970s, deflationary policies caused the collapse of salary indexation, financial markets, and exchange rates. Additionally, the surge in international market interest and the suspension of capital loans to Latin America, triggered by Mexico's debt default, culminated in the economic crisis that Brazil would then face.

The military regime transitioned to a democratic government, which then adopted neoliberal-oriented policies. Since this shift, economic growth has been rather modest. If Brazil continues with its average yearly per capita increase of 0.27%, it will take approximately 250 years to double. Income inequalities are escalating and have never been a pressing priority for the country. Brazilian educational standards are below the Latin American average. This is concerning given that European and Asian economic development experiences have underscored education's significant role in boosting social mobility.

Brazil is a young nation and is yet to fully form. It is one of the world's largest countries, with an estimated area of 8.5 million km^2 and a population of 212 million at the start of 2021. Currently, the natural population increase is less than 1%, and approximately 87% of inhabitants live in urban areas. The majority of Brazilians reside in large metropolitan areas such as São Paulo (approximately 21 million), Rio de Janeiro (roughly 12 million), Belo Horizonte (around 6 million), Brasilia, Porto Alegre, Salvador, Recife, Fortaleza, and Curitiba, with respective populations descending from 4.2 to 3.5 million.

The sizable Brazilian population is concentrated relatively well across the capitals of the 26 states and 1 Federal District. While all citizens are deemed Brazilians, their ethnological backgrounds are quite varied, even within the same region. As per the IBGE (2024), 48% of Brazilians claim European ancestry, predominantly Portuguese, Italian, German, and Spanish.

The Portuguese arrived during colonial times when the Imperial Family relocated from Portugal to Brazil in 1808. The Portuguese, French, and Dutch arrived during the colonial period and intermixed with enslaved individuals from diverse African countries, as well as multiple indigenous ethnicities (approximately 300) and languages (about 275) in the region. Japanese, Arabs, and other immigrants from a variety of countries and races arrived in Brazil later, but in comparatively smaller numbers.

Portuguese is the official language, spoken from the north to the south of the country. The Community of Portuguese Language Countries, or the Lusophone community, comprises the former colonies of Portugal, with Brazil as the largest. Other countries where the language is official, albeit not spoken by the entirety of their populations, include Angola, Mozambique, Cape Verde, East Timor, Guinea-Bissau, Equatorial Guinea, and São Tomé and Príncipe. Among better-educated

Brazilians, English is the most spoken foreign language. Due to its similarity to Portuguese, Spanish is also well-understood, particularly within the business community.

The first Brazilian Constitution of 1824, enacted following Brazil's declaration of independence from Portugal, declared the Roman Catholic Church as the country's official religion. Although other religions were privately practiced by the predominant population of enslaved individuals and indigenous people since the fifteenth century—when the country was "discovered"—public worship was restricted. Religious freedom was ultimately recognized after the Proclamation of the Republic in 1889, as outlined in the second Brazilian Constitution of 1891.

Deodoro da Fonseca, the first military president of Brazil, mandated the separation of the church from the state. This separation was enshrined in six Brazilian constitutions (1934, 1937, 1946, 1967, 1969, and 1988). Regardless of this decree, the Catholic tradition has been influential since the colonial period, with other religions, primarily of African origin, becoming legalized in 1950. More recently, commencing in the 1980s, many Neo-Pentecostal churches have broadened their presence in the country.

The country still has a high illiteracy rate, around 12%, with a Human Development Index (HDI) of 0.755. This final metric consolidates per capita income, life expectancy, literacy rate, enrollment, and attendance ratio in educational establishments. Overall, Brazil ranks 75th out of 188 countries on the HDI. According to the IBGE (2024), nearly 100% of the population has electricity access, and over half are Internet users.

Following Maddison (2000), the GDP of Brazil—the indicator that measures the fluctuation in the value of goods and services within a country over a certain period—averaged 5.7% from 1929 to 1980. This period represents the most economically dynamic era in which the country experienced its "economic miracle." World Bank data indicates that Brazil's average GDP was 10.9% between 1968 and 1974, with 1973 being the most dynamic of those years, as its GDP growth reached 13.9%.

Over this half-century of development, Brazil transitioned from a focus on primary agricultural production and mineral extraction to a more dynamic industrial sector, which is yet to be fully consolidated. This economic vitality was largely buoyed by state companies' intense participation in the domestic market, as well as government measures for its protection. Several financial plans directed these transformations; however, with the oil crisis of the 1970s, industrialization lost some of its drive.

The 1980s is often referred to as the "lost decade." The subsequent decade witnessed the most extensive privatization ever seen in either Brazil or the world. Various economic sectors were liberalized in 1990. In the first decade of this century, a "commodity boom"—prompted by high prices for agricultural and mineral product exports to China—benefited the economy. However, income inequalities remain prevalent, necessitating the implementation of significant and structural changes to address current challenges.

To Further Research and Reflect

- Highlight the advantages and disadvantages of populational concentration for economic growth purposes.
- How many constitutions have been implemented in your country? When was the church separate from the state in Brazil and your country?

2.3 IBGE and Data on the Brazilian Population

One of the initial steps in studying a country or region involves searching for reliable sources and information. Each country has certain organizations responsible for providing accurate information to its citizens. For example, the Census Bureau in the USA provides quality data on its population and economy. Conversely, on the other side of the globe, Japan maintains the e-Stat, a portal site where the Japanese government publishes the nation's statistics. Similarly, Brazil has the IBGE, whose institutional mission is "to portray Brazil with information necessary for the knowledge of its reality and the exercise of citizenship."

The legacy of the IBGE, in providing data and information, dates back to colonial times. With the advent of the Republic, its activities significantly expanded, particularly when the registration of vital events became compulsory. The institute's name was formalized in 1937, following the establishment of the Brazilian Council of Geography and its integration with the National Institute of Statistics (INE), created in 1934 after the National Statistics Department was abolished. Today, the IBGE represents the most extensive and comprehensive data repository on Brazilian geography, population, and economic activities, inspiring both awe and respect.

The IBGE demonstrates its commitment to public service through its educational portal, IBGE Educa, which disseminates data and information to children, youth, and teachers. Among its many activities, this portal offers a user-friendly interface for accessing the IBGE's wealth of data. For instance, the projection of the Brazilian population in March 2021 was 213 million. Furthermore, the 2019 PNAD Contínua—the National Continuous Household Sample Survey—highlighted that 48% of men and 52% of women reside in Brazilian territory. The portal also showcases Fig. 2.1, which visually represents the distribution of the Brazilian population by age and gender.

The Brazilian age pyramid, derived from the IBGE's data, offers critical insights into birth rates, the population's average age, and lifespan. Figure 2.1 illustrates that, in 2019, the population of Brazil was proportionally older than it was in 2012. This shifting demographic can be discerned from the reduced percentage of the youngest age groups (identified at the base of the pyramid) in 2019 compared to the oldest individuals (occupying the top). A downward trend could be observed in the country's resident population distribution by age group, specifically among individuals under 30.

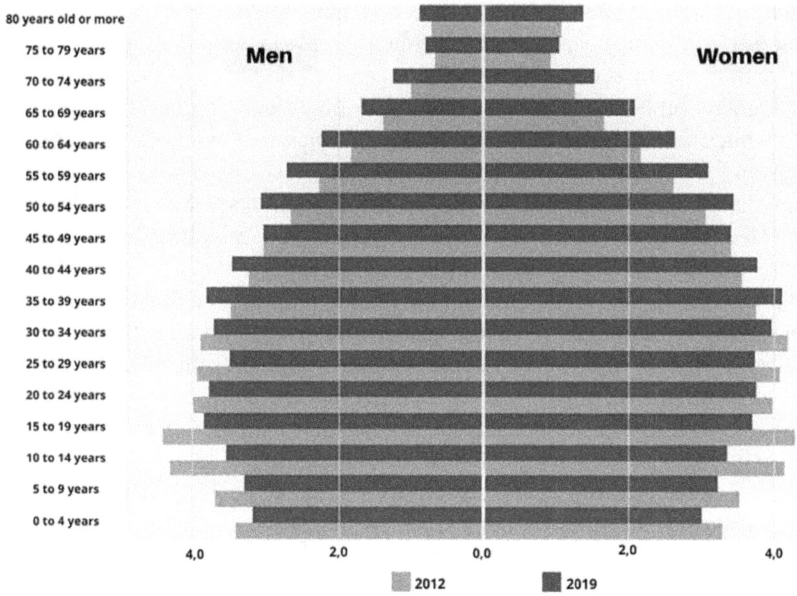

Fig. 2.1 Brazil: population gender and age. Source: IBGE (2019)

Access to quality education is integral to the development of citizenship and the expansion of democracy. The IBGE says a person is considered literate if they are capable of writing a basic note. According to this guideline, the 2023 census indicates a reduction in illiteracy among Brazilians aged 15 and above. Despite this progress, there remains a staggering 9.3 million illiterate individuals in the country, a number higher than the total population of many countries.

By 2023, nearly 55% of individuals aged 25 and over had completed at least secondary school—meaning, they had finished primary education. Nonetheless, those aged 15 and over with less than 5 years of formal education are deemed functionally illiterate, comprising 30% of Brazilians. Given Brazil's population size, this percentage represents an alarming number—more than 40 million functionally illiterate individuals.

Functional illiteracy refers to the incapacity of an individual to effectively use reading, writing, and calculation skills in everyday life despite having completed primary education. It is a more encompassing concept than merely not being able to read or write. Functionally illiterate people may struggle to understand and execute basic tasks of reading, writing, comprehending, and effectively participating in modern society. There can be multiple causes for functional illiteracy, including inadequate or substandard education, limited access to educational resources, learning disabilities, or cognitive impairments.

In Brazil, nursery school is not compulsory. Education is only mandatory from 4 years old. Before this, the decision to enroll is up to the families. However, the state must ensure that there are spaces available for everyone who wishes to attend. It is important to note that Brazilian legislation mandates school attendance from the ages of 4 to 17. In 2023, nearly 29 million young people ranging from ages 15 to 29 did not participate in school or attend a vocational or pre-university education course. A higher number of black or brown individuals were in this situation compared to whites, and there were significantly more men than women. The primary reason given for not studying was the need to work.

The majority of Brazilians (85%) reside in urban settings, while a smaller percentage (15%) inhabit rural areas. During the 1970s and 1980s, Brazil experienced an intense exodus from rural areas. Increased agricultural mechanization forced many workers out of the countryside, prompting them to relocate to cities in search of employment opportunities. This movement from rural to urban areas continues today, albeit at a reduced rate. The intense process of urbanization in Brazil has led to rapid metropolitan growth. Urban occupation has expanded beyond traditional city confines, leading to the establishment of large metropolitan centers such as São Paulo, Rio de Janeiro, Porto Alegre, Salvador, Goiânia, and Manaus.

The IBGE generates reports on the color or race of the Brazilian population using self-classification criteria. Individuals are requested to classify themselves into one of five colors: white, black, brown, indigenous, or yellow. According to the 2019 PNAD, 43% of Brazilians identified themselves as white, 47% as brown, 9% as black, and 1% as yellow or indigenous.

The IBGE has identified 305 distinct indigenous ethnic groups within Brazil. The key tribes among these groups include the Macro-Jê (Boróro, Guató, Jê, Karajá, Krenák, Maxakali, Ofayé, Rikbaktsa, Yatê) and Tupi (Arikém, Awetí, Jurúna, Mawé, Mondé, Mundurukú, Puroborá, Ramaráma, Tuparí, Tupi-Guarani). According to the 2010 Census, 274 indigenous languages are spoken within Brazil, with the majority of indigenous territory inhabitants conversing in their indigenous language at home. Importantly, 77% of individuals identified as belonging to an indigenous ethnic group can comprehend and converse in Portuguese.

To Further Research and Reflect

- What is the institution in charge of providing reliable data on the population and economy of your country? Are the statistics these organizations produce reliable?
- Population aging is a global phenomenon. Briefly summarize how your society is dealing with the increasing number of older adults in your country.

2.4 Lack of Education

The lack and disproportionate number of inadequately trained professionals is a historical deficit that has characterized the development of Brazil. Education, as a social practice, aims to leverage the potentialities, skills, and competencies of humans. It is not limited to just the school environment but refers to the broader scope of human development through teaching and learning. Enhancing the intellectual capacity of each individual is a primary objective of the educational systems in all countries. This process is intrinsically associated with the realms of school, family, and social education. It is important to denote that education goes beyond mere instruction and knowledge dissemination, as it also involves the development of autonomy and critical thinking.

According to the Federal Constitution, education is a right for all individuals. The Federal Constitution outlines three primary educational objectives: (a) to ensure the full development of the individual, (b) to prepare the individual for the practice of citizenship, and (c) to qualify the individual for the job market. It also stipulates that education is the responsibility of the Federal Government, to be delivered by the Ministry of Education, the states, the municipalities, and the Federal District.

The expansion of primary schooling within the public school network began in the early 1980s. However, of the 65 countries participating in the Program for International Student Assessment (PISA), Brazil ranks 53rd. As of 2019, data from the National Household PNAD survey confirmed that the illiteracy rate for individuals aged 15 years or older was estimated to be over 6%. This translates to 11 million illiterate adults in Brazil. Illiteracy rates across different regions in Brazil can be seen in Fig. 2.2.

The country is still far from achieving its goal of teaching all children to read and write by the time they are 8 years old. It struggles with low performance according to the Basic Education Development Index (IDEB), an instrument created by the federal government to gauge the quality of education in public schools. IDEB data from 2017 indicates that the average score is 5.8 in the early years of primary school, 4.7 in the final years of primary school, and only 3.8 in high school. Only 17% of individuals aged 25 years or older have completed a higher education degree. The educational levels of the economically productive workforce are outlined in Fig. 2.3.

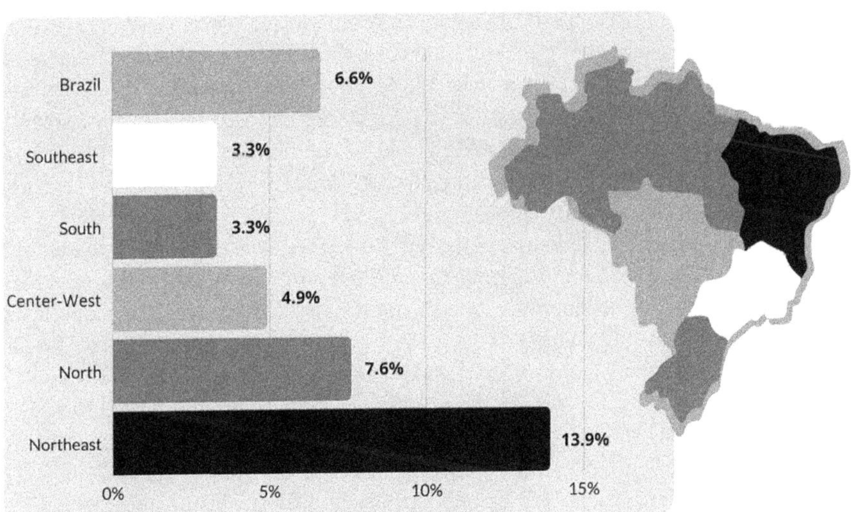

Fig. 2.2 The illiteracy rate among people aged 15 years and older (2019). Source: IBGE (2019)

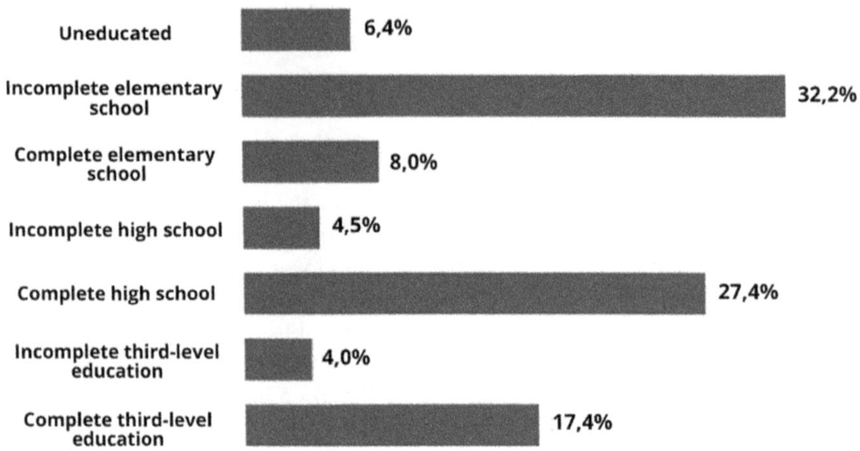

Fig. 2.3 Education level of people aged 25 years or older in 2017. Source: IBGE (2019)

Access to quality education is a fundamental right, vital for the cultivation of citizenship and the growth of democracy. However, for those with low incomes, the pressing need to enter the labor market often results in a truncated educational experience, with diminishing enhancements in learning as students progress through primary and secondary education systems. No reform or transformation can be truly effective without enhancements to teacher qualifications. Students must develop critical thinking skills to interpret the data and information readily available in numerous areas of knowledge and must be enabled to incorporate these inputs into their growing wisdom.

Digital education has become a significant responsibility for educational systems today. About three-quarters of Brazilian students have Internet access at home, which is crucial for accessing educational resources and maintaining connections with their peers and teachers. However, the Covid-19 pandemic has posed significant challenges to school learning in Brazil. Participating in a considerable research project, "The State of E-Learning in Higher Education in the Era of the Pandemic: How Do We Move Forward?," Masalimova et al. (2022) unveiled the many facets of transitioning from face-to-face education to virtual means.

During the Covid-19 pandemic, countries worldwide have striven to broaden the scope of distance education and mandate its use. However, this shift has been accompanied by many technological challenges, including difficulties in operating complex systems. Initially, students' attitudes towards distance learning were positive because it facilitated learning anytime and anywhere. Still, it also led to psychological health issues, such as fear, anxiety, stress, and decreased attention spans. Additionally, many schools lacked the necessary infrastructure to transition to online schooling effectively. Although alternatives to traditional distance learning have been introduced, their lack of interactivity and linearity has not equaled the benefits gleaned from face-to-face teaching and has, thus, failed to adequately replace it.

The low level of education in the Brazilian workforce has long been a critical barrier to the country's economic development, perhaps for decades or even centuries. This deficiency, combined with mismanagement in the health and various financial sectors, highlights the unsustainable nature of Brazil's development. According to OECD (2024) data, mandatory instruction time in Brazil falls short of the OECD average. Meanwhile, the Brazilian government's expenditure per student in public institutions is US $4300, significantly less than the nearly three times higher investment (US $11,500 in 2020) by OECD member states.

Less than 20% of students aged 18–24 are enrolled in universities. Accessing and studying at Brazilian universities presents significant challenges. A recurring issue with university admission in Brazil is the students' substandard education during their high school years. It is virtually impossible to reduce dropout rates in both high schools and universities for Brazilian students who need to work to support themselves. Generally, the need for survival takes precedence over acquiring knowledge at all educational stages.

Government programs intended to motivate students to attend college have been implemented. At the national level, the ENEM (National High School Exam) offers students the opportunity to compete for slots in the SISU (Unified Selection System), Prouni (University for All Program), and FIES (Student Financing Fund). However, merely improving access appears to be insufficient. Local initiatives are more modest, struggling to overcome the challenges of incorporating more students into the education system.

Despite efforts to democratize higher education, inequalities persist in access to it, particularly for low-income, black, and brown students. Once admitted to university, these students often grapple not just with academic challenges, but also with the burden of balancing work and study. Many must work to fund their education and support their families. The Covid-19 pandemic has only further highlighted and deepened Brazil's social, economic, and educational disparities.

To Further Research and Reflect

- What measures were implemented in your country to end illiteracy, and which ones would you recommend for Brazil?
- Compare the primary skills of your country's workforce in the three essential economic sectors: agriculture, industry, and services. Which ones would you apply to similar Brazilian sectors?

2.5 Economic and Spatial Inequalities

Social and economic inequalities have been a principal characteristic of Brazilian development since imperial times, and persisted with the establishment of the Republic in 1889 by way of a political-military coup d'etat. Military governments have often prioritized economic growth (an increase in the production of goods and services within an economy) over economic development (policies and initiatives

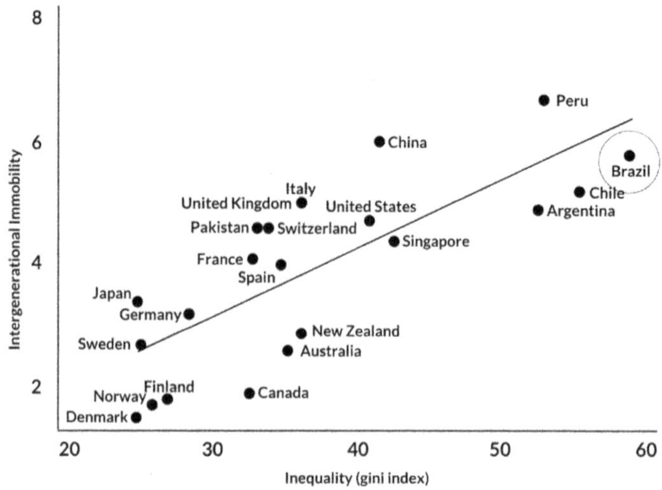

Fig. 2.4 Equality and mobility in selected countries. Source: Corak (2016)

aimed at improving income, employment, infrastructure, education, and living standards) during their periods in power. The concentration of wealth has remained constant. IBGE (2019) data reveals that the wealthiest 10% of Brazil's population possess approximately 43% of the country's income, while the poorest 10% hold less than 1%.

As corroborated by Fig. 2.4 from Corak (2016), Brazil (like other Latin American countries, such as Chile, Peru, and Argentina) is marked by low social mobility and high societal inequality. In contrast, nations like Denmark, Norway, Finland, and Sweden exhibit a more equitable distribution of wealth and per capita income. This suggests that social inequalities are more a matter of policy than a natural phenomenon. Looking Eastward, several Asian countries have managed to elevate their per capita income through rapid industrialization, concurrently improving the standard of living for their populace and maintaining a relatively equal society.

Numerous minimum wage or universal basic income programs have been deployed globally to curb economic disparities. These initiatives are often referred to as conditional or unconditional cash transfers, poverty alleviation, income security, or the promotion of social justice. More than two decades ago, Brazil instated its most significant social program, Bolsa Familia. However, critics of these programs voice concerns about work disincentives and the quest for productivity enhancements. Conversely, some contend that these programs enable individuals to pursue education, training, entrepreneurship, and other activities that can contribute to individual well-being and overall economic output.

Governments worldwide have extensively used various programs during the recent global pandemic. The advent of the Covid-19 global pandemic, which led to millions of citizens losing or downgrading their jobs, exacerbated wealth concentration. Despite their short-term efficacy, these programs did not help reduce global wealth disparity. These structural phenomena have undergone rigorous study, and several proposed measures have been voiced.

Milanović (2019), for instance, advocates for a people's capitalism that taxes the wealthiest incomes and inheritances with the intent of redistributing capital to decrease inequality and enhance mobility. According to him, the economy would persist as a capitalist establishment, as most of its production would utilize privately owned resources. The majority of workers would earn wages, and decisions on production and pricing would predominantly be made by companies in a decentralized manner. Piketty (2019) and Saez and Zucman (2019) also strongly suggest the taxation of large fortunes as a solution to persistent inequalities in the twenty-first century.

Numerous changes unfolded in the economic system during the twentieth century. Nonetheless, the impetus of self-interest and the desire to own properties fueled a decentralized wealth generation system. According to Hall and Soskice (2001) the multiple forms of capitalism, ranging from those governed by liberal market economies, such as the USA, UK, Canada, Australia, New Zealand, and Ireland, to those of coordinated market economies like Germany, Belgium, the Netherlands, Scandinavian countries, and Austria, significantly improved the standard of living for their citizens. This drive for wealth also gained momentum in the early development of the diverse and substantial Brazilian economy.

In terms of territory, Brazil is larger than Europe. It is approximately 2.6 times the size of India. The Brazilian states of Bahia and Minas Gerais are larger than France and Spain, the biggest countries in Europe. The states of Amazonas (1.560 million km^2) and Pará (1.246 million km^2) are larger than Mongolia and Angola. While these states are rich in natural resources, they rank among the lowest on the HDI within Brazil, with scores of 0.674 and 0.646 in 2010, respectively. The Amazon has a population density of just 2.23 people per square kilometer. The Amazon Forest itself is larger than the next two biggest rainforests combined—the Congo Basin and the Indonesian islands.

During the so-called "economic miracle" period (1968–1974), when Brazil was under a dictatorship, the country's GDP grew by an average of 11% per year. This was achieved by significantly investing in infrastructure, including the globally ambitious Trans-Amazonian Highway project. The original plan was to construct a fully paved highway stretching 5000 km from João Pessoa, located on the coastline of the Paraiba state in the Northeast region, all the way to the Peruvian border. However, due to the rainy season as well as a lack of funds and engineering capabilities, these plans were not fulfilled. While some stretches near urban areas have been paved, significant portions of the highway remain incomplete.

In 2015, the governments of China, Brazil, and Peru signed a memorandum of understanding to develop a project—the Transcontinental Railway. The proposed route began in Campinorte de Góias, traversed Mato Grosso, Rondônia, and Acre, before reaching the Peruvian border. Following its crossing of the Amazon region and the Andes, the railway intended to reach a port on the Pacific coast.

The ambitious project also envisions links to the FIOL (West-East Railway in the East) and the FNS (North-South Railway in the North), extending to the Atlantic coast. The total length of the route is 4919 km. The Peruvian segment spans 1629 km, while the planned Brazilian railway covers 3290 km. Estimated project costs total US $70 billion, with approximately US $40 billion attributed to the mountainous Peruvian route and US $30 billion earmarked for the Brazilian side.

Large infrastructure projects are crucial for integrating vast sections of Brazilian territory. Roads, railroads, ports, and airports have propelled the dynamism of national economies—both economic growth and human development. Almost everything in the country is massive. However, to ignite sustainable and persistent economic development, other influencers should also be considered, such as human capital—the knowledge and skills of people (reflected in the population's educational levels)—and sound economic policies, among others.

Policymakers and managers involved in these projects must take into account their potential to enhance human development and improve sanitation, health, education, and environmental protection. The integration of new and extensive regions of the Brazilian territory, such as the Amazon region, is crucial for human development. However, it presents significant challenges in guaranteeing environmental protection. The previous experiences of economic growth from Brazil and other countries have not effectively constructed a more equal and inclusive society.

To Further Research and Reflect

- What have been your country's most significant infrastructure programs, and how have private or public agents financed them? What similarities do they share with the projects developed in Brazil?
- How should countries sustainably integrate an almost unpopulated territory into the national and international economic system without worsening income inequalities and environmental degradation?

2.6 Brazilian Earnings and Social Indicators

Researchers and journalists frequently use the National Continuous Household Sample Survey—PNAD Contínua—by IBGE (2019) to discuss developments or setbacks in Brazil's main social indicators. The survey reported that 131.2 million (63%) out of Brazil's 210 million people reported earning some income in 2019. A majority source their income from work (44% of the total population), while a smaller portion earn their income from other sources (25%). The latest Brazilian Census, conducted in 2022, indicates that the Brazilian population is around 203 million, but the percentages relating to earnings did not show significant change. For updated statistics, refer to the IBGE (2024) for socioeconomic and agribusiness indicators.

Other sources of income are typically not derived from employment and can include retirement or pension funds, unemployment insurance, savings-derived income, government income transfer programs, and alimony. The average monthly income for Brazilians aged 14 and older who are employed was about 400 dollars in 2019. Nevertheless, the subsequent survey in 2020 revealed a notable decline, with the average income dropping to roughly 250 dollars. This dramatic decrease in average income levels, which is a direct result of Brazil's response to the Covid-19 pandemic, emphasizes the urgency and importance of this challenging issue. The financial figures were converted based on the exchange rates of March 2021.

Half of Brazilians receive an average of 150 dollars per month. On the other hand, those in the top 1% of the population, in terms of income, receive an average monthly payment of 5400 dollars. This figure is 36 times more than what half of the population earns as a minimum wage salary each month. Significant income disparities are evident across different regions of the country. In 2019, the southern region had the highest average real monthly income. Conversely, the North and Northeast regions recorded the lowest values.

Income disparities are particularly striking when examined by gender, race, and educational level. Among the employed population in 2019, men reported an average monthly income of 450 dollars, while women reported an average of 350 dollars. Women earned 77% of what men did. When considering everyone earning a wage, the average total monthly pay for white individuals was higher than that for brown and black individuals. The differences are significant, with the figures, respectively, being 530 dollars versus 300 and 290.

The average income of white individuals is 30% higher than the national average, while the incomes of brown and black individuals are 25% and 27% lower, respectively. When comparing based on the level of education, individuals with a complete college education have an average monthly income of approximately US $900. This figure is almost six times higher than that of workers without formal schooling, who earn around US $160. Figure 2.5 depicts these disparities.

Before the Covid-19 pandemic, nearly 46 million Brazilians—about 24% of the population—reported having some level of difficulty in at least one of the examined skills (i.e., seeing, hearing, walking, or climbing steps) or possessed mental/

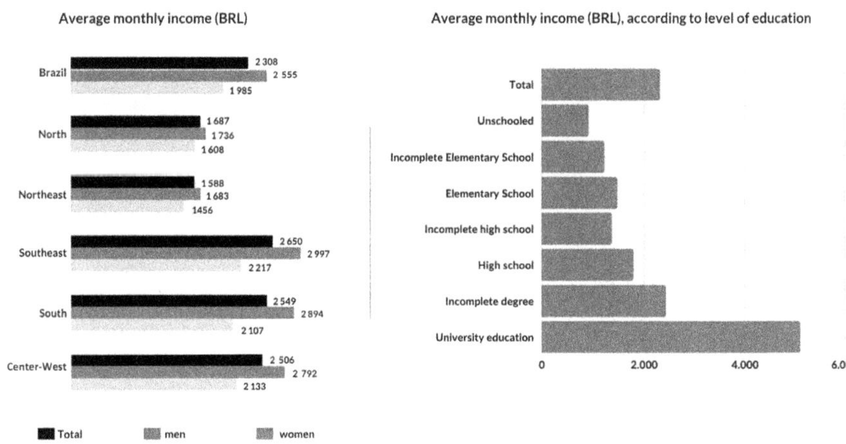

Fig. 2.5 Income differences by region, gender, and education. Source: IBGE (2019)

intellectual disabilities. In posing this question, the IBGE aimed to grasp the public's perception of their difficulties, even if they used aids such as glasses/contact lenses, hearing aids, or canes.

According to international guidelines, "people with disabilities" are defined as individuals who report having difficulty with certain abilities. Efforts were made in the survey to identify intellectual and mental disabilities by assessing the respondents' performance in typical activities. However, this questionnaire did not take into consideration mental disorders, diseases, or disturbances such as autism, neurosis, schizophrenia, and psychosis.

In addition to examining the population with disabilities, the IBGE periodically surveys municipal services through the Municipal Basic Information Survey (Munic) to determine whether they are adapted for individuals with mobility challenges. Data from the 2017 survey indicates that out of 1679 municipalities equipped with intra-municipal bus public transport services, only 12% had their fleets fully adapted for accessibility by people with disabilities or reduced mobility. Meanwhile, 49% had fleets that were only partially adapted. These statistics highlight that public infrastructure is not adequately adapted for these citizens.

According to the IBGE (2019), there are 72 million permanent homes in Brazil. Of this total, 86% are houses, 14% are apartments, and the remaining 0.2% comprise other types of dwellings such as rooming houses or tenements. Among these homes, 73% are owned, 18% are rented, and 9% are occupied under lease agreements. In addition to the number and characteristics of residents and households, the PNAD Contínua also collates information on essential sanitation services, including water supply, bathroom facilities, sewage systems, garbage disposal, and electricity provision.

Monitoring the provision of these services is paramount. They ensure improved living conditions and healthcare for the population. The survey revealed that 85% of households relied on the public distribution network as the primary source of water supply. Additionally, water is also supplied by deep or artesian wells (7%); shallow wells, underground wells, or waterholes (3%); fountains or springs (2%); and other methods (2%).

In 2019, 98% of homes had private bathrooms. The proportion of homes with private bathrooms varied across regions in the country. For instance, 90% of homes in the North had private bathrooms compared to nearly 100% in the South. When we look at the access to the public sewage network, the disparities become more pronounced. The North (27%) and Northeast (47%) regions exhibited the lowest levels of sewage access, while the Southeast (89%), the South (68%), and the Center-West (60%) exhibited the highest.

The primary destination for waste from Brazilian households is direct collection by sanitation services. This is supported by the PNAD Contínua, which indicates that the proportion of households with collected waste has been gradually increasing. In certain instances, sanitation services collect trash from dumpsters (7.0%), or households burn their garbage on their property (7%), or dispose of it elsewhere (1%). In 2019, virtually all homes (99%) had access to electricity, either from the public grid or alternative sources. That same year, the public grid supplied almost all households (99%) with electricity. A significant proportion of households in all regions had access to electricity, with only a modest variation of 1% between different areas.

To Further Research and Reflect

- Contrast some Brazilian income indicators with your country's income averages and suggest ways of improving incomes based on your nation's efforts to leverage the earnings of low-income people.
- Based on any other country's experience, suggest some policies for Brazilian authorities to reduce income differences among its population's highest and lowest income levels.

2.7 Agribusiness: Global Commodity Supplier

Despite the low earnings and wealth disparities among Brazilians, the country boasts one of the most dynamic agribusiness sectors worldwide. This sector, which represents a significant portion of both the domestic and global economies, contributes to nearly one-third of the Brazilian economy. It spans the entirety of the agricultural production ecosystem, encompassing services, techniques, and equipment. Brazil is the world's largest exporter of chicken meat, coffee, and sugar, the second-largest exporter of beef, and the fourth-largest exporter of pork. The agribusiness sector also involves an intertwined relationship among the primary (agriculture), secondary (technology and raw material transformation industries), and tertiary (transportation and commercialization of products derived from crops) sectors of the economy.

Since colonial times, Brazil has provided raw materials and natural resources for both domestic and international markets. More recently, from the 1970s onwards, the country has experienced significant growth in its agro-industrial sector, particularly in the production and export of coffee, soy, oranges, sugar, and livestock. According to the Brazil Agriculture and Livestock Confederation (CNA, 2020), the transformative impact of the agricultural revolution over the past 40 years is without doubt the most significant event in Brazil's recent economic history. This ongoing revolution is continually shaping the country's future development and fostering optimism regarding the potential of Brazil's agribusiness.

Agriculture, the linchpin of Brazilian agribusiness, holds the largest share among its areas, followed by livestock farming. Soybeans and cattle rearing form the pillars of Brazilian agriculture, accounting for a quarter of all production. This is followed by beef cattle, corn, milk, sugar, chicken, coffee, and cotton. These activities fuel the economy and have a significant role in the nation's labor market, employing over 30% of the Brazilian workforce, thus highlighting the social impact of agribusiness.

In 2019, agribusiness accounted for over 40% of Brazil's export earnings, playing a pivotal role in maintaining a trade balance surplus (when exports surpass

Table 2.1 Brazilian primary agribusiness production

	Sugar	Coffee	Orange Juice	Soy	Chicken	Beef	Corn	Pork
Produces	29,5 Ml t (2°)	3,8 Ml t (1°)	1,3 Ml t (1°)	117 Ml t (2°)	13,3 Ml t (2°)	9,9 Ml t (2°)	101 Ml t (3°)	3,7 Ml t (4°)
Exports	19,6 Ml t (1°)	1,9 Ml t (1°)	1,2 Ml t (1°)	75,4 Ml t (1°)	3,6 Ml t (1°)	2,0 Ml t (1°)	39,0 Ml t (3°)	0,7Ml t (4°)
Share	36%	27%	76%	51%	38%	22%	20%	10%

Source: Adapted from CNA (2020)

Table 2.2 Brazilian rural establishment by area (2017)

Classification	Establishments	Total area (ha)	Average area (ha)
Total	5,073,324	351,289,816	69
Small	4,672,051 (92%)	96,597,717 (27.5%)	21
Medium	231,430 (4.6%)	66,332,617 (18.9%)	287
Big	92,806 (1.8%)	188,359,482 (53.6%)	2030
No area declaration	77,037 (1.5%)	...	

Source: IBGE (2017)

imports). With revenues in 2018 nearing US $100 billion, Brazil ranked as the world's fourth-largest exporter of agricultural and livestock products, trailing just behind the European Union, the USA, and China. As presented in Table 2.1, Brazil is the largest exporter of orange juice, soybeans, beef, and chicken, as well as the third-largest corn exporter. Notably, it is also the world's leading producer of coffee and orange juice; it ranks second in sugar, soybeans, beef, and chicken production and third in corn production.

Despite being a main pillar of the Brazilian economy, agribusiness raises concerns due to its social and ecological impact, including the unequal distribution of generated wealth. These criticisms are intrinsically tied to rural social movements, which accuse agribusiness of exacerbating land concentration, a process where the majority of land is held by a small number of investors. In 2017, Brazil's Gini index for rural establishments was 0.867. Like other Gini measures, a value closer to zero indicates improved income distribution, whereas a value close to one signifies increasing inequality (Censo Agro, 2017). Table 2.2 presents the fiscal structure of the rural establishments, along with their average area in hectares.

According to the Censo Agro of the IBGE (2017), only 502,000 farms (1%) in Brazil have irrigated water. Almost half of the rural area is utilized for cattle raising. Brazil's geographic dimensions are of continental proportions. Table 2.2 reports the distribution of land use across 851 million hectares of the territory. Some parts of the territory are cultivated twice yearly due to favorable climatic conditions. Almost half of the land currently used in farming consists of unexploited areas that are unavailable for agricultural conversion without clearing new regions in the Amazon rainforest.

Brazil possesses natural advantages in agribusiness compared to other large countries such as China and the USA. In addition to having abundant land enriched with numerous rivers, lakes, and aquifers, and the benefit of consistent rainfall, the duration and intensity of sunlight favor agribusiness activities, requiring minimal technology use across most regions of the country. Even in the driest area of the Northeast region, some agribusiness activities thrive.

The Brazilian agribusiness sector accounts for around 40% of exports, contributes to 20% of the country's GDP, and employs one-third of the workforce. Given the enormous influence of this sector, there is an ongoing debate over the necessity of state-led support. This discussion gets even more heated within the industry, as traditional producers and those enthusiastic about incorporating novel techniques and technological tools for productivity growth differ over the allocation of federal government resources. Typically, the majority of the cattle are grazed on extensive farms. Yet, only a small percentage of the country's farms utilize modern technologies for cattle raising, which are resource-intensive and involve cultivating various crops.

Among these innovative resources, technologies like sensors are increasingly being adopted. These sensors collect data from plantations, including information on soil and climate conditions, enabling tasks to be commanded automatically from a distance and in real time. Drones transmit aerial images that assist agribusinesses in monitoring crop growth. Similar to sensors and other management software, these tools aid producers in reducing costs and enhancing productivity.

In addition to introducing information technology tools, the implementation of biotechnologies is another emerging trend in the Brazilian agribusiness sector. Genetically improved seeds and the introduction of genes that result in better plant adaptation to each specific location are being used to explore what has become known as "precision farming." Precision farming considers spatial and temporal variations essential for maximizing production. This includes data on soil variability, pest occurrence, and weather conditions within the property to design and improve farming practices.

However, the modernization of the agribusiness sector in Brazil and the consequent productivity increase are also producing negative costs. One of these is the displacement of numerous rural workers from agriculture. Governments have been severely criticized for their "failure" to address unjust land distribution in the country by NGOs, the Catholic Church, and, one of the most globally significant landless workers' movements, the *Movimento dos Sem Terra* (MST). They condemn the still considerable number of unproductive landholdings (referred to as "latifundium"), the replacement of workers with advanced technologies, and the substantial influence of large international companies in the sector.

Furthermore, there is a conflict between ruralists (large landowners and pro-agribusiness politicians) and environmentalists concerning Brazil's disorderly

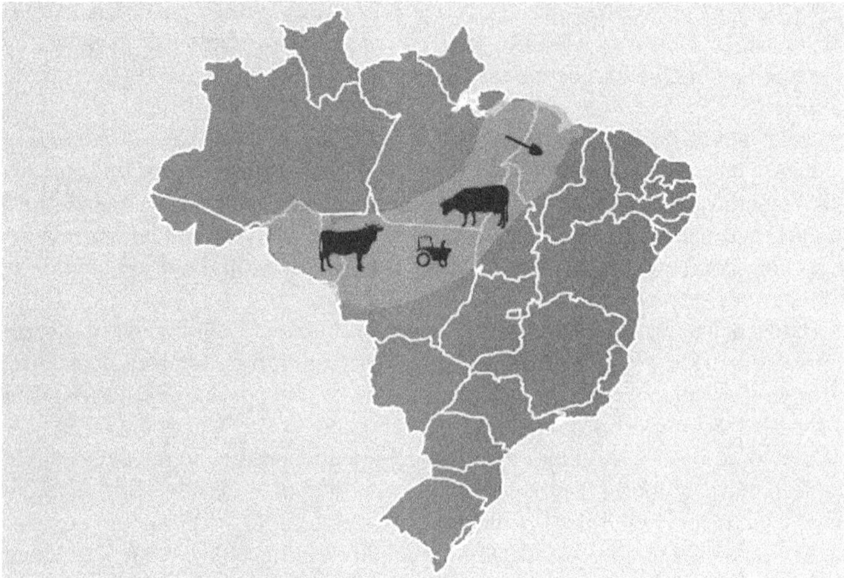

Fig. 2.6 Brazilian "Arc of Deforestation." Source: Radio PUC (2024)

expansion of cultivable land. Rural entrepreneurs are extending the agricultural frontier, decreasing the number of environmental reserves and green areas. According to Radio PUC (2024), Brazil has an "Arc of Deforestation" in which the agricultural boundary advances towards the forest, and the highest deforestation rates in the Amazon are observed. This area corresponds to 500,000 km^2 of land from the eastern regions of Brazilian North and north parts of Center-West, as shown in Fig. 2.6.

To Further Research and Reflect

- Describe the pros and cons of an effective land ownership reform. How can social movements effectively call for agrarian reform to ensure subsistence for the landless population?
- Briefly consider the employment of advanced agribusiness technologies in your country of origin and what Brazilians can learn from it.

2.8 Challenges Facing the Brazilian Economy Today

The Brazilian economy faces various challenges, including recovering from economic downturns, fostering innovation and entrepreneurship, addressing socioeconomic disparities, and navigating complex international trade relationships. The country has been particularly impacted by the mismanagement of the Covid-19 pandemic, which has significantly hindered its growth and development. As Brazil strives to recover from this severe economic downturn, it must also tackle long-standing issues such as income inequality, unemployment, and underinvestment in crucial sectors such as education and healthcare.

Brazil's path to recovery has been slow and uneven, involving significant policy disputes. However, the Brazilian government has demonstrated a praiseworthy understanding of the role of innovation and entrepreneurship in driving economic growth. Despite the challenges, the government has initiated programs like the First Innovative Enterprise (Prime), which hold immense potential for fostering innovation and entrepreneurship. While the effectiveness and long-term viability of these initiatives are still under scrutiny, their existence underscores the government's commitment to ongoing evaluation and potential adjustments.

The Prime concept holds enormous potential for developing innovative mechanisms within industrial enterprises. Its focus on enhancing cost structures could notably improve, particularly in manufacturing products like colorless, odorless, and tasteless noble gases (inert gases). By examining basic value components such as energy costs, equipment maintenance, and wages, Prime aims to reduce expenses, amplify profits, and improve the overall efficiency of industrial enterprises. This approach highlights the potential of innovation in optimizing production processes and boosting competitiveness in the market.

Competition policy and antitrust regulation are not just regulatory measures, but also crucial drivers of innovation, consumer welfare, and fair market competition. Antitrust laws are primarily designed to curb monopolistic practices and maintain a competitive market environment. They oversee mergers, acquisitions, and business activities that could potentially undermine competition. The effective enforcement of these laws is a cornerstone for promoting innovation, as it continually compels companies to enhance their products and services to remain competitive.

The interplay between competition policy and innovation is intricate. Specific collaborations between companies, like joint R&D projects, have the potential to promote innovation. Policymakers must navigate this complexity with caution, balancing the need to fuel competition with the advantages of allowing cooperative endeavors that cultivate technological advancements and economic growth. This calls for a nuanced approach that weighs the long-term benefits of innovation against the immediate necessity to sustain competitive markets.

Competition authorities grapple with novel challenges in regulating large tech platforms exerting significant market power in the digital era. There's an active debate over whether ex post antitrust enforcement or ex ante regulation is more potent in this context. Supporters of ex ante rules contend that they more aptly address the unique traits of digital markets, whereas detractors caution about the potential risks of overregulation. These discussions underscore issues about the spread of "fake news" and misinformation in cybernetic spaces, a trend that is notably prevalent during political campaigns and natural disasters.

Galvão et al. (2023) note that fake news, exacerbated by the rise of social and digital networks, has become an acute issue, particularly during the Covid-19 pandemic in Brazil. This misinformation has compromised the quality of scientific health communication, negatively affecting citizens' lives. Fake news about vaccines and the SARS-CoV-2 virus in Brazil has negatively impacted public health efforts, undermining adherence to vaccination campaigns. Social media platforms such as WhatsApp, Facebook, and Instagram play a crucial role in propagating fake news. This can sabotage global health interventions and erode trust in scientific expertise, particularly in countries like Brazil, where confidence in public institutions is low.

The importance of regulatory frameworks in addressing misinformation and the need for collaborative efforts among various stakeholders to combat the spread of fake news in Brazil is evident. It is also clear that competition policy and antitrust regulation must evolve to address emerging economic realities, all while upholding the principles of free and fair competition. Striking the right balance is crucial for fostering innovation, protecting consumers, and ensuring long-term market economy health.

Brazil's antitrust regime has evolved significantly, transitioning from a strictly controlled economy to a more competitive market environment. Despite this progress, the country confronts challenges in implementing effective competition policies, particularly in merger control and cartel enforcement. Enhancing regulatory frameworks and improving enforcement mechanisms continue to be vital for fostering a fair and competitive economic landscape.

Merger control pertains to the regulation and supervision of mergers and acquisitions, ensuring they do not significantly hinder effective competition within a market. The primary goals of merger control are to forestall the creation of monopolies or dominant firms that could potentially abuse their market power and to safeguard consumer welfare by preserving competitive market structures. Companies engaged in mergers or acquisitions typically need to notify competition authorities before the transaction's completion. These authorities then review the proposed merger to evaluate its prospective influence on competition.

Competition authorities examine factors including market share, concentration levels, potential entry barriers, and the merger's impact on prices, quality, and innovation. Depending on their evaluation, authorities may approve the merger, sanction it with conditions (such as divestitures or behavioral remedies), or disallow the merger if it is deemed to significantly erode competition. Their responsibilities encompass identifying, probing, and penalizing collusive agreements between competitors—the creation of cartels.

Cartels generally involve price-fixing, market-sharing, bid-rigging, and output restriction. These are significant violations of competition law as they damage consumers by raising prices, limiting choices, and suppressing innovation. To remedy these problems, it is essential to enhance regulatory frameworks and bolster enforcement mechanisms to encourage a fair and competitive economic environment in Brazil.

Competition authorities employ various strategies to detect cartels, which include leniency programs (allowing participants to self-report in return for lesser penalties), whistleblowers, market monitoring, and collaboration with other domestic and international enforcement agencies. When a suspected cartel is identified, the authorities carry out in-depth investigations that involve dawn raids, document examinations, interviews, and other evidence-collecting methods. Upon confirmation of a cartel, the involved parties may face stern penalties, such as hefty fines, individual criminal charges, and actions to break down the cartel's operations. These sanctions aim to deter anticompetitive conduct and encourage adherence to competition laws.

Robust merger control and cartel enforcement are essential for fostering Brazil's competitive and dynamic economy. The country can learn from international best practices, such as implementing comprehensive and transparent merger review processes and strengthening penalties and sanctions to deter anticompetitive behavior. Additionally, detection and investigation capabilities can be enhanced through advanced analytical tools and international cooperation. A culture of compliance and ethical business practices can be promoted through education and advocacy programs.

Galvani (2018) contends that socioeconomic disparities in Brazil, particularly those between rich and poor municipalities, present significant challenges to policy implementation and regional development. Despite the counterintuitive findings suggesting poor municipalities outperform wealthier ones in the execution of specific programs, it is crucial to address these disparities to foster inclusive growth. As indicated by Schio Junior (2017), family businesses contribute significantly to Brazil's economy and inclusive growth. However, these entities frequently encounter issues pertaining to succession planning, interference from family members, and conflicts.

To Further Research and Reflect

- Are you in favor of regulating social media platforms? How is your country addressing the issue of "fake news"?
- Describe a successful socioeconomic growth program in your country in any economic sector and provide recommendations for how Brazilian authorities could adapt and implement this program to benefit their economy.

References

CNA—Brazil Agriculture and Livestock Confederation. (2020). *Panorama do Agro*. Available at: https://www.cnabrasil.org.br/cna/panorama-do-agro.

Corak, M. (2016). *Inequality from generation to generation: The United States in comparison* (IZA Discussion Paper No. 9929).

Galvani, F. (2018). Bridging the implementation gap in poor areas: A study of how municipal socio-economic characteristics impact intergovernmental policy implementation. *Social Policy & Administration, 52*, 408–433.

Galvão, T., Noll, P. R. E. S., Silveira, E. A., & Noll, M. (2023). Fake news and misinformation in Brazil: Critical analyses regarding scientific information in pandemic times. *Journal of Human Growth and Development, 33*(3), 493–500.

Hall, P., & Soskice, D. (Eds.). (2001). *Varieties of capitalism: The institutional foundations of comparative advantage*. Oxford University Press. 540 p.

IBGE. (2017). *Censo Agro*. Available at: https://censoagro2017.ibge.gov.br/.

IBGE. (2019). *Pesquisa Nacional por Amostra de Domicílios Contínua—PNAD Contínua*. Available at: https://www.ibge.gov.br/estatisticas/sociais/trabalho/17270-pnad-continua.html?=&t=o-que-e.

IBGE. (2024). *Dashboard of indicators*. Available at: https://www.ibge.gov.br/en/indicators.html.

Maddison, A. (2000). *Brazil economic performance since 1500: A comparative view.* Paper presented at XIII Fórum da Liberdade, 4 April 2000, on Brazil's 500th Anniversary. Instituto de Estudos Empresariais. Porto Alegre, Rio Grande do Sul.

Masalimova, A. R., Khvatova, M. A., Chikeleva, L. S., Zvyagintseva, E. P., Stepanova, V. V., & Melnik, M. V. (2022). Distance learning in higher education during Covid-19. *Frontier in Education, 7*. https://doi.org/10.3389/feduc.2022.822958.

Milanović, B. (2019). *Capitalism, alone: The future of the system that rules the world.* The Belknap Press of Harvard University Press. 304 p.

OECD. (2024). *Brazil*: Overview of the education system (EAG 2023). Retrieved April 30, 2024, from https://gpseducation.oecd.org/CountryProfile?primaryCountry=BRA&treshold=10&topic=EO.

Piketty, T. (2019). *Capital et Idéologie*. Éditions du Seuil. 1232 p.

Radio PUC. (2024). Construção de estradas e agronegócio intensificam o desmatamento na Amazônia. Available at: http://www.radiopuc.vrc.puc-rio.br/cgi/cgilua.exe/sys/start.htm?from%5Finfo%5Findex=10&infoid=254&sid=16.

Schio Junior, L. E. (2017). Understanding the family businesses: A case study from Brazil. Available at: https://dspace.mit.edu/handle/1721.1/111455.

Saez, E., & Zucman, G. (2019). *The Triumph of Injustice: How the Rich Dodge Taxes and How to Make Them Pay.* W. W. Norton & Company. 232 p.

Chapter 3
Sustainable Development in Brazil

3.1 Introduction

The Sustainable Development Goals (SDGs) of the United Nations (UN) prioritize reducing hunger and poverty, and various countries have been implementing these goals through diverse social programs. With more than 170 nations, 2500 non-governmental organizations, and nearly 8000 journalists in attendance, the Earth or Rio Summit of 1992 was one of the largest UN conferences since the publication of "Our Common Future" in 1987. Brazil has been a key participant in international discussions and the pursuit of sustainable development. However, Brazil's adherence to the 2030 Agenda for Sustainable Development to Transform the World—established at the 2015 UN Summit in New York—has been inconsistent.

The coronavirus disease 2019 (Covid-19) pandemic has significantly impacted poverty trends in Brazil and globally, reversing the historic trend of poverty reduction. Over 10% of the population earn less than US $1.90 per day, with the most vulnerable groups being children and women. They are the main beneficiaries of Bolsa Família, a program providing direct income transfers to families in extreme poverty, which caters to approximately 14 million families across the country. Government data from 2019 reveal that for 13.5 of Brazil's 73 million families (accounting for 19% of the total), the elderly are the only source of income. Brazil's economy has struggled to regain its earlier dynamism since the 1980s, which was marked by an import-substitution strategy.

Industrialization has been a critical driver of economic growth and development for many nations in the last century, with various mixes of inward-looking and outward-looking tactics. Once seen as a newly industrialized economy, Brazil is experiencing an early deindustrialization process. Despite being the world's tenth most developed industrialized region, the Southeast area of Brazil is still in the early

G. Masiero, *Brazilian Socio-Economic Dynamics*, Contributions to Economics,
https://doi.org/10.1007/978-3-031-87685-1_3

stages of this process. Industrialization is the best approach to boosting economic growth and development, as demonstrated by the development experiences of other industrialized nations.

Today's economic development and expansion must be sustainable. Since 2015, 169 targets across 17 SDGs have guided substantial progress in promoting sustainable human development. Economic development involves improving the population's standard of living and quality of life, whereas economic growth is a result of a nation's productive activity. Data concerning Brazil's situation suggest that, upon examining 145 of the 169 global SDG targets, there has been no improvement in 88% of the environmental goals. The pandemic severely impacted the government's push towards sustainable progress. A roadmap featuring 25 research priorities was established by the UN (2024b) to foster equity, resilience, sustainability, and progress towards the SDGs.

Achieving the SDGs is no mean feat for any nation. It requires robust international cooperation, predominantly for developing vast regions. Take, for instance, 60% of the Amazon region is in Brazil, with the remaining portion spread across eight other South American countries: Peru, Colombia, Bolivia, Ecuador, French Guiana, Guyana, Suriname, and Venezuela. Since 2008, the Brazilian Development Bank (BNDES) has administered a global fund to conserve the Amazon rainforest. Norway (93.8%), Germany (5.7%), and the Brazilian State Company Petrobras (0.5%) have made the majority of the contributions. The Amazon boasts one of the world's most diverse yet incompletely cataloged collections of flora and fauna. Various ethnic groups, including many that are isolated, inhabit Amazônia.

Brazil is requesting that the UN extend an additional 2.1 million km^2 exclusive economic zone (EEZ) over the Atlantic Ocean to its "Blue Amazon." If this area is added to the current 3.6 million km^2 of EEZ, the "Blue Amazon" would have a total marine area of 5.7 million km^2. This represents a more than 50% expansion of Brazil's sovereign area. In addition, Brazil is appealing to the UN to extend its borders to the limits of the continental shelf, thus increasing the maritime zone to around 4.5 million km^2, which is half of Brazil's land area. To enhance the technological capabilities of its Navy and secure the oceanic borders, Brazil is building five submarines, one of which is nuclear-powered. At the end of 2020, the Brazilian Central Bank (BACEN) successfully introduced PIX to the financial sector as an instant payment method, enabling funds to be transferred between accounts in seconds, anytime.

The country is also creating cyber-physical environments to consolidate its expansive territory, where information and operational technology intersect. Since 1996, Brazil has utilized electronic ballot boxes for national, regional, and local elections. This device is a light, portable, and sturdy microcomputer. Online banking and mobile phones account for approximately 70% of transactions. Smartphones are rapidly surpassing other payment methods as the preferred option for customers of the Brazilian National Financial System, with growth rates nearing 20%.

3.2 Brazil and Global Sustainable Development

The use of advanced technology in Brazilian agricultural activities should take into account current discussions on climate change and sustainability. Since the establishment of the Conference on the Human Environment (UNCHE) in 1972, the creation of the World Commission on Environment and Development (WCED) in 1983, and the Rio Summit in 1992, global attention has been increasingly focused on environmental issues. More recently, the Millennium Development Goals (MDGs) of 2000 and Rio+20 in 2012 have amplified the understanding that environmental conservation and economic development can indeed be mutually reinforcing.

As Barbier and Burgess (2019) point out, the vast majority of low- and middle-income economies are resource-dependent. These countries have a significant concentration of primary products, which account for a large share of their exports and contribute heavily to their economies. This dependency increases stress on the environment and freshwater resources. Brazil is one such country. Accordingly, there are ongoing discussions about how it can best meet the challenge of achieving elevated levels of economic development while simultaneously preserving the environment.

In 1972, the UN Conference on the Human Environment (UNCHE), held in Stockholm, recognized the importance of environmental management. This meeting represented a significant step forward in discussions on sustainable development. As research has progressed, societies worldwide are realizing that environmental issues must be considered in economic planning. Around the same time as this conference, a group of influential businesspeople and politicians met in Rome. This small gathering, mostly comprising scholars from the Massachusetts Institute of Technology (MIT), was later known as the Club of Rome. These scholars published a report, created using mathematical models, to illustrate the potential impact of a rapidly growing world population and finite resource supplies on future generations.

Meadows, Randers, and Meadows (2005) published an updated study, *Limits to Growth: The 30-Year Global Update*, underscoring the impact of humanity on the climate, water quality, and natural resource exhaustion. Both the original and updated studies emphasize that modern industrial society surpasses the sustainable ecological limits of the global environment. Global warming has since become a widely discussed issue in scientific and corporate spheres.

By the late 1970s, following two significant global oil crises, the need to consider the environment and development concurrently grew more apparent. The term "eco-development" emerged to supersede previous studies which focused on "environment and development" and "development without destruction." In 1983, the WCED was founded. This commission published a renowned report, "Our Common Future," in 1987. Gro Harlem Brundtland, the then-Prime Minister of Norway, coordinated the research that formed the basis for this final report. The Commission underscored the connection between poverty alleviation, environmental protection, and social equity via sustainable economic growth.

These themes were intensely discussed at the successive UN Conference on Environment and Development (UNCED). The largest UN Conference, the Earth Summit or Rio Summit, was held in 1992. It brought together over 170 governments, 2500 non-governmental organizations, and 8000 journalists. The conference aimed to discuss and create awareness about the principles and actions needed to ensure sustainable development. Its main outcome was the promulgation of Agenda 21, which highlighted the importance of each country's engagement at both local and global levels to find solutions for socio-environmental problems. Agenda 21 comprises 40 chapters, split into 4 main sections. Since the 1992 Rio Summit, there has been increased pressure on governments from local authorities to develop policies that would make Agenda 21 a feasible reality.

In 2000, the UN, building upon its previous conferences and summits, established the MDGs—a declaration urging a 15-year global effort to reduce extreme poverty. According to the UN (2021a), these goals aim to reduce child mortality, enhance maternal health, and combat HIV/AIDS, malaria, and other diseases. Moreover, the goals strove to uphold environmental sustainability, establish global partnerships for development, seek methods to eradicate extreme poverty and hunger, and achieve universal primary education.

In 2012, another significant summit, Rio+20, was organized in Rio de Janeiro to assess the progress made towards building a more eco-friendly society over the past two decades. This summit reviewed the advancements and implementation challenges of Agenda 21, proposing further actions to ensure that the original objectives were achieved. Brazil, which chaired the meeting, led discussions emphasizing the principle of non-regression. This principle refers to the non-acceptance of any setbacks to previously assumed international concepts and commitments.

In Brazil, the discussions at the Rio+20 enhanced the link between the broad objectives encapsulated in the concept of sustainable development and the nation's economic development plans. To enhance and spread the concept of a "green economy," Brazil proposed adopting the concept of an "inclusive green economy." This emphasized the significance of the social pillar (over the economic and environmental pillars) at the Rio+20 summit.

The outcomes of these, as well as other UN conferences and summits, have significantly underscored and driven the implementation of environmental sustainability principles by public and private businesses globally. These principles can be encapsulated as follows: preventative measures are more effective than resolving problems post-occurrence, and long-term environmental and economic costs should be accounted for in financial systems. The quality of economic, social, and environmental factors should be prioritized over their quantity, and both nature and the rights of future generations must be considered and respected.

Sustainability metrics, indices, or indicators of sustainable development that incorporate these principles have been established. These include the Daly Rules, Ecological Footprint Analysis, Global Reporting Initiative, and Life Cycle

Assessment (LCA). Boulanger (2008) proposes that indices, which compete with and complement the GNP as an indicator of development, should be utilized. They should consider the domains or pillars (economy, society, and environment), the resources and productive assets (manufactured, natural, human, and social capital), human well-being (needs, capabilities), and norms (efficiency, fairness, and prudence).

New indicators for sustainability or happiness, including the politically controversial Gross Domestic Happiness (GDH) index, were constitutionally enacted in 2008 by the Bhutanese government. These are not universally accepted. Despite this, UN Conferences have continued to promote discussions on the creation of eco-friendly societies. The UN (2021b) states that its Commission for Social Development in 2015 recognized the need to strengthen the social aspect of sustainable development and suggested that member states enhance policy coherence.

Within social sectors, such as methods to enhance access to high-quality education, primary healthcare, safe drinking water, sanitation, and procedures specific to groups like youth, elderly, people with disabilities, and indigenous peoples, policies that support employment, decent work, and social inclusion have been strongly advocated. These policies combine economic and environmental viewpoints into social policymaking and integrate social policy perspectives into broader, more complex policymaking processes.

The UN Summit in New York in 2015 established *The 2030 Agenda for Sustainable Development*, to transform the world. Building on the MDGs, a list of 17 SDGs with 169 associated targets became the focus of sustainable development policies for governments. These ambitious 17 goals are depicted in Fig. 3.1. Countries around the world, including Brazil, are actively implementing measures to achieve these goals, despite varied progress and occasional setbacks.

Fig. 3.1 The SDGs of the agenda 2030. Source: United Nations (2024b)

To Further Research and Reflect

- Describe three eco-friendly measures your country is implementing and consider the feasibility of their implementation in Brazil.
- Select at least one SDG that has yet to be accomplished and discuss how your national government allocates resources to finance the activities necessary to reach the goal in your territory by 2030.

3.3 Poverty in the World and Brazil

What is poverty? Numerous institutions have strived to formulate more precise definitions and metrics to encompass this concept. Simply put, poverty is the lack of access to essential services, such as basic sanitation, healthcare, education, and electricity, among others. It also pertains to a shortage of consumer goods, particularly food, and basic material possessions required to sustain life. This restricted access is typically associated with an individual's or household's income. Beyond this basic definition, various interpretations emphasize certain aspects and characteristics.

For example, the World Bank (2021) uses a set of monetary values to identify individuals living in poverty or extreme poverty. These values, expressed in dollars, are regularly adjusted in response to the international economic climate and the purchasing power evident in the world's poorest countries. The percentage of the population living below this estimated monetary threshold is designated as being under the poverty line.

Living on less than US $1.90 a day is considered extreme poverty. According to the World Bank (2021), it was estimated that 35.9% of the population lived below the poverty line in 1990. However, by 2017, this figure had dropped to 9.2%. When calculated using purchasing power parity at US $1.90 a day, the number of impoverished individuals was estimated to be about 1.912 billion in 1990, falling to 689 million by 2017. Unfortunately, this decreasing trend has reversed due to the impact of the Covid-19 pandemic.

For the UN, daily per capita income and access to essential services are determinants of poverty, hunger, malnutrition, discrimination, and social exclusion. Furthermore, poverty can be defined as either absolute or relative. Absolute poverty is determined by a scarcity of resources and is calculated based on objective parameters, such as lack of income. On the other hand, relative poverty involves comparing the living standards of individuals, families, or groups (including countries), in relation to how income distribution occurs within society.

As reported by the UN (2021a), in 2018, four out of five individuals living below the international poverty line resided in rural regions. Children constitute half of this impoverished population. In many regions, a significant majority of individuals living in poverty are women. Seventy percent of the world's impoverished, aged 15 and above, have no primary education. The majority are residents of Sub-Saharan

Africa, in countries such as Tanzania, Ethiopia, Madagascar, Nigeria, and the Democratic Republic of the Congo.

Covid-19 has pushed many people back into extreme poverty in urban areas, where lockdowns and mobility restrictions have been enforced. Workers involved in informal services have been significantly impacted. In response, many countries have deployed emergency cash and in-kind rescue packages, primarily focused on the pandemic's initial months. The human and economic toll resulting from the extended pandemic is expected to persist until 2030, the target year for reducing the global absolute poverty rate to below 3%.

Pandemics and various structural economic and social issues significantly hinder efforts to reduce poverty. For instance, focusing on Brazil, the abolition of slavery served to exacerbate the existing social inequalities within the newly formed nation by leaving freed slaves to fend for themselves, without any state support. Additionally, Brazil has always been heavily dependent on foreign aid and began its modernization process quite late. This led to the exclusion of a large portion of the population, subsequently exacerbating social and income inequalities.

One of the reasons for poverty in Brazil is urbanization. A sharp rise in urbanization corresponded with the development of rural areas, gaining momentum in the 1970s and 1980s. Many migrants to the cities, due to their lack of professional training, became underemployed or unemployed. Some of these migrants also settled in less expensive houses on the city outskirts. The number of people living in poverty typically increases significantly during national and international economic crises, with most of these individuals residing in Brazil's urban centers. However, in Brazilian favelas, there may also be a decrease in the availability of essential urban services, which is a common occurrence.

The registered poverty rates in Brazil have significantly dropped since the 1970s. From 1970 to the 2000s, Brazil's poverty rate fell from 68 to 25% of the population. The most substantial decrease, however, has happened since 2003. The social inclusion and income transfer programs initially began at the end of the 1990s and were unified from 2003 onwards with the establishment of the Bolsa Família. These initiatives are integral reasons for this meaningful progress.

As a direct income transfer program, this initiative primarily targets families living in poverty and extreme poverty to help them break the cycle of vulnerability. Its key objectives are to ensure access to food, education, and health services for these families. As noted by Baroni et al. (2021), the program assists families with a per capita income of approximately US $18 per month. For pregnant women or children up to 17 years old, the financial aid may vary up to a maximum of US $35.

Despite the existence of income transfer programs, the Covid-19 pandemic has accentuated profound inequalities and escalated unemployment nationwide. Over a quarter of Brazil's total population was living on less than US $5.5 a day. In response to the crisis, an Emergency Cash Transfer Program (Auxilio Emergencial) was implemented to provide financial assistance to the most vulnerable sectors of the populace. Offering amounts ranging from US $120 to US $240, specifically for single mothers, this temporary program effectively reduced extreme poverty levels. However, the situation worsened post-pandemic due to deepening social inequalities and a drastic income reduction for the poorest 40% of the population.

The poverty line is adopted to identify the population living in poverty and extreme poverty in Brazil, aligned with the metric used by the World Bank. In current values, an individual subsisting on less than US $90 per month is considered poor in Brazil. Conversely, extreme poverty is characterized as living on less than US $30 per month, encompassing roughly 6.7% of Brazilians, equating to almost 14 million people.

Despite the emergency aid rescue package, a segment of the "invisible" population did not receive financial aid, owing to their absence in the federal government's databases of transfer programs such as the Unified Registry. The poorest states in Brazil are predominantly found in the northern and northeastern regions, based on data from the Atlas of Human Development in Brazil, which collates data from the National Household Sample Survey (PNAD). Maranhão has the highest poverty rate, with 30% of its population living in poverty.

Historically, the concentration of poverty in Brazil is primarily found in its interior and on the outskirts of its large coastal urban centers. By contrast, the state with the least concentration of poverty is Santa Catarina, located in the South region, with less than 3% of its population living below the necessary subsistence minimum. During the pandemic, poverty has more severely impacted families with children and older adults. However, contradicting common perceptions, research suggests that before the pandemic, unemployment was less prevalent among the elderly than the youth, with older people providing economic support for millions of families (Nery et al., 2018).

To Further Research and Reflect

- Given that the United Nations' first Sustainable Development Goal (SDG) is to end poverty globally by 2030, what are at least three specific policies that the public and private sectors should implement to achieve this critical objective?
- How does your country ensure social protection for older adults and the most economically vulnerable families? Can you highlight strategies or programs offering valuable insights and lessons for Brazil to enhance its social protection initiatives?

3.4 Brazilian Economic Development Through Industrialization?

In 2009, 2013, 2019, and 2021, *The Economist* dedicated special issues to striking stages of Brazil's economic performance—these issues featuring noteworthy front cover pages. These covers serve to summarize significant recent historical events. Initially, Brazil is portrayed as experiencing exponential growth, taking off at an impressive pace. However, subsequent covers reflect trends from the final first decade of this century. They depict Brazil weighed down in an escalating economic crisis, thereby reversing its trajectory as an economic powerhouse.

This trend has even been characterized as a national threat. By 2021, a special report from *The Economist* mused upon "Brazil's dismal decade," highlighting that few countries have spiraled economically as rapidly as Brazil has. The socioeconomic disparities have only grown larger.

In the first decade of the 2000s, Brazil experienced a stable macroeconomic environment, marked by fiscal balance, consistent inflation, and a trade surplus. High earnings were driven by agricultural and mineral commodities, owing to favorable prices stimulated by China's robust demand in the trade sector. Brazil then invested in infrastructure projects related to renewable resources, aiming to modernize the country's energy matrix, and implemented social inclusion programs to expand credit and raise the minimum wage. These policies contributed to an economic path characterized by dynamism.

Traditionally, Brazil has been an exporter of low-value-added commodities, simultaneously importing industrialized products. As per the OECD (2021), Brazil's foremost exports in 2019 comprised soybeans, of which it is the world's preeminent exporter, petroleum, iron, corn, and sulfate chemical wood pulp. The primary purchasers of these exports were China, the USA, Argentina, the Netherlands, and Japan. As for top imports, these included refined petroleum, vehicle parts, crude petroleum, integrated circuits, and pesticides, sourced primarily from China, the USA, Germany, Argentina, and South Korea.

Since the beginning of the nineteenth century, industries have been concentrated in countries like the USA, Canada, Japan, and various European nations, notably the UK, Germany, Italy, Belgium, and France. However, starting in 1950, industrialization expanded across the globe. Countries that underwent industrialization after the 1950s are known for different classifications. The taxonomy of developed and underdeveloped was modified to less developed countries and newly industrialized countries, and more recently, the latter are referred to as emerging economies.

Gabriel et al. (2020) posit that the manufacturing industry is viewed as the primary sector of tradable goods that promotes higher real per capita income growth in developing countries. They suggest that the further a country is from the world's technological frontier, the more positive the impact of a competitive real exchange rate on income growth becomes. In such instances, the manufacturing production multiplier on the total economy often surpasses that of other sectors.

Economists concur that industrializing a country is an exceedingly effective method for augmenting income and enhancing well-being. Nevertheless, some burgeoning countries, like Brazil, are starting to experience the deindustrialization of their economies. A large part of this novel phenomenon is commonly credited to another one: China's progressively rapid industrialization.

Cano (2008) provides compelling evidence for the significant dismantling of the industrial sector in Brazil. In the 1980s, manufacturing comprised 33% of gross domestic product (GDP); today, it represents 16%. The proportion of manufactured goods in total exports peaked at 59%; it currently hovers around 40%. In this unfavorable context, private investment has been inadequate. National authorities are faced with the task of managing exchange rates, increasing tariffs, monitoring the inflow of dollars into the domestic market, reducing interest rates, and augmenting public investment.

Although Brazilian livestock and agriculture constitute 26% of Brazil's exports, their progress yields fewer spillovers than the industrial sector. While the agricultural machinery sector has advanced, it has not led to job increases or sparked significant growth in the rest of the economy. Mining presents even fewer spillovers due to its minimal backward linkage effects. The forward results from extraction are also limited and would only increase if these activities were connected to processing in a metallurgical plant. When minerals are exported without processing, as is often the case in Brazil, job creation is not promoted. Petroleum is a similar example whereby unless extraction is paired with petrochemical processing plants, job generation for the local economy remains restricted.

Though Brazil boasted the eighth-largest industrial park, its industrialization was hampered by a foreign debt crisis in the 1980s. This period saw rampant hyperinflation, an economic opening, and a lackluster performance in the 1990s. After economic stabilization was achieved through the Real Plan, high interest rates coupled with an overvalued exchange rate escalated public debt and stifled investment. This resulted in halted industrial progress in numerous sectors. Concurrently, China's swift industrialization had a profound impact on production processes in almost every country worldwide, notably those not yet industrialized or unable to compete with China's labor costs, like Brazil.

Most economists and policymakers believe that "latecomer" developing countries have two alternative strategies to modernize their economies: inward-looking and outward-looking. In the first scenario, the emphasis is on import substitution, which implies that economies focus on producing imported goods domestically. Through this approach, countries can conserve foreign exchange and eventually become exporters of manufactured products, once they master the production process.

Governments may impose measures to regulate domestic markets, including tariffs, quotas, and subsidies to protect and foster "infant industries." In the latter case, the emphasis is on an outward-looking strategy stressing resource allocation to kindle export-oriented industries. Policies are not biased towards production-oriented for either domestic or foreign markets, and international markets determine prices. Both approaches have their pros and cons.

Since the beginning of the last century, particularly after World War II, many nations have started to look for strategies to industrialize their economies instead of exploiting primary commodities and natural resources. One benefit of adopting industrialization policies is that a consumer market for industrial products already exists. Domestic industries replace imported goods, and it is often easier to protect domestic markets than negotiate with developed countries to secure lower trade barriers.

Moreover, this policy bolsters incentives for multinational companies to establish their factories in less developed countries as a measure to counter high tariffs, thus fostering local job creation. However, there are disadvantages, which include the lack of incentive to enhance efficiency due to protection from foreign competition, the absence of economies of scale and scope, and insufficient resources to develop highly value-added technologies and products. Furthermore, it poses a challenge for any government to discern which sectors of the economy should be promoted and the duration of such promotion.

Wade (2003) explains that success in Asian countries with small domestic markets was driven by "governing markets" and outward-looking development strategies. Many countries implemented import-substitution policies to lessen their reliance on imports. However, only a few, such as the so-called Asian Tigers—South Korea, Taiwan, and the city-states of Singapore and Hong Kong—were prosperous. These governments promoted labor-intensive sectors, and macroeconomic balancing policies further assisted these nations in developing other more capital-intensive industries.

Outward-looking strategies involve keeping markets open and offering subsidies to successful exporters, which may include credit guarantees and infrastructure facilities. Companies continue to exploit their long-term comparative advantages to enhance their productivity through methods such as learning by doing and "reverse engineering" in the global market competition. Reverse engineering is a process that deconstructs a product to comprehend its functions, intending to duplicate or improve it in production.

Advocates of these policies firmly believe that competing in international markets fosters efficiency and modernization in companies. Additionally, by accessing global markets, companies can secure economies of scale by selling their products in larger markets. These proponents also highlight that this strategy promotes the transfer of more advanced technology. However, developed nations typically protect their established, more competitive industries and erect barriers to technology transfer.

In the nineteenth century, the primary economic activity in Brazil was the production and export of coffee. This plant, originally from Asia, served as the driving force of the economy in imperial times and was crucial for the birth of the nation's industrial economy in the early twentieth century. Coffee facilitated capital accumulation in the Southeast, favoring significant private investments in the then-budding industrial sector. Brazilian industrialization reached its peak in the 1970s, having started half a century earlier, primarily in the Southeast region.

The Southeast region boasts a large industrial park, primarily located in São Paulo. Although this region is South America's most industrialized, it still relies heavily on the exportation of its raw materials. São Paulo produces most of the sugarcane in the country, making it the largest exporter of sugar worldwide and the second-largest producer and exporter of ethanol, surpassed only by the USA. In the neighboring state of Minas Gerais, the world's largest mining company, Vale, paves the way for mineral exports. Meanwhile, Rio de Janeiro stands as the country's top oil-producing state, closely followed by Espírito Santo, with the Brazilian oil company Petrobras leading investment and petroleum development in both states.

To Further Research and Reflect

- Considering the objectives of employment generation and improving income distribution, what would be the best strategies for less developed countries to ignite economic growth and accelerate it faster than others to catch up with developed countries?
- Consider at least two reasons a nation might want to implement an inward or an outward strategy to develop itself. What strategies have been implemented in your country, and what industries can fuel economic growth in a large country such as Brazil?

3.5 Brazilian Progress Towards SDGs

Despite the capacity of many countries to develop themselves through industrialization, the depletion of natural resources and pollution have emerged as severe problems to address. Sustainable development has become a central issue in climate change negotiations. Since 1990, most countries have engaged in debates and implemented measures to combat or mitigate climate change, particularly following the signing of the Kyoto Protocol in 1997 and the Paris Agreement in 2015.

Although countries concur on the scientific evidence supporting climate change, they differ in their opinions regarding which countries are primarily responsible—developed or developing—and on how to establish emission-reduction targets. The USA's wavering dedication to the Paris Agreement has stoked significant concerns. Many experts remain concerned, anticipating disastrous implications tied to climate change. They predict dramatic heatwaves and floods in the approaching years, underscoring the imperative of global cooperation and action.

To address the challenges of climate change, the adoption of the 2030 Agenda for Sustainable Development was orchestrated. Since 2015, governments and organizations worldwide have striven to implement 17 goals along with their 169 targets. The 2030 Agenda embodies hope, offering a chance for alignment and the creation of a minimal consensus towards economic growth and development. It stands as a testament to our collective commitment to a sustainable future. However, it is important to note that the 2030 Agenda is goal-setting, not a rule-making mechanism.

While the 2030 Agenda for Sustainable Development represents a significant stride towards global sustainability, it is not without its critics. Some argue that it does not adequately address urgent environmental issues or interrogate the production and distribution of wealth. Additionally, it does not openly critique nations' dependence on economic growth through the exploitation of national resources. Notably, the 2030 Agenda does not suggest specific alterations to multilateral decision-making or governance, leaving nation-states individually accountable for achieving their targets.

Multilevel governments must monitor progress in the implementation of the 2030 Agenda's goals across different economic sectors, requiring interagency coordination and accurate data. These actions become even more complex and essential to national coordination in a large and diverse territory like Brazil. Brazil has made significant strides since 2016, facing unique challenges and opportunities. A National Commission has served as a crucial institutional coordination mechanism for reviewing and addressing the SDGs within Brazil. The Commission has scrutinized the SDGs' goals in line with Brazilian realities; established national priorities; analyzed legislation, plans, and projects in light of the SDG goals; and mapped public policies.

To implement the 2030 Agenda across the 5565 municipalities of Brazil, the Commission stresses the importance of engaging the private sector, academia, and civil society. Indeed, the immense challenge lies in integrating and mobilizing various government and economic sectors along with social agents towards the recognition of the SDGs and the necessary steps required for their achievement. The National Commission, which is comprised of 32 high-level representatives from federal government ministries, state governments, and the private sector, coordinates initiatives with society and other branches of government. This Commission, established in 2016, was dissolved by Presidential Decree 9.759 in April 2019, and its responsibilities were subsequently delegated to different government institutions. Despite these changes, both government and civil society initiatives continue to endorse the planning and dissemination of the SDGs in Brazil. Furthermore, the Civil Society Working Group for the 2030 Agenda (2020) persists in monitoring the progress of Brazil's SDGs.

The fourth report from the group draws attention to the devastating impact of the Covid-19 pandemic and the actions of former President Jair Bolsonaro. Since taking office in 2019, the President has not made progress on the 2030 Agenda. This edition is based on the analysis of 145 out of the 169 global SDG targets. It concludes that there has been no progress made in 88% of environmental goals. More than one-third of these goals are regressing; another one-third are either threatened or stagnant, and 17% lack data for evaluation.

The report reveals a 35% increase in deforestation in the Amazon region from June 2019 to June 2020, along with a 30% rise in the tropical Atlantic Forest. Despite preservation efforts, encroachments have resulted in approximately 75% of this area getting depleted. The Civil Society Working Group for the 2030 Agenda (2020:8) assessed the first of the 17 SDGs for Brazil and concluded, "Brazil was already failing to meet targets for poverty eradication—in the last 5 years, the country has experienced setbacks or a lack of information in virtually all targets of this SDG."

This situation has been exacerbated by the Covid-19 pandemic. The mishandling of the crisis has amplified ongoing economic and social inequality in Brazil. Among the significant issues, grand corruption scandals involving Brazilian elites are frequently cited as a primary concern. A report from Transparência Internacional (2021) reveals that Brazil ranked 106th out of 180 nations in 2019. It emphasizes that there have been critical regressions in the country's battle against corruption, decrying the manipulation and loss of independence of its primary anti-corruption organizations. The report also notes setbacks within the judiciary, Congress, and investigative journalism sectors, which obstruct further advancement in corruption prevention.

Since 2014, an extensive investigation called "Car Wash" led by the Federal Police has uncovered numerous criminal activities conducted by senior politicians and wealthy entrepreneurs in Brazil. This marked the first instance in Brazilian history when wealthy and upper-echelon politicians faced prosecution, were found guilty, and were incarcerated (although many of them did not remain imprisoned for extended periods). However, by the end of 2020, with President Bolsonaro and his family members (who are also traditional politicians from Rio de Janeiro) under investigation, the efforts of prosecutors and the federal police were discontinued.

Two decades after the initial World Summit in Rio de Janeiro—the ECO-92—most of the sustainable development targets negotiated with previous Brazilian governments in multilateral forums have recently been rescinded. The Covid-19 pandemic has further underscored the unsustainability of Brazil's long-standing development trajectory. As pointed out by Seixas et al. (2020), the country appears to be moving in a direction contrary to the future envisaged by the 2030 Agenda.

To Further Research and Reflect

- Select three SDGs and contrast the measures taken by your nation and the Brazilian government, adding your comments about the degree to which the goals were accomplished.
- Check the Research Roadmap for Covid-19 (UN, 2024a) and select 3 of the 25 research priorities for which you would like to see researchers in your country partner with Brazilian counterparts.

3.6 The Amazon Fund: A Brazilian or an International Issue?

Even with some setbacks, awareness of sustainable development is increasing. The UN report "Our Common Future," published in 1987, defines sustainable development as a strategy "that meets the needs of the present without compromising the ability of future generations to meet their own needs." Five years later, in 1992, more than 100 heads of state convened for the first international Earth Summit in Rio de Janeiro. The summit's outcome was the formal recognition of the Convention on Climate Change and Biological Diversity.

The leaders endorsed the Rio Declaration and the Forest Principles, adopting Agenda 21 to achieve sustainable development in the twenty-first century. Section I of this agenda established social and economic dimensions. It called for international cooperation to accelerate sustainable development in developing nations, combat poverty, and alter consumption patterns. It also emphasized demographic dynamism and sustainability, the protection and promotion of human health, and the integration of environmental considerations into decision-making processes.

In subsequent decades, sustainable development emerged as a significant goal for most nations. The SDGs came into existence in 2015, calling for universal action aimed at eradicating poverty, protecting the planet, and ensuring peace and prosperity for all by 2030. However, these discussions and reports have faced substantial criticism for their top-down approach and lack of joint preparation by key stakeholders. Redclift (2005) contends that the concept of sustainable development is an oxymoron due to the ambiguity of the assumptions and conclusions found in these discourses.

Complex environmental and social issues do not foster widespread consensus. However, a fundamental agreement on reducing emissions from deforestation and forest degradation appears to have placed the world's largest forest—the Amazon—under the scrutiny of several organizations. Multilateral agencies, national governments, various corporations, and numerous non-governmental organizations (NGOs) have been steering the region's development from an exploratory to a more sustainable practice. In this context, the Amazon Fund was initiated and can be considered a tool for establishing an equitable and integrated society.

The Amazon rainforest, also known as Amazônia, is the world's largest untouched land territory. It spans 7 million km^2, out of which 5.5 million km^2 (2.1 million square miles) comprises the rainforest in Northern Brazil. Although 60% of the Amazon rainforest resides in Brazil, it also spans eight other South American countries: Peru, Colombia, Bolivia, Ecuador, French Guiana, Guyana, Suriname, and Venezuela.

Ten percent of global greenhouse gas emissions result from the deforestation of tropical forests, which store over 100 billion tons of carbon. This important public good warrants our preservation efforts. Approximately 60% of these emissions, predominantly in the Brazilian Legal Amazon, arise from deforestation and associated burning for large-scale agriculture, extensive low-productivity cattle ranching, human settlement expansion, mining, pig iron production, and unsustainable logging.

These fossil fuel-based development activities tend to be more profitable for producers, at least in the short term, than forest preservation. The driving force behind deforestation is economics, while preservation (for others and for the "future generations to meet their own needs") is a political matter. How can the international community and national authorities address this issue?

According to Fundo Amazônia (2024), the Amazon Fund attracts non-reimbursable investments intended to protect the Amazon biome. Established in 2008, the Amazon Fund (AF) is a Brazilian initiative governed by the BNDES, aiming to support initiatives to Reduce Emissions from Deforestation and Forest Degradation (REDD+). The most contentious issues throughout AF's years of operation have revolved around its governance, allocation of funds, and the evaluation and monitoring of concerns, as gleaned from newspapers, TV interviews, and social media.

The AF was established on August 1, 2008, by Brazilian presidential decree 6.527. Since then, the regulations concerning endowments have been revised by the decrees of 2016, 2019, 2020, and 2023. While the fund has been the subject of amiable discussions in mainstream media, little of it has been systematically organized by either foreign or domestic researchers. As of 2021, the Government of Norway has been the most significant contributor, accounting for roughly 94% of all donations. It has been followed by the Federal Republic of Germany (5%) and the Brazilian corporation Petrobras (0.5%) as the major donors.

Projects in the region, sponsored by the Fund, should follow the guidelines of a national action plan. These guidelines cover the management of public forests, environmental control, monitoring, inspection, sustainable forest management, and the promotion of economic activities arising from the sustainable use of forests. Moreover, they also address the issues of territorial planning, land-title regularization, conservation and sustainable utilization of biodiversity, and restoration of deforested areas.

All sponsored projects must comply with both the National and the Fund's guidelines, demonstrating their contribution to reducing deforestation and degradation. The AF has funded 102 projects as of 2021, courtesy of over US $1.3 billion in donations. The governmental sector originated most of these projects (61%), while the private sector accounted for 38%, and nations outside the Amazon region constituted 1% (Fundo Amazônia, 2024). The majority of projects and resources have been approved for execution by regional states, with NGOs coming next in line.

Overall, a significant portion of the project has been dedicated to the borders of indigenous lands (28 projects), conservation units (28), land registration (19), settlements (16), and combatting illegal fires and burns (6). The project's collaboration with other government measures helps keep deforestation rates in the Brazilian Amazon under control (Fig. 3.2). However, these measures are insufficient for sparking sustainable economic development across such an extensive territory. Recent data released by mainstream media indicate that Amazon deforestation has risen over the past 2 years.

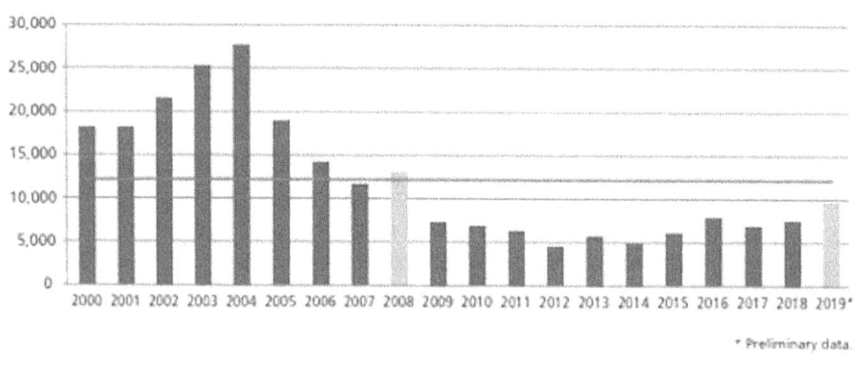

Fig. 3.2 Annual deforestation rates in the Brazilian Amazon (km²/year). Source: Amazon Fund (2020)

To Further Research and Reflect

- The logic of deforestation in the Amazon Forest or the Cerrado region is economical, and preservation is political. How can the international community and Brazilian national authorities solve this apparent contradiction?
- What is your country doing to preserve the forests, and what are your suggestions for expanding the Amazon Fund?

3.7 The Blue Amazon: Brazil Wants to Be Bigger

Amid the Sea of Japan, two seemingly small islets sit almost equidistant between Japan and Korea. As reported by Genova (2018), South Koreans view a trip to these minute islands, the Dokdo Islands, as a civic duty. The area of these islands is no larger than that of Grand Central Terminal in downtown Manhattan, New York. These land masses, also known as the Liancourt Rocks, Dokdo, or Takeshima Islands, depending on who is asserting ownership, have been at the heart of a diplomatic dispute between Japan and Korea for over 300 years.

Long-standing conflicts are also prevalent in South America. For instance, Argentina and the UK disputed over the Malvinas or Falkland Islands in 1982. Another military conflict occurred between Ecuador and Peru in 1995 to gain control over the Cordillera del Cóndor border area. In 2023, the ongoing territorial dispute over the Essequibo region escalated, with Venezuela laying claim to this area governed by Guyana. This dispute dates back over a century. Since 2004, Brazil has been diplomatically demanding the expansion of its EEZ in the Atlantic Ocean.

The UN has implemented a comprehensive legal framework for territorial disputes, acknowledging the territorial sea, which stretches up to 12 nautical miles (22 km) from the coast. Within this sea section, the coastal state primarily exercises full dominion over the water mass, the overhead airspace, and the underlying bed and subsoil. A coastal state may exercise the requisite control to halt or suppress violations of its customs, fiscal, immigration, and sanitary laws and regulations within its territory or territorial sea in the immediately following 12 miles, known as a contiguous zone. However, the UN may grant recognition to an EEZ extending up to 200 nautical miles (370 km), originating from the baselines agreed upon by a coastal state. This legal framework, serving as the cornerstone of Brazil's appeal to enlarge its EEZ, is a vital component to comprehend within the sphere of territorial disputes.

The potential of the continental shelf, encompassing the submerged areas adjacent to the territorial sea, is immense. It includes the bed and subsoil of the submarine areas that extend beyond its territorial sea. States including Brazil are competing for sovereignty over their continental shelf to harness the vast resources in its waters, soil, and subsoil. Recent discoveries of deep-water oil on Brazil's coastline have merely scratched the surface of its potential. Other studies indicate the presence of economically valuable metals such as nickel, copper, cobalt, and manganese at great depths, around 4000 m. This could potentially revolutionize Brazil's economy, promising a bright future.

In the EEZs, any state is permitted navigation and overflight rights and can also lay submarine cables and pipelines. Within these zones, the coastal state holds sovereign rights for exploration, exploitation, conservation, and management of the natural resources, whether living or non-living, found in the waters overlying the seabed and its subsoil. The EEZ can be utilized for economic purposes such as water and wind energy production. Additionally, the coastal state has jurisdiction regarding the placement and use of artificial islands, installations, and structures, in addition to marine scientific research and the protection and preservation of the marine environment. Figure 3.3 depicts the three areas of the Blue Amazon: Brazil's coastal sovereign demarcations.

The maritime territory of Brazil encompasses the marine areas under its sovereignty or jurisdiction, which includes inland waters, the territorial sea, the contiguous zone, the EEZ, and the continental shelf. The country is developing an advanced

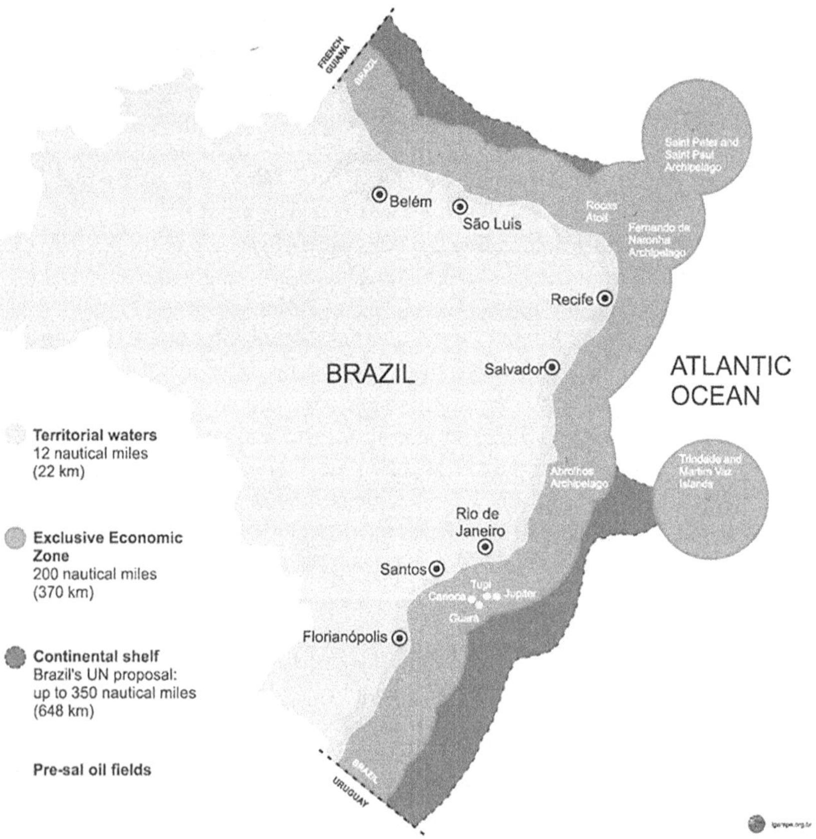

Fig. 3.3 Brazil's Blue Amazon. Source: Thompson and Muggah (2015)

surveillance system to monitor the Blue Amazon, supporting its claims. As reported by Thompson and Muggah in 2015, the objective of this Blue Amazon Management System is to utilize a combination of satellites, radar, drones, naval vessels, and submarines for the surveillance of its extensive coastline, which spans over 4600 miles.

With a coastline of 7400 km, Brazil has jurisdiction over 3.5 million km^2 of maritime space. Since 2004, Brazil has petitioned the UN Commission on the Limits of the Continental Shelf (CLCS) to expand its EEZ by an additional 2 million km^2. This area encompasses the Brazilian territorial sea (12 miles), in addition to the EEZ (188 miles) and the continental shelf, also known as the "Blue Amazon" due to its evident wealth. Clearly, the name emphasizes the idea that this oceanic territory is akin to the Amazon Forest.

Brazil is seeking a new outer limit for its continental shelf in five areas: the Amazon Cone, the Northern Brazilian Chain, the Vitória and Trindade Chains, the São Paulo Plateau, and the South Continental Margin. A study concerning the Outer Limit of the Brazilian Continental Shelf was submitted to the UN, calling for an additional 2.1 million km^2 to be added to Brazilian territory. Incorporating this area into the existing 3.6 million km^2 of the EEZ, the "Blue Amazon" would span a maritime area of 5.7 million km^2. In essence, Brazil is advocating for an upward expansion of its national territory by over 50%.

The pre-salt reserves are situated within the "Blue Amazon." From these reserves, 85% of oil and 75% of natural gas are extracted. Additionally, this territory provides 45% of the fish harvested in Brazil. Other natural resources and a rich biodiversity present in the area remain unexplored. In 2019, Brazil had a portion of its claim approved by the UN, which resulted in the incorporation of an extra 170,000 km^2 into the Brazilian continental shelf located in the southern region.

The country is still awaiting the UN's analysis of requests from the equatorial and eastern/meridional regions. As noted in the *Dossiê Amazônia Azul*, Castro et al. (2017) observe that despite the vast potential of resources in the "Blue Amazon," the understanding of Brazilians regarding their sea and its resources remains in its infancy. While the Brazilian population may not view this territory as strategic, the Brazilian Navy holds a different perspective. Since 1989, the Navy has pioneered the development of the Continental Shelf Survey Plan to assess the potential of living and non-living resources in marine areas under national jurisdiction and adjacent spaces.

The Navy is the main advocate for expanding Brazilian maritime territory in the "Blue Amazon." To safeguard both the current and newly enlarged territories, the Navy requests access to first-generation ships and robust floating, air, and amphibious means in adequate quantities. According to Marinha do Brasil (2021) this will ensure a continuous naval presence in the "Blue Amazon." In addition to modernizing its fleet, the Brazilian Navy has been implementing the Submarine Development Program (Prosub) since 2011. This program involves the construction of five submarines, including one nuclear-powered. It is the most comprehensive military technology development program undertaken by the Brazilian Armed Forces.

To Further Research and Reflect

- Consider the advantages and disadvantages of the imminent expansion of the Brazilian maritime territory under the aegis of three significant aspects: (1) economic, (2) scientific, and (3) sovereignty.
- What are your country's territorial disputes, and why has the UN not been able to deliberate on the rights asserted by Asian countries over small islands? Consider the case of the Dokdo or Takeshima Islands.

3.8 Digitalizing the Country: Some Initiatives

What is the digital economy? It is a realm in which digital platforms such as Amazon, Uber, Alibaba, and Airbnb have not merely revolutionized business models, they have become their very essence. These platforms—along with social media giants like Facebook, Twitter (now X), Instagram, and LinkedIn—have transformed the way we connect and interact. They are data-driven entities that use technology to create virtual marketplaces, facilitating peer-to-peer interactions on a global scale. Moreover, they have harnessed the power of economies of scale and built trust among strangers.

The digital revolution's core consists of infrastructures like 5G networks, cybersecurity measures, data protection protocols, artificial intelligence, and the Internet, powering the vital activities of the digital economy. A few years ago, digitization primarily involved transforming mechanical products, such as watches, into digital formats. It now covers various technologies that enhance connectivity, security, and data management, fundamentally altering how businesses operate and people interact.

The digital revolution has extended well beyond mere analog to digital broadcasting replacement. It has also transformed how we communicate and conduct business globally. Electronic platforms have encouraged peer-to-peer activities, leading to disruptive transformations and productivity gains. Such transformations are so significant that countries worldwide are now prioritizing the development of their economies based on Industry 4.0 initiatives.

This industry, known as the Fourth Industrial Revolution, encompasses advancements in connectivity, artificial intelligence, and flexible automation. It aims to create cyber-physical environments that integrate information and operational technologies including the Internet, big data, cloud computing, additive manufacturing, advanced robotics, virtual reality, and other developments in artificial intelligence. These technologies have been gradually incorporated into Brazil's contemporary industrial sectors.

However, the OECD (2020) states that 23% of adults in 2018 reported never having accessed the Internet. Brazilian businesses utilize digital technologies less frequently than those in developed nations, especially micro businesses. According to the OECD's evaluation, Brazil has significantly modernized its policies and institutions over the last 20 years to foster innovation, research, and development. In certain sectors, such as oil and gas, aviation, agriculture, and health, the country's innovation system has advanced to a level of excellence. However, in other areas like productivity improvements, augmented competitiveness, or a stronger position in global value chains, it continues to fall behind.

Numerous companies in the Brazilian market adapt to the digital economy by incorporating digital tools into their operations. The Brazilian government too proactively incorporates technological advancements into its primary activities. A significant example is the 1996 introduction of the electronic ballot box. This innovative system, developed using a robust, lightweight microcomputer, is utilized for national, regional, and local elections and voting systems. The electronic ballot box comprises two terminals: the clerk's terminal, used to identify and authorize the voter to vote (in some models, voter's identity verification occurs via biometrics), and the voter's terminal, where the vote is numerically logged.

Three small visual signals aid the clerk, indicating whether the terminal is available to the voter, whether the vote has already been completed, and whether the electronic ballot box is connected to the power supply or running on an internal battery. The voter terminal features a numeric keyboard for entering the vote and a liquid crystal display that presents instructions guiding the voter in recording their vote. If a problem arises with the electronic ballot box during voting, contingency procedures are implemented.

According to UNCTAD (2019), various drivers have led the expansion of the digital economy. The digital sector encompasses the information and communications technology (ICT) segment. This comprises significant innovations in crucial devices such as semiconductors and processors, as well as the development and enhancement of core technologies like computers and telecommunication equipment. The digital economy embraces digital platforms, mobile applications, and payment services. The growth of enabling infrastructures, notably Internet and telecommunication networks, has also proven instrumental.

The digitalized economy is comprised of segments where goods and services are increasingly employed in digital business models, such as e-commerce, and new organizational structures like start-ups. Just as in non-digital societies, countries exhibit different levels of development and certain changes take time for implementation. A limited number of countries, for instance, are experimenting with electronic voting technologies in national or local elections. The Brazilian Electoral Court (TSE) provided electronic voting machines for official elections or pilot tests in Paraguay, Argentina, the Dominican Republic, Ecuador, and Mexico from 2003 to 2005.

The share of the digital economy in global GDP has been increasingly driven by the advantages of scale and scope, and the imperatives of social distancing imposed during the Covid-19 pandemic. Before the crisis, the digital economy's contribution to Brazil's GDP was approximately 22%. This percentage underscores the significance of this burgeoning economy as a driver of economic growth. Brasscom—Brazilian Association of Information Technology and Communication Companies(2019), representing more than a hundred companies and institutions, reports that the digital transformation sector generated 1.52 million jobs.

New start-ups and business models are emerging with the growth of Brazil's digital economy; this involves developments such as application programming interfaces and various standard e-commerce activities. These elements have triggered the rise of online commercial exchange platforms, characterized by decentralized digital networks. E-commerce has taken an increasingly central role in the economy, boasting an annual growth rate of more than 10% and engaging thousands of users. In terms of e-commerce, Brazil is considered the most developed market in Latin America.

Consumers worldwide are increasingly becoming digitally connected. Pre-dating the health, economic, and social crises, the Central Bank of Brazil (BACEN 2019) stated that smartphones were ubiquitously used for various tasks such as banking interactions, shopping, payments, and social media. This modality is preferred among users of the Brazilian National Financial System (SFN) and showed the most substantial growth compared to 2017, at 18.5%. Internet banking follows in second place, accounting for 21.9 billion transactions, marking a 6.3% increase over 2017. Combined, smartphone and Internet banking represent nearly 70% of total transactions. In 2020, the Central Bank successfully introduced PIX as an instant payment method in the Brazilian market.

In the non-digital economy, various challenges exist, including optimizing regulatory frameworks and city infrastructures. Moreover, there is a lack of suitable mechanisms to manage economic activities, particularly in terms of tax collection. To further the digitalization of the economy, Michel Temer, the former President of Brazil, signed a law (Decree 9612) in 2018 to regulate the country's digital economy. The digital economy appears to be rapidly enhancing productivity in every industry. However, it is also hastening the ongoing process of wealth concentration. Taxes, if properly implemented, may serve as a countermeasure to this phenomenon, especially when there is social pressure in this direction.

To Further Research and Reflect

- As Brazil has effectively used an electronic ballot box since 1996 in its elections, explain how the elections in your country are performed and the pros and cons of the different systems.
- Consider the advantages and disadvantages of increasing the digitalization of economic activities in the education sector and the spread of "fake news" and prejudices through digital technologies.

References

Amazon Fund. (2020). *Projects portfolio*. Available at: http://www.fundoamazonia.gov.br/en/carteira-de-projetos/.

Bacen. (2019). *Uso de Smartphones Já Supera Internet Banking nas Transações por Meio Eletrônico*. Available at: https://www.bcb.gov.br/detalhenoticia/374/noticia.

Barbier, E., & Burgess, J. (2019). Sustainable development goal indicators: Analyzing trade-offs and complementarities. *World Development, 122*(C), 295–305.

Baroni, L., Alves, R. F. S., Boccolini, C. S., Salles, R., Gritz, R., Paixão, B., & Boccolini, P. M. M. (2021). Database on the coverage of the "Bolsa-Família" conditioning cash-transfer program: Brazil, 2005 to 2021. *BMC Research Notes, 14*, 435.

Boulanger, P. (2008). Sustainable development indicators: A scientific challenge, a democratic issue. *SAPIENS—Surveys and Perspectives Integrating Environment and Society, 1*(1).

Brasscom—Associação Brasileira das Empresas de Tecnologia da Informação e Comunicação. (2019). *Relatório Setorial Brasscom 2019*. Available at: https://brasscom.org.br/relatorio-setorial-de-tic-2019/.

Cano, W. (2008). *Desconcentração Produtiva Regional do Brasil 1970-2005* (3. ed. rev. e ampl.). Unesp. 304 p.

Castro, B. M., Grandini, F. P., Dottori, M., & Fortes, J. F. (2017). A Amazônia Azul: Recursos e Preservação. *Revista USP, São Paulo, 113*, 7–26.

Civil Society Working Group for the 2030 Agenda. (2020). *2030 Agenda for sustainable development spotlight report*. Synthesis IV-Brazil. Available at: https://brasilnaagenda2030.files.wordpress.com/2020/08/en_sr_2020_web.pdf.

Fundo Amazônia. (2024). *Fundo Amazônia*. Available at: http://www.fundoamazonia.gov.br/pt/fundo-amazonia/.

Gabriel, L. F., Ribeiro, L. C. D. S., & Oreiro, J. L. (2020). Manufacturing, economic growth, and real exchange rate: Empirical evidence in panel data and input-output multipliers. *PSL Quarterly Review, 73*(292), 51–75.

Genova, A. (2018). Two nations disputed these small islands for 300 years. *National Geography*. Available at: https://www.nationalgeographic.com/history/article/history-dispute-photos-dodko-rocks-islands.

Marinha do Brasil. (2021). *Prosub—Programa de desenvolvimento de submarinos*. Available at: https://www.marinha.mil.br/prosub/revistas_prosub.

Meadows, D., Randers, J., & Meadows, D. (2005). *Limits to growth: The 30-year update*. Earthscan. 338p.

Nery, P. F., Tenoury, G. N., & Shikida, C. (2018). Probabilidade de desemprego por faixa etária: implicações para idade mínima e políticas de emprego. Senado Federal, Consultoria Legislativa. Textos para discussão n. 253. 51 p. Available at: http://www2.senado.leg.br/bdsf/handle/id/549866.

OECD. (2020). *A Caminho da Era Digital no Brasil*. Available at: https://www.oecd.org/digital/a--caminho-da-era-digital-no-brasil-45a84b29-pt.htm.

OECD—The Observatory Economic Complexity. (2021). *Brazil*. Available at: https://oec.world/en/profile/country/bra.

Redclift, M. (2005). Sustainable development (1987–2005): An oxymoron comes of age. *Sustainable Development, 13*, 212–227.

Seixas, C. S., Prado, D. S., Joly, C. A., May, P. H., Neves, E. M. S. C., & Teixeira, L. R. (2020). Environmental governance in Brazil: Towards the sustainable development goals (SDGs)? *Cadernos Gestão Pública e Cidadania, São Paulo, 25*(81), 1–21.

Thompson, N., & Muggah, R. (2015). *The Blue Amazon: Brazil asserts its influence across the Atlantic*. Instituto Igarapé. Available at: https://igarape.org.br/the-blue-amazon-brazil-asserts-its-influence-across-the-atlantic/.

Transparência Internacional. (2021). *Brazil: Setbacks in the legal and institutional frameworks (2020 update)*. Available at: https://transparenciainternacional.org.br/retrocessos/.

UNCTAD—United Nations Conference on Trade and Development. (2019). *Digital economy report 2019. Value creation and capture: Implications for developing countries*. United Nations. Available at: https://unctad.org/en/PublicationsLibrary/der2019_overview_en.pdf.

United Nations (UN). (2021a). *Millennium development goals*. Available at: https://www.undp.org/content/undp/en/home/sdgoverview/mdg_goals.html.

United Nations (UN). (2021b). *Ending poverty*. Available at: https://www.un.org/en/sections/issues-depth/poverty/.

United Nations (UN). (2024a). *UN research roadmap for the COVID-19 recovery: Leveraging the power of science for a more equitable, resilient and sustainable future*. Available at: https://www.un.org/en/pdfs/UNCOVID19ResearchRoadmap.pdf.

United Nations (UN). (2024b). *Sustainable development goals*. Available at: https://www.un.org/sustainabledevelopment/.
Wade, R. (2003). *Governing the market: Economic theory and the role of government in East Asian industrialization*. Princeton University Press. 496 p.
World Bank. (2021). *Understanding poverty*. Available at: https://www.worldbank.org/en/understanding-poverty.

Part II
Brazilian Contemporary Realities

Chapter 4
Entrepreneurship and SMEs in Brazil

4.1 Introduction

Entrepreneurs are known to be passionate, innovative, and capable of overcoming adversity. They possess a high degree of open-mindedness, exceptional work capacity, and the flexibility to change direction as needed. One of Brazil's most prominent entrepreneurs, Viscount de Mauá, exemplified these traits as an open-minded business person, extending his influence from the north to the south of Brazil, and even onto Uruguay, Argentina, and London. Indeed, the history of such outstanding Brazilian entrepreneurs continually inspires new generations of creators.

Aside from possessing desirable personal traits to become an entrepreneur, contextual adversities must be addressed. Significantly, Brazil holds the 124th position among 190 economies in the World Bank's Doing Business publication. This ranking presents an extensive analysis of worldwide business regulation, establishing it as a crucial benchmark for Brazil's business environment.

Government institutions have been aiding companies in increasing their size and competitiveness. Institutions such as the Brazilian Development Bank (Banco Nacional de Desenvolvimento Econômico e Social - BNDES), Bank of the Northeast of Brazil (Banco do Nordeste do Brasil - BNB), Amazon Bank (Banco da Amazonia S.A. - BASA), Bank of Far Southern Development (Banco Regional do Extremo Sul - BRDE), and Funding for Studies and Projects (Financiadora de Estudos e Projetos - FINEP) provide financial incentives and investment support to all companies operating in Brazil, with particular emphasis on those engaged in research and innovation activities. In addition, certain regulatory laws favor entrepreneurs and their companies. The country also backs two significant research corporations: Embrapa and Embrapii.

Founded in 1973, the Brazilian Agricultural Research Corporation, also known as Embrapa, has been a crucial driving force in agribusiness research advancements. Recognizing its significant impact, the Brazilian Company of Industrial Research

G. Masiero, *Brazilian Socio-Economic Dynamics*, Contributions to Economics,
https://doi.org/10.1007/978-3-031-87685-1_4

and Industrial Innovation, Embrapii, was established in 2013. Embrapii strives to boost research and technological development within Brazil's industrial sector, fostering innovation and competitiveness on a national scale.

Despite government support, one in three companies in Brazil declares bankruptcy before their second year of operation. Notably, micro and small enterprises account for 99% of businesses in the country. They play a critical role in contributing to 30% of gross domestic product (GDP) and generating 55% of the total jobs. Entrepreneurs from various sectors actively pursue innovative strategies in products, processes, value, management, and business models. They demonstrate resilience and adaptability in the face of challenges.

Typically nestled within environments designed for the growth of new businesses—known as incubators—start-up companies organize and implement their operations to develop novel products, solutions, or processes. Brazil is currently home to 369 business incubators, 90 initiatives for technology parks, and 35 accelerators. The inaugural Brazilian incubators emerged in the 1980s, backed by the National Council for Scientific and Technological Development (CNPq), a government institution that supports scientific and technological development at the national level.

Start-ups, micro, and large companies in Brazil benefit from the services provided by the S-System. This system comprises nine entities: National Service of Industrial Learning (Serviço Nacional de Aprendizagem Industrial - SENAI), Social Service of Industry (Serviço Social da Industria - SESI), National Service of Commercial Learning (Serviço Nacional de Aprendizagem Comercial - SENAC), Commerce Social Service (Serviço Social do Comércio - SESC), National Rural Learning Serviçe (Serviço Nacional de Aprendizagem Rural - SENAR), National Cooperative Learning Service (Serviço Nacional de Aprendizagem do Cooperativismo - Sescoop), Social Service for Transportation (Serviço Social do Transporte - SEST), National Service for Learning in Transportation (Serviço Nacional de Aprendizagem do Transporte - SENAT), and the Brazilian Micro and Small Company Support Service (Serviço Brasileiro de Apoio às Micro e Pequenas Empresas - Sebrae).

These organizations play a significant role in training Brazilian workers and providing healthcare and leisure activities. SENAI and SESI are affiliated with the National Confederation of Industry (CNI), the main representative body for the Brazilian industry. SENAC and SESC, on the other hand, fall under the National Confederation of Trade in Goods, Services, and Tourism (CNC), which represents the commercial, service, and tourism sectors. Notably, the Brazilian agriculture and cooperative sectors also have their own organizations that serve their members.

All member companies of the aforementioned entities, operating in various sectors of the economy, depend on credit. This challenge has stalled the country's economic development. State banks such as Banco do Brasil, Caixa Econômica Federal, and the Brazilian National Economic and Social Development Bank (BNDES) have fueled Brazilian economic dynamism in the agricultural, housing, and industrial sectors, respectively. Banco do Brasil is one of the largest and oldest public banks worldwide.

Banco do Brasil was established in 1808 when Brazil was still a Portuguese colony. BNDES, similar in size and activities to the World Bank, is also a significant institution. These large banks are strictly regulated by the Brazilian Central Bank (BACEN), which also has the responsibility of controlling inflation. During the inflationary years of the 1980s and 1990s, Brazilians experienced seven economic plans, popularly referred to as "economic packages," and circulated four different currencies: the Cruzado (1986–1989), Cruzado Novo (1989–1990), Cruzeiro (1990–1993), and Real (1993–1994 to the present).

The Brazilian financial sector is experiencing a surge in the current landscape, with inflation being managed effectively. Specifically, digital banks have exhibited a remarkable annual growth rate of approximately 60% in Brazil, particularly in terms of new bank accounts. However, despite this expansion, it is noteworthy that an estimated 45 million Brazilians remain unbanked. Nevertheless, digital banks have significantly fostered financial inclusion by facilitating access to banking services for previously underserved populations.

Despite the rapid growth of digital banks and fintechs, the Brazilian financial market remains largely concentrated. Only five major banks—comprised of two state-owned and three private institutions—dominate over 80% of the country's economic transactions. Caixa Econômica tops the list with 23 million customers, followed by Bradesco with 18 million, Itaú with 16 million, Banco do Brasil with 13 million, and Santander with ten million customers. These statistics highlight one of the world's most significant banking concentrations.

4.2 Brazilian Entrepreneurs and How to Do Business in Brazil

Brazil, being a young and emerging country, offers more entrepreneurial opportunities than many mature and developed societies. Marcovitch (2012) systematically gives a brief history of some successful entrepreneurs. These individuals are identified as men and women who are passionate, are innovative, and possess the ability to overcome adversity. They are characterized by their open-mindedness, their extraordinary capacity for work, and their flexibility to alter strategies or courses when necessary. Besides establishing successful companies or business groups that have propelled the country's development, they have engaged with social or philanthropic projects with equivalent energy and resilience. They have braved risks and seized the opportunities of their era despite crises and uncertainties.

Marcovitch (FEA, 2024) has written a three-volume series detailing the history of selected Brazilian entrepreneurs, delineating the pivotal roles these standout figures played in the country's development. Spanning nearly two centuries of business history, from Antonio Prado's ventures in 1820 to the present day, when enterprises have gained global traction, these publications underscore the journeys of varied entrepreneurs. Included among these are Nami Jafet, Família Prado,

Francesco Matarazzo, Ramos de Azevedo, Jorge Street, Roberto Simonsen, Júlio Mesquita, Leon Feffer, Irineu Evangelista de Sousa, Luiz de Queiroz, Attilio Fontana, Valentim Diniz, Guilherme Guinle, Wolff Klabin, Horácio Lafer, José Ermírio de Moraes, João Gerdau, Curt Johannpeter, Herman Lundgren, Luiz Tarquínio, Bernardo Mascarenhas, Delmiro Gouveia, Roberto Marinho, Augusto Trajano de Azevedo Antunes, Samuel Benchimol, and Edson Queiroz.

The trilogy emphasizes the prevailing traits of entrepreneurship exhibited by these leaders. Collectively, these individuals possessed a vision for the future, a robust and consistent capacity for innovation, and a keen sensitivity to strategic trade-offs. Key entrepreneurs emerged at various stages of Brazilian development. For instance, the Prado Family was instrumental in Brazil's shift from a development phase centered on coffee production to the onset of industrialization, a process led by Irineu Evangelista de Sousa, also known as Visconde de Mauá. Other notable figures include Matarazzo, a dominant industrialist in São Paulo; Feffer, who focused on technology; and Jafet, a pioneer in retail.

The country's economic development was not solely driven by male entrepreneurs. The trilogy also comprises biographies of 8 female pioneers, supplementing the list of 24 male pioneers. Ermelinda Queiroz, Índia Vanuíre, Irmã Dulce, Mãe Aninha, Nise da Silveira, Dona Veridiana, and Waldisa Russio are acknowledged as exceptional entrepreneurial pioneers. In varying ways, whether through their attitudes, life actions, or representativeness, these women have left significant legacies that persist in inspiring the younger generation.

The first and most inspiring Brazilian industrialist was Irineu Evangelista de Sousa, Viscount of Mauá. Caldeira (1995) demonstrated that this entrepreneur was an open-minded businessman who extended his influence to Uruguay, Argentina, and London. He established his first company in the UK with his former employer, who previously owned a company in Rio de Janeiro. In 1830, he was accepted into the Scottish import company of Richard Carruthers, where he learned English and accounting. Subsequently, in 1840, he founded one of his initial ventures, Carruthers de Castro & Cia.

His initiatives introduced gaslighting to the streets of Rio de Janeiro and connected Brazil to Europe via a submarine telegraph cable. After constructing the first railway in Magé, Rio de Janeiro, Mauá was granted the title of Baron in 1854. Twenty years later, in 1874, Emperor Dom Pedro II bestowed upon him the title of Viscount. He was a crucial proponent of Brazilian industrialization, having established a foundry, a shipyard, a railway, the first large bank, and a regular shipping company with operations spanning the Amazon in the North to the Guaiba River in the South.

Viscount of Mauá was an accountant, economist, business administrator, legislator, and provincial deputy, representing the state of Rio Grande do Sul for nearly two decades. Owing to his extensive business connections abroad, he functioned as an informal diplomat for the Empire. Although he was Brazil's first great entrepreneur, he could not continue to expand his enterprises due to political and economic crises, including the end of slavery and the monarchy in Brazil. These changes significantly impacted his entrepreneurial activities. He passed away in Petropolis, Rio de Janeiro, in 1889, just before the Republic's Proclamation.

Before taking her vows, Sister Dulce (1914–1992), also known as Maria Rita, was renowned as one of Brazil's leading philanthropic entrepreneurs. She converted her home into a service center and, at the age of 22, founded Bahia's first Christian workers' movement. In subsequent years, she played a pivotal role in establishing numerous philanthropic institutions. Among these initiatives was a health complex called Obras Sociais Irmã Dulce. Sister Dulce was nominated for the Nobel Peace Prize in 1988 and beatified by the Pope in 2009. In 2019, she was canonized and is now known as Saint Dulce of the Poor.

Like Viscount of Mauá or Sister Dulce, with a long-term perspective, it is easy to envision numerous opportunities to become a successful pioneer entrepreneur in the urbanized areas of Brazil or its vast remote regions in the North. Indeed, today, several of Brazil's successful entrepreneurs are billionaires. These include Jorge Paulo Lemann, with an estimated fortune exceeding US$ 25 billion. There are also prominent female entrepreneurs, such as Luiza Helena Trajano Inácio Rodrigues (with an estimated fortune of roughly US$ 5 billion), who operates the retail store chain Magazine Luiza and other companies.

Djankoy et al. (2007) endeavored to discover what contributes to the success of an entrepreneur in the Brazilian setting. Their research found that an entrepreneur's family origins have been consequential in their success, particularly coming from well-educated households. Coupled with individual intelligence, their entrepreneurial drive often flourished due to familial aid. Nonetheless, these authors also demonstrated that overconfidence can be detrimental to business success.

Reflecting on the past, Marcovitch (2012) identifies several common factors, while acknowledging innumerable differences among the most successful Brazilian entrepreneurs. They demonstrated an interest in innovation and possessed a clear vision of the future, powered by a strong work ethic and an emphasis on achieving superior results. They also exhibited an authentic interest in the "other" and an unceasing quest for a meaningful life that could turn adversities into advantages.

Possessing favorable personal traits to become an entrepreneur in Brazil can help one surmount many contextual challenges. In a World Bank ranking that evaluates business environment regulation across 190 economies, Brazil holds 124th place (Doing Business, 2020). The country ranks 138th on the index for company initiation, which gauges the number of procedures, costs, and time necessary for a company to officially start its operations. In the taxation category, Brazil sits at 184th place. For the indicator that scrutinizes the acquisition of credit and financing operations, the country takes the 104th position. Figure 4.1 showcases the relative ranking of Brazil compared to its competitors across key indicators for conducting business.

While there are considerable challenges to doing business in Brazil, international companies operating within its borders generate nearly one-third of its GDP. As a major economy, virtually all global consulting firms have experts available to assist international investors in establishing themselves in Brazil. Along with legal and market considerations, these companies often advise attention to the Brazilian

Fig. 4.1 Doing Business in Brazil. Source: Doing Business (2020)

business mindset, relationships, and understanding of local culture and habits. Initiating a chat over *cafezinho* and sharing news about football or TV stars can be a good starting point, as personal relationships are as crucial as business relations in Brazil. However, in this control-oriented, hierarchical society, the organization's top-ranking individual typically makes almost all decisions, even minor ones.

To Further Research and Reflect

- What are your aspirations and goals for developing a fulfilling career? Have you considered pursuing entrepreneurship as a path to success?
- Could you summarize a successful business initiative in your domestic market with solid potential for implementation in the Brazilian context?

4.3 Supporting RD&I—Embrapa and Embrapii

Setting up a business anywhere demands meticulous consideration of various factors. However, Brazil distinctively encourages innovative companies, presenting numerous opportunities for expansion and success. Like any other country, Brazil also requires human capital, adequate infrastructure, tax incentives, subsidies, and accommodation for regulatory hurdles, along with opportunities for technological partnerships.

Brazil's commitment to science and technology is not merely a paper strategy but a reality propelling its development. The country concentrates on fostering investments via targeted innovation programs and institutes, which have seen notable success. This approach acknowledges the pivotal role of science and technology in all productive sectors, aiming to promote economic growth and competitiveness.

Vasconcellos and Neto (2012) highlight that the partnership programs between the Brazilian Space Agency (Agência Espacial Brasileira - AEB) and the National Aeronautics and Space Administration - (NASA) stand as a testament to Brazil's global collaboration capabilities. Such collaborations have fostered technology transfers and established certain organizational arrangements and supportive elements for these transfers. This underscores the significance of dynamic relationships between social actors in the innovation sector and space production, further augmenting Brazil's reputation in the global innovation arena.

The pharmaceutical industry, a critical economic player in Brazil's health sector, has significantly benefited from programs promoting technological development. For instance, the Institute of Drugs Technology (Farmanguinhos) of the Fundação Oswaldo Cruz (Fiocruz) plays a crucial role in regulating drug prices. It has been striving to streamline costs and optimize project deadlines through improved project management processes. Through targeted innovation programs and institutes, Brazil's proactive approach to science and technology has fostered growth and competitiveness across diverse sectors, including space exploration, pharmaceutical development, and education.

With regard to sector-specific incentives, the so-called Lei do Bem (No. 11196) of 2005 provides tax incentives to companies engaged in technological innovation activities and projects across Brazil. The most common expenses that can be used to offset tax payments are Research, Development, and Innovation (RD&I) expenditures. These include salaries for researchers, payments to university and scientific suppliers, technology and innovation institutions, outsourcing costs, and travel expenditures.

Building on earlier legislation passed in 2016, Decree 9283/18 structures various methods to boost innovation in Brazil. It does this by enabling cooperation projects between companies, research institutes, and non-profit private organizations using public funds. Consequently, companies can commission technological research and innovation development projects from these entities, using the funds transferred to these institutions as a source of tax benefits.

Law 13,755/18 applies to the automobile industry and advocates for technological development, competitiveness, innovation, vehicle safety, environmental protection, energy efficiency, and the quality of automobiles, trucks, buses, motor chassis, and auto parts. This statute instates a novel policy for the automotive sector, replacing the previously established Inovar-Auto (a program to encourage technological innovation and densification of the automotive vehicle production chain). Among the revisions, the legislation presents mandatory requirements for selling vehicles in Brazil. It also establishes the highly successful Rota 2030 Program, which has produced a significant impact on mobility and logistics and a taxation system for auto parts not manufactured within the national borders.

Since the 1980s, Brazil has been seeking ways to stimulate the development of the country's information and communication technology sector. The Informatics Law, seen as a beacon of hope, encourages training and competitiveness in information technology by offering tax benefits. In return for these tax incentives, beneficiary companies are required to invest in R&D activities. The Informatics Law was recently amended by Law 13,969/19, which provides financial credits to companies investing in RD&I activities within the information and communication technology sector.

Brazil has a lengthy history of state programs that provide financial incentives and investment institutions. This includes the Brazilian Development Bank

(BNDES), which was established in 1952, and the Funding Authority for Studies and Projects (FINEP), created in 1962. Regional initiatives, such as the Banco do Nordeste (BNB), the Banco da Amazônia (BASA), and the Regional Bank for Development of the Far South (BRDE), have also been set up. Furthermore, regional and municipal governments have set up programs to stimulate innovative businesses by offering subsidies or fiscal incentives.

Mazzucato and Penna (2016) categorize all primary agents of the Brazilian Innovation System and propose its transformation into a mission-oriented system. They advocate for the implementation of a systemic policy plan that inspires both public and private actors to collaborate in accomplishing specific objectives outlined in a comprehensive strategic innovation program. For these authors, merely promoting technology development is insufficient. Instead, they argue that any innovation policy or program must articulate "missions" capable of mobilizing production, distribution, and consumption patterns across various economic sectors.

Innovation policy is not solely about stimulating technology and individual sectors. According to the aforementioned authors, it is essential to identify and articulate missions that would inspire production, distribution, and consumption patterns across industries. Dynamic partnerships among the state, academia, and the business sector not only create and shape new markets but also provide explicit technological and sectoral guidance. This results in productivity increases, superior jobs, and higher tax revenues.

Etzkowitz (2003) posits that innovation is increasingly based on a "triple helix" of interactions among universities, industries, and government. Beyond teaching and research, universities have expanded academic knowledge and fostered technology-based firms following an interactive, primarily linear, innovation model. Companies perpetually strive to elevate their technological capabilities, forge closer ties with universities, and promote higher levels of training and knowledge-sharing. Governments, in addition to setting the rules as traditional regulators, also participate in public entrepreneurship and venture capital.

While Brazilian reality is complex, there are limited successful examples in its recent history. A key challenge Brazil faces is the absence of a consistent long-term strategic plan to guide scientific research and private entities in their innovation pursuits. During the Brazilian dictatorship, efforts to centralize agricultural research were made by creating a single organization—much like the US agrarian research institutions. Embrapa (2024), mentions that the Brazilian Agricultural Research Corporation, or Embrapa, was founded by the Ministry of Agriculture, Livestock, and Supply in 1973, and since its establishment, it has consistently been a technical innovation institution dedicated to producing information and technologies for Brazilian ranching and agriculture.

The company and its partners have endeavored to develop the National Agricultural Research System—Sistema Nacional de Pesquisa Agropecuária (SNPA). This system is an authentically Brazilian model of tropical agriculture and livestock, targeting the technological expansion of food, fiber, and energy production. Embrapa was responsible for integrating the *Cerrado* into the Brazilian grain production system. Since its inception, it has augmented the supply of beef, pork, and chicken to the domestic market and contributes almost 10% of these products to the international market.

Based on Embrapa's success in the primary sector, a similar organization was designed to foster innovation in the industrial sector. The Brazilian Company of Industrial Research and Innovation (Embrapii) was established in 2013 to promote innovations in both the industrial and service industries. According to Embrapii (2024), this institution was founded as a social enterprise through a joint initiative of two ministries, namely, Industry and Education.

Despite being funded by the federal budget, Embrapii operates as an autonomous organization that independently allocates its resources. This organization works with scientific and technological research institutions, centering on business needs and targeting risk-sharing in the pre-competitive phase of innovation. Through sharing project risks with companies, Embrapii seeks to encourage the industrial sector to undertake high-intensity technological innovation, thereby bolstering the competitive capacity of Brazilian companies.

The Brazilian Micro and Small Enterprises' Support Service (Sebrae) is the main entity that assists small and medium companies with their management challenges. It emphasizes that the primary reasons companies fail in their initial years are due to a lack of planning and business management. These elements are crucial in understanding the market, such as knowing the companies' customers, competitors, and suppliers. In general, all the S-System and business incubators intervene and invest to enhance the management of small companies and support new ideas.

Partnering with various entities, Sebrae has been developing the Pesquisa GEM (2024). The most recent survey highlights that owning one's own business is the third most common dream among Brazilians. The percentage of women, low-income individuals, and those who initiate businesses "out of necessity" has decreased. Conversely, the proportion of men, those with higher education and income, those who start a business "for opportunity," and those motivated "by necessity" has seen an increase. The same survey draws attention to certain areas, namely, credit, bureaucracy, technology, and entrepreneurial education at the secondary or technical level. These are the most frequently cited and not yet solved issues

To Further Research and Reflect

- Describe how innovation activities are supported in your country of origin. Give an example of an innovative industrial product developed in your country that has not yet been commercialized in Brazil.
- Contrast your country's research and technology development institution initiatives with two of Brazil's most significant: Embrapa and Embrapii.

4.4 Small Businesses and Incubators in Brazil

Customer satisfaction and differentiation are more than just buzzwords in the retail industry; they are the pillars of success. For a business to succeed, it needs to attract customers, generate sales, and earn loyalty. This holds particularly true for small businesses and incubators in Brazil, where intense competition is prevalent. If a company falls short of its customers' minimum quality expectations, it will likely experience a decline in sales, diminished profits, and an escalated risk of closure. This scenario highlights the importance of customer satisfaction and differentiation in the business environment, motivating entrepreneurs to incorporate these elements at the heart of their business strategies.

Brazil's retail industry, especially in clothing and accessories, represents a unique economic activity. It boasts the most significant number of registered companies in the country, ranging from small stores on the streets to large shopping malls and galleries in cities of all sizes and commercial districts. This diversity is not confined to the physical environment; business strategies and customer interactions also differ, making it a fascinating sector to explore.

Small businesses, often considered the backbone of the retail industry, display remarkable resilience in large shopping malls or specialized commercial streets—familiar sights in major Brazilian cities. As noted by Moda Center (2021), a standout example is the Santa Cruz shopping mall in Pernambuco, Brazil's largest wholesale apparel center, hosting over 10,000 retail outlets. During peak shopping periods, the mall attracts over 200,000 weekly visitors from across the country, exemplifying Brazil's vibrant retail scene and robust consumer culture.

Exploring the retail landscape in Brazilian cities can be a fascinating journey. For instance, in São Paulo, 25 de Março Street stands as an exceptional model, boasting over 800 stores that cater to popular commerce. In a similar vein, in the historical center of Rio de Janeiro, 11 streets adjacent to Rua da Alfândega provide a unique shopping experience. These streets, coupled with the Mercado Público present in nearly all provincial capitals, are bustling historical places in the downtown area with stores selling food, artisan crafts, vegetables, fruits, and other daily consumer products.

Fostering relationships with customers does not only occur in a physical environment. In Brazil, the majority of small businesses also maintain a digital presence on social media. Instagram is the predominant social media platform used for this purpose, with half of all Brazilians having used it to discover new products or services. Companies employ strategies like collaborating with influencers and posting daily updates to attract customers and convince them to make purchases through Instagram.

Instagram has proven to be an excellent promotional channel. According to D'Angelo (2021), entrepreneurs can communicate with a wide customer base while spending less money (given that around three-quarters of Brazilians use the app, and 84% report logging into Instagram at least once daily). While Instagram is the most frequently utilized digital platform for attracting new customers and showcasing products, WhatsApp serves as the go-to application for facilitating direct customer-company interactions, thereby concluding sales. Consequently, businesses often engage with customers via WhatsApp.

WhatsApp is installed on practically 100% of mobile phones in Brazil, with around 30% of consumers making purchases via the app. It is primarily used by small businesses and freelancers since it is a free, user-friendly tool. Small entrepreneurs do not need to invest in e-commerce platforms or have a deep understanding of technology to facilitate their sales. Customers usually discover the product that they want to buy via Instagram and make purchases via WhatsApp. From the customer's perspective, WhatsApp allows for a more intimate interaction between sellers and consumers. The customers can freely exchange information, receive real-time photographs, and negotiate prices—a common practice in Brazil.

After negotiating via WhatsApp, the entrepreneur is then required to receive the payment and proceed with the delivery. It is unusual for small businesses in Brazil to have online payment platforms such as a website or payment services like PayPal. As such, customers commonly pay companies through bank transfers. Since 2020, a new service in Brazil named PIX has permitted individuals and businesses to transfer funds between bank accounts instantaneously without incurring any charges, unlike conventional bank transfers. PIX has revolutionized the way Brazilians pay for their purchases made via WhatsApp or Instagram due to its simplicity and speed. It is now more prevalent than traditional transfers for small-scale commercial transactions.

The tools such as Instagram and WhatsApp are accessible and straightforward to use. Yet, attracting customers and securing a digital sales market can be challenging for small businesses. Many business owners fail to educate themselves professionally on utilizing social networks effectively. Neither do they comprehend their customers' interests to effectively offer products and services in both physical and digital environments. Merely offering the best outcome is inadequate. If a business wishes to avoid bankruptcy, undertaking professional tactics on social media and understanding the specifics of the chosen customer segment is crucial. Continuous innovation is essential.

Entrepreneurs undertake a variety of productive activities, emphasizing product innovation, process modification, value creation, management, and business model transformation. According to the Oslo Manual (2018), product innovations are defined as new or improved goods or services introduced to the market, which are significantly different from the company's preexisting offerings. Process innovations encompass the introduction of new or substantially enhanced production and distribution methodologies. Value innovations denote the alterations made to the attributes of goods and services to distinguish them from other products available in the market.

Management innovation refers to implementing new practices, processes, structures, and administrative techniques to accomplish organizational objectives. Innovation in business models seeks either radical or incremental changes in how the organization captures value and selects market segments to generate revenue within a given value chain. The focus is on executing cost and profit management

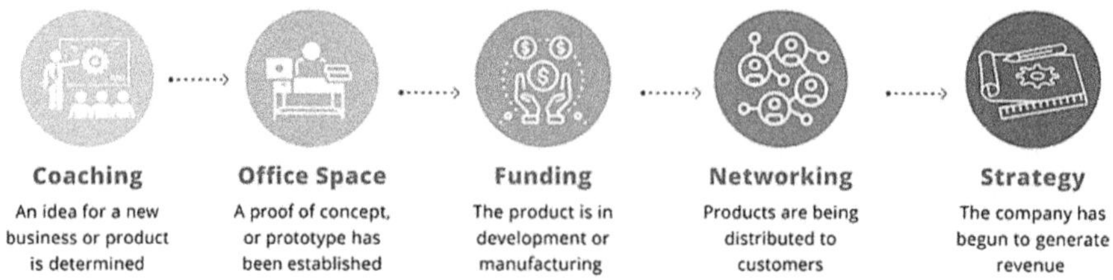

Fig. 4.2 The main functions of a business incubator. Source: Workbox (2024)

strategies arising from relationships with suppliers and consumers. Furthermore, organizations should implement both cooperative and competitive strategies to outperform competitors.

These activities are standard for any company but are emphasized more in start-ups. Ries (2011) views start-ups as entities that, from their embryonic stages, focus on organizing and implementing their operations to create something new. Their goal is to develop at least one innovative, repeatable, rapidly expanding, and highly profitable business model. Most of these businesses are fostered in supportive environments for new businesses, known as business incubators. A business incubator is an organization whose purpose is to strengthen and support micro and small companies in their early stages, to enhance their survival prospects in the market. Figure 4.2 illustrates some of its functions.

Business incubators first emerged in the USA when a family purchased a large facility from Massey Ferguson that had ceased operations in 1956 in Batavia, New York. Unable to lease the facility to a single entrepreneur, the family subdivided the space and rented lots to multiple small-business owners. The effectiveness of the Batavia Industrial Center was quickly demonstrated, and soon, similar initiatives proliferated in technology parks, research hubs, and innovation centers. In Brazil, the first incubators surfaced in the 1980s, sponsored by CNPq—the National Council for Scientific and Technological Development—Brazil's primary institution for supporting science and technology development.

São Paulo Research Foundation (Fundação de Amparo à Pesquisa do Estado de São Paulo - Fapesp), a research foundation in the state of São Paulo has played a vital role in sponsoring innovative research. Its primary focus on research and technological innovation is within higher education centers. Some of the most prominent Brazilian business incubators include the Center for Innovation, Entrepreneurship, and Technology at the University of São Paulo (Cietec); Genesis Institute (PUC-Rio); Inova (Incubator of Technological Projects and Companies at National Institute of Metrology Standardization and Industrial Quality - Instituto Nacional de Metrologia, Qualidade e Tecnologia - Inmetro); or the Technological Development Park (Parque de Desenvolvimento Tecnológico - Padetec).

Brazil hosts 369 business incubators, around 90 technology park initiatives, and 35 accelerators—organizations that link experienced entrepreneurs and investors to assist early tech companies in enhancing their business strategies. Since 1987, the

National Association of Entities Promoting Innovative Enterprises (Associação Nacional de Entidades Promotoras de Empreendimentos Inovadores - Anprotec) has backed such initiatives. The most notable business incubator is Cietec, a non-profit private association established to foster innovative entrepreneurship, emphasizing the conversion of knowledge into valuable market products and services.

Cietec has developed methodologies and expertise in the selection and monitoring of technology-based start-ups. The incubator aids entrepreneurs in organizing incubation processes and in the creation and management of innovative habitats. It facilitates the promotion of activities and identification of public and private capital through "angel investments," "seed capital," and "venture capital." It aims to bolster the technological, marketing, and organizational efforts of start-ups.

The primary advantage of business incubators in Brazil, as well as globally, is that they mitigate the failure rate of companies in their initial years. Incubators typically offer pre-incubation, incubation, and post-incubation programs for these companies. With both the incubation and post-incubation programs, the businesses have the option to establish themselves as resident companies at the incubator's premises or remain non-residential. Regardless of their choice, the businesses are provided with support and guidance to aid in their growth. This administrative assistance can strengthen start-up companies, enabling them to navigate the challenges of launching a new business successfully.

To Further Research and Reflect

- Could you outline some of the prominent programs in your country aimed at supporting innovative businesses? Could you offer insights into the advantages and shortcomings associated with the responsibility for implementing such initiatives?
- What are the primary distinctions between inventions and innovations? Additionally, could you provide examples of both developed in your country and discuss their potential for commercialization in Brazil?

4.5 The S-System—SENAI, SENAC, SESC, SESI, SENAR, SESCOOP, SEST, SENAT, and SEBRAE

Brazilian Business Federations play an integral role in shaping the country's economic landscape since they serve to represent and advocate for the interests of various industries. Organizations like the National Confederation of Industry (Confederação Nacional da Indústria - CNI), the Brazilian Confederation of Agriculture and Livestock (Confederação da Agricultura e Pecuária do Brasil - CNA), and the Brazilian Federation of Banks (Federação Brasileira de Bancos - Febraban) are crucial intermediaries bridging the gap between businesses and the government. They exert influence on policy making, labor laws, and trade regulations to foster a favorable environment for economic growth. By channeling a unified voice for their members, these federations ensure the concerns and needs of different sectors are duly noted and addressed at both the national and international levels.

Moreover, Brazilian Business Federations play a key role in promoting innovation, sustainability, and competitiveness in their respective industries. These federations facilitate research and development initiatives, support educational programs, and foster partnerships between businesses and academic institutions. For example, the CNI's Institute for Industrial Development Studies (Instituto de Estudos para o Desenvolvimento Industrial - IEDI) conducts research designed to pinpoint both challenges and opportunities within the industrial sector. Simultaneously, the CNA invests in technological advancements to enhance agricultural productivity and sustainability. Additionally, through the S-System, these federations provide training programs, resources, and networking opportunities. By helping businesses adapt to changing market conditions and global trends, they ensure long-term growth and resilience within Brazil's diverse and dynamic economic landscape.

The establishment of the S-System in 1942 marked a pivotal moment in Brazil's history, testifying to the country's forward-thinking approach. At a time when Brazil had a visionary outlook, it sought to create an education network to boost labor productivity and provide cultural and leisure services. This network was uniquely designed to operate with guaranteed funding, without depending on public management. Today, the S-System continues to be a significant entity, encompassing nine institutions that represent professional categories protected by the Brazilian Constitution, underscoring its lasting impact.

The S-System financing, a direct result of fees levied on the salaries of companies' workers within the corresponding category, is a tangible demonstration of the system's steadfast commitment to workers' social welfare. These funds, a direct investment in the workforce, are then funneled to their respective entities to finance activities designed to enhance professional performance. Each entity has a specific mission and a corresponding set of actions, all aimed at boosting the workforce and ensuring a direct and tangible benefit for the workers.

The National Service of Industrial Learning (Serviço Nacional de Aprendizagem Industrial - SENAI), a vital component of the S-System, offers training courses and technical advice. Conversely, the Social Service of Industry (Serviço Social da Indústria - SESI) enhances the system with cultural, recreational, health services, and sports options. Both entities are key to the CNI. According to CNI (2021), the Confederation was established in 1938 and currently represents 1280 trade unions to which nearly 700 thousand companies are affiliated. As a potent industry representative, CNI plays a pivotal role in dialogue with the Brazilian Executive, Legislative, and Judiciary branches.

SENAI, one of the world's five largest professional education complexes and the largest in Latin America, is a source of national pride. It operates through a decentralized system of local units, consisting of local branches and national and regional administrative bodies created under the supervision of CNI. The Ministries of Education, Labor, and Social Security, along with labor union representatives, serve on the organization's board, further underscoring its importance and influence.

The organization boasts a network of 208 laboratories across the nation, offering comprehensive technical and technological services to businesses. In collaboration with Brazil's Ministry of Foreign Relations, it leads workforce training initiatives in several countries including Cape Verde, Guinea Bissau, Guatemala, Paraguay, East Timor, Mozambique, Peru, Jamaica, São Tomé and Príncipe, and Haiti.

Established in 1946, SESI operates 1304 units across Brazil. It oversees libraries, theaters, cultural spaces, and schools that offer primary education, supporting workers and their dependents in education, artistic pursuits, leisure activities, and training for both youths and adults. SESI offers sports, social integration, and disease prevention programs to maintain or reestablish the health of workers and families associated with national industries.

The National Confederation of Trade in Goods, Services, and Tourism (Confederação Nacional do Comércio de Bens, Serviços e Turismo - CNC) was established in 1945. This organization represents the commercial and service sectors, managing the Confederative System of Trade Union Representation (Sistema Confederativo da Representação Sindical do Comércio - Siscmércio). In line with CNC (2021), the entity represents over a thousand unions in the commerce and services sector, amounting to around five million companies and approximately 25 million jobs.

Additionally, CNC administers two significant social development entities, SESC and SENAC. These entities are integral components of the S-System. Established in the 1940s, SESC and SENAC have significantly contributed to enhancing the quality of life and improving job prospects for countless Brazilians via their programs.

CNC operates over a thousand stationary and mobile units nationwide, surpassing conventional educational offerings. In addition to professional training, it provides comprehensive support in healthcare, sports, leisure, and cultural activities to commerce workers and their families. Moreover, these programs are accessible to the broader population, contributing significantly to societal well-being.

The National Rural Learning Service (Serviço Nacional de Aprendizagem Rural - SENAR) engages in activities related to agribusiness. Founded in 1951, it is part of the CNA. This Confederation represents small, medium, and large Brazilian rural producers, totaling approximately five million individuals and more than 2000 unions. On a national scale, it advocates for agricultural interests.

SENAR was established in 1991 and modeled after SENAI and SENAC. The board comprises an equal number of councilors from both the workforce and the agribusiness sector. Additionally, CNA operates the CNA Institute, a non-profit civil association founded in 2009. The Institute produces studies and conducts research in both social and agribusiness sectors, aiming to meet the needs of the CNA/SENAR System. SENAR specializes in professional development and social advancement for rural men and women. Meanwhile, the CNA Institute focuses on conducting research in the social and agribusiness realms.

The Organization of Brazilian Cooperatives (Organização das Cooperativas Brasileiras - OCB) was founded in 1969 (OCB, 2021). Today, it comprises two entities that are dedicated to expanding cooperative activities in Brazil. These are the National Cooperative Learning Service (Serviço Nacional de Aprendizagem do Cooperativismo - Sescoop) and the CNCoop (National Cooperative Confederation - Confederação Nacional das Cooperativas). Each organization actively promotes collaborative business activities throughout Brazil.

Brazil is home to more than 6800 formally registered cooperative enterprises, represented by the OCB. The OCB's mandate is to advocate for the sector's interests within the three branches of power. These cooperatives encompass 14.2 million members and spawn approximately 400,000 direct jobs. Established in 1999, Sescoop oversees the organization, administration, and execution of professional training for cooperatives and their employees. Registered in 2011 with the Ministry of Labor, CNCoop is accountable for managing the sector's industrial relations.

The National Transport Confederation (Confederação Nacional dos Transportes - CNT) was established in 1954 to represent the Brazilian transportation sector, encompassing 155 thousand companies and 2.2 million workers. The CNT system also oversees SEST and SENAT and Institute of Transportation and Logistics (ITL).

All the aforementioned entities have national offices overseeing their state branches. These organizations receive funding from contributions collected by the federal government from businesses based on their payrolls. For instance, industries contribute 1% of their payroll to SENAI and 1.5% to SESI. Commercial companies contribute 1.5% to SESC. These contributions are subsequently transferred from the federal government to these entities.

Sebrae, another crucial component of the S-System, stands out due to its unique structure and origins. Established in 1972, this institution operates under private management, yet maintains links to the federal government. Initially dubbed the Brazilian Center for Support to Micro and Small Companies, it evolved into an autonomous social service in 1990, as indicated by the shift from "C" for center to "S" for service.

The genesis of all these organizations and their financial frameworks can be traced back to the mid-1940s, with only four entities—Sescoop, SENAR, SEST, and SENAT—emerging after the enactment of the 1988 Federal Constitution. Rooted in a vision of societal improvement, these institutions are dedicated to offering Brazilian workers opportunities for leisure, cultural enrichment, and professional development at subsidized or no-cost rates.

Since their inception, these organizations have played essential roles in the democratization of access to critical services and opportunities for the Brazilian population. By offering a broad range of programs and resources, they aim to enhance the quality of life for individuals from various socioeconomic backgrounds. From vocational training to recreational activities, these initiatives strive to equip citizens with the tools and skills necessary for personal and professional growth.

Furthermore, these entities epitomize a focused endeavor to bridge the gap between aspiration and achievement, especially for those from marginalized or underserved communities. Through strategic partnerships and innovative approaches to service delivery, they strive to eliminate barriers to entry and promote a more inclusive and just society. With a commitment to accessibility and affordability, they demonstrate a dedication to harnessing the full potential of every Brazilian citizen, regardless of their background or situation.

The debate about discontinuing mandatory financing for the S-System has continued over multiple administrations. A significant portion, representing more than 66% of received federal funds, is allocated to provide free activities for the general public. However, the level of federal government involvement in the System varies, with changes in the percentage of funds transferred to affiliated entities. This allocation ratio is vital to ensure the ongoing supply of complimentary activities for Brazilian workers and the wider population.

To Further Research and Reflect

- Briefly describe the institutions in your country responsible for workers' training and leisure activities, including their funding sources.
- What are the most innovative ideas and capabilities implemented in workforce training in your country? Discuss how these could be adapted and applied in the Brazilian context.

4.6 The Brazilian Financial System

The role of banks in bolstering economic development in Brazil is a topic of debate, just as is the contribution of the nation's financial system. Nevertheless, it is vital to emphasize that the Brazilian National Financial System (Sistema Financeiro Nacional - SFN) is not merely a part of this debate. Indeed, it is a critical player in promoting the country's balanced development and serving the interests of the community. The SFN is a network of entities mobilizing financial resources from national citizens and foreigners alike. Additionally, it is in charge of distributing and circulating currency and overseeing Brazil's financial processes. The System consists of regulatory, supervisory, and operational organizations, each carrying out distinctive functions.

The regulatory agencies, which are a vital component of the SFN, are tasked with defining rules that ensure the healthy functioning of the national financial market. These agencies include the National Monetary Council (Conselho Monetário Nacional - CMN), the National Private Insurance Council (Conselho Nacional de Seguros Privados - CNSP), and the National Supplementary Pension Council (Conselho Nacional de Previdência Complementar - CNPC). Their role is to ensure fair and transparent operation of the financial market while protecting the interests of institutions and citizens. For instance, the CMN sets monetary policy, the CNSP regulates the insurance market, and the CNPC oversees the supplementary pension system.

The operational subsystem of the SFN is a complex network of organizations that directly interacts with the public, facilitating financial transactions. These organizations form the backbone of the SFN and include banks and savings institutions, consortium administrators, stock exchanges, insurers and reinsurers, pension funds, credit unions, brokers and distributors, commodities and futures exchanges, open social security entities, payment institutions, non-bank institutions, and capitalization companies. Each entity plays a unique role in the financial system, contributing to its overall functioning and effectiveness.

The organizations overseen by national regulatory and supervisory institutions, alongside those guided by international agreements issued by the Basel Committee on Banking Supervision (BCBS), are crucial for maintaining the stability and integrity of the banking sector. The BCBS, in particular, plays a pivotal role in outlining the capital levels that banks should maintain, taking into account the risks associated with assets on their balance sheets. The original agreement, established in 1988, underwent revisions in 1995 and 2004. It is currently embodied in the third version, Basel III, reflecting the committee's commitment to ensuring the soundness of the banking sector.

The oversight and regulations of BCBS are crucial in guaranteeing that banks uphold suitable capital levels to counter risks effectively. These standards and guidelines set by the BCBS enhance the resiliency of the banking system and shelter it from financial crises. The evolution of BCBS, starting from the original Basel Accord to the present Basel III, indicates a continuous effort to adapt to shifting market dynamics and enhance the potency of global banking regulations.

In the domestic market, the CMN holds the highest authority within the financial system. It is responsible for formulating currency and credit policies to secure currency stability and promote economic and social development. The CMN's three primary responsibilities are as follows: adapting the volume of means of payment to meet the real needs of the national economy and its development process; regulating the internal value of the national currency to prevent or correct inflationary episodes of internal or external origins, economic depressions, and other imbalances resulting from cyclical events; and regulating the external value of the currency and the country's balance of payments to optimize the use of foreign currency resources.

The CNSP establishes the guidelines and rules for private insurance policies. Some of its responsibilities include regulating the constitution, organization, operation, and inspection of entities under its domain, and applying sanctions if there is non-compliance. The CNSP is also tasked with setting general characteristics for insurance, private pensions, capitalization, reinsurance contracts, and guidelines for reinsurance operations. Moreover, this entity acts as a disciplinary authority for insurance brokerage firms and professionals.

The CNPC regulates the supplementary retirement allowance scheme operated by closed additional pension entities and funds in Brazil. These entities are also subject to oversight by the Central Bank, which is responsible for controlling inflation and setting monetary policy, including interest rates. BACEN's role in establishing interest rates, such as the Special System for Settlement and Custody rate (Sistema Especial de Liquidação e de Custódia - SELIC), significantly impacts the financial sector.

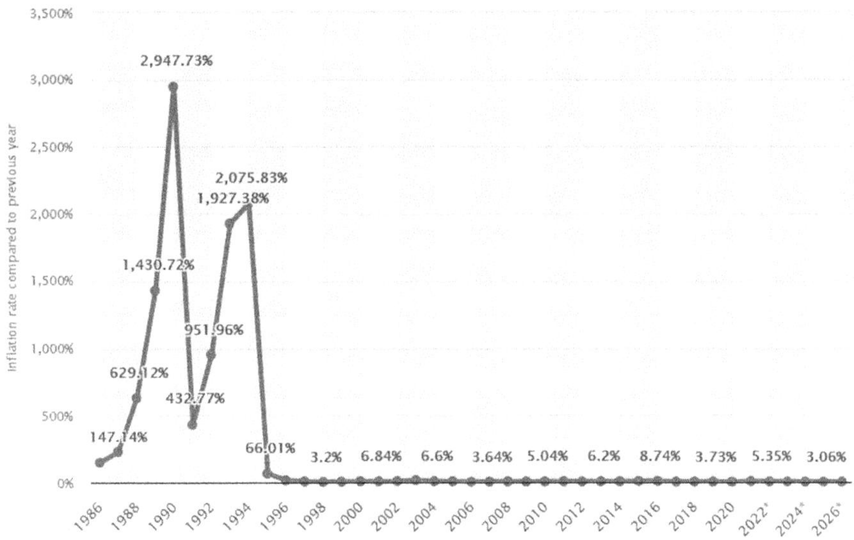

Fig. 4.3 Inflation rates in Brazil from 1986 to 2026. Source: Statista (2021)

Regulating inflation is complex in a country that experiences frequent economic crises and instabilities. For instance, in the early 1990s, inflation rates soared to nearly 3000% in 1990 and 2000% in 1994 (Fig. 4.3). During these volatile periods, the country underwent seven economic plans, colloquially referred to as "economic packages," and transitioned through four different currencies: the Cruzado (1986–1989), Cruzado Novo (1989–1990), Cruzeiro (1990–1993), and the Real (1994 to the present).

However, only the last of these plans, the Real Plan, succeeded in ending the high price volatility (along with the price rise) of essential products and a drastic devaluation of the national currency. Technically, hyperinflation corresponds to an annual inflation rate exceeding 100%. More recently, inflation has spiked during the coronavirus disease 2019 (Covid-19) pandemic, even though it is nowhere near those historic exponential rates.

BACEN regulates the quantity of money in the economy for financial and price stability. It oversees and supervises financial institutions. Among the many tasks the bank undertakes, it issues paper money and coins, carrying out the services related to their circulation. The Central Bank is known as the bank of banks because it receives both compulsory and voluntary payments from other financial institutions.

It authorizes operations and supervises rediscounts, loan operations, and clearing services. BACEN carries out transactions to purchase and sell federal public securities, controls credit, and establishes the conditions for exercising management positions in financial institutions. It also monitors other companies' interference in the capital markets.

One of the Central Bank's most critical and politically debated functions is controlling foreign capital flows. As Reuter (2012) explains, regulating these flows is crucial due to concerns related to global money laundering, transfer pricing, and tax evasion issues. Tobin (1978) proposed an international tax to manage capital movements, known as the Tobin tax.

The primary concept of the Tobin tax is to impose a fixed-rate tax on all transactions in the foreign exchange market. This rate would significantly affect short-term investments' returns, while its impact would be less substantial in the long term. The net outcome would be the discouragement of short-term capital movements (both illicit and speculative) while leaving long-term foreign investment flows undisturbed.

The Monetary Policy Committee (Comitê de Política Monetária - Copom) of BACEN is responsible for establishing the primary interest rate target. Copom was created in June 1996, and since then, it has achieved a more stable and transparent process for the country's monetary policy decision-making. Currently, Brazil's interest rates are not as high as in inflationary periods. However, these rates continue to fluctuate frequently. Over the past two decades, they have averaged 10%. Increased costs for capital borrowing are often cited as one reason for limited investments in many sectors of the Brazilian economy.

Another crucial institution assisting BACEN in governing the economy is the Securities and Exchange Commission (Comissão de Valores Mobiliários - CVM). This body is tasked with supervising, standardizing, enforcing rules, and developing Brazil's securities market. Securities are documents, issued by either companies or other entities (be it public or private), which exemplify a host of rights and obligations for their owners, and are bought and sold in the securities market—these include shares, bonds, certificates, debentures, etc. If the Central Bank or the CVM imposes a penalty on a financial system agent, the entity can appeal to the National Financial System Resource Council (Conselho de Recursos do Sistema Financeiro Nacional - CRSFN) to modify the decision.

In the insurance market, the Superintendence of Private Insurance (Superintendência de Seguros Privados - SUSEP) is in charge, diligently overseeing and inspecting the markets for insurance, open private pensions, capitalization, and reinsurance. Moreover, the National Superintendence of Supplementary Pension Plans (Superintendência Nacional de Previdência Complementar - PREVIC) is an autonomous body that carefully supervises and inspects closed supplementary pension entities and policies for the additional pension schemes operated by these entities. Both bodies perform a myriad of critical duties related to maintaining the liquidity and solvency of companies, monitoring investments, and protecting consumer interests in their respective markets. They are unwavering in their mission to safeguard the accumulation of popular savings through insurance, open private pensions, capitalization, and reinsurance operations.

Large private and public financial institutions hold a significant stake in managing Brazilian savings and development projects. A prime example is Caixa Econômica Federal (CEF), a federal savings bank with a pivotal role. It finances the construction of houses and other sanitation projects by diligently managing

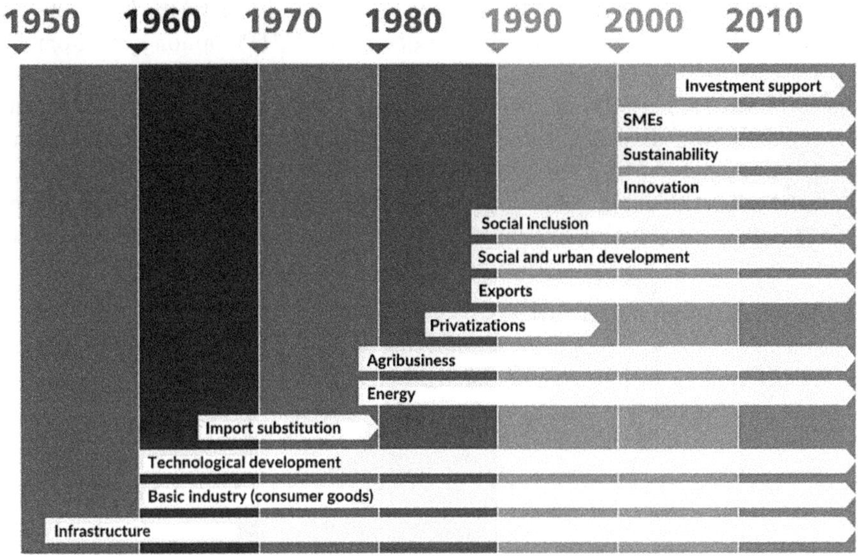

Fig. 4.4 BNDES investment priorities from 1950 to 2010. Source: Adapted from Barboza et al. (2018)

workers' contributions to their Guarantee Fund for Length of Service (Fundo de Garantia por Tempo de Serviço - FGTS).

CEF's involvement in low-income housing projects has evolved over the decades. In the past, the bank's role was more centralized, with the National Housing Bank (Banco Nacional da Habitação - BNH) managing housing finance through state-owned housing companies (Companhia de Habitação - Cohab) until 1986. Since 1999, CEF has participated in the Residential Leasing Program (Plano de Ações Articuladas - PAR), adopting a different land and urban strategy with joint management between the Union, municipalities, and private entrepreneurs.

The BNDES oversees numerous funds, including the Amazon Fund, and offers loans to bolster the advancement of the Brazilian economy. Established in 1952, the bank has been touted as a catalyst for Brazil's economic expansion. Figure 4.4 illustrates the progression of the bank's priorities during its over half-century of operations.

The National Bank for Economic and Social Development (Banco Nacional de Desenvolvimento Econômico e Social - BNDES) was founded in 1952. In the 1980s, its mission broadened to underscore a more socially oriented approach, symbolized by an "S" added to its name. This federal autarchy is tasked with formulating and implementing a national economic development policy. Over time, the bank aided in developing the Brazilian economy across different governmental regimes, eventually becoming more influential than the World Bank. The BNDES' loan portfolio was comparable to that of the World Bank by the mid-2000s and had grown to over three times larger by 2013.

The significant expansion of the bank was primarily driven by the influx of new resources, resulting from SELIC interest rates and the R$500 billion loans from the Treasury to BNDES. As a result, BNDES's total liabilities skyrocketed from less than 10% in 2007 to 60% in 2014, indicating a substantial increase in its dependence on Treasury funds. In recent years, BNDES has undertaken a restructuring process characterized by a multidimensional retreat from operations. This strategic shift was influenced by investigations into the bank's alleged involvement in corruption scandals, triggering a reevaluation of its activities and a reassessment of its operational focus.

To Further Research and Reflect

- Detail your country's approach to financing development and explore the pivotal role of state-owned banks compared to private investment banks in fostering growth, particularly in remote and expansive regions.
- What are your thoughts on implementing an international taxation system akin to the one advocated by Tobin?

4.7 Virtual Banks and Fintechs in Brazil

Digital banks are gaining substantial traction in Brazil. According to Poder 360 (2021), the number of accounts in digital banks hit 82 million in mid-2021, marking a significant growth of roughly 66% in just 1 year. Prominent players in this market include industry titans such as Nubank, holding over 40 million accounts, and InterBank, Original Bank, C6 Bank, Agibank, Neon, and Next. The advent of digital banks in Brazil dates back to 2014, a relatively recent but swiftly growing phenomenon in the nation's financial landscape.

These banks leverage advanced technology and an efficient cost structure, allowing them to provide fee-free services that traditional financial institutions generally charge for. With an estimated 45 million unbanked Brazilians, digital banks are essential in promoting financial inclusion. This inclusion extends beyond mere statistics and offers tangible benefits to people, including easier access to credit, simplified business transactions, and streamlined bill payments.

One of the primary benefits of digital banks is their convenience. Unlike traditional banks, they operate without physical branches, providing all services via online channels. Account opening, contract signing, and document validation are all executed virtually, whether through an app, website, or even WhatsApp messages. The sole service that necessitates a physical presence is cash withdrawal, achievable through InterBank 24-hour ATMs.

As reported by Money Times (2021), findings from a survey conducted by C6 Bank/Ipec in April 2021 revealed that 57% of Internet users in Brazil hold at least one digital bank account, with 10% having transitioned away from traditional banking services. Moreover, regarding demographics, the survey highlighted a notable preference for digital banks among younger age groups. Specifically, 51% of

Brazilians aged 16 to 24 reported having an account with a digital bank, compared to 41% opting for traditional banking services.

Other companies in Brazil deliver financial services through apps and digital tools, such as credit, payment options, accounting, and investments. These companies are known as fintechs. Over the past 5 years, fintechs have experienced a sevenfold growth in Brazil. The market was regulated in 2018 with the BC+ program, created by BACEN to enhance the efficiency of the national financial system through modern legislation and lower-cost credit. The growth of fintechs has been driven by this new regulatory environment and the perception that Brazil's highly concentrated financial system is inefficient.

In addition to regulation and opportunity, several other factors have contributed to the growth of fintechs. Digitization is one such factor: people have increasingly sought improved services from financial institutions, specifically online, faster solutions. Another contribution was the increased access to big data. By accessing users' economic histories, service providers can offer heightened personalization for each individual, thereby enhancing the user experience with their services.

One of the primary characteristics of Brazilian fintechs is their focus on a single or limited number of functions. For instance, banks such as Nubank or Banco Inter do not maintain a broad product portfolio compared to traditional banks. Creditas and TuTu Digital concentrate on offering credit, while Mercado Pago and Vindi deliver payment solutions for individuals and businesses. Meanwhile, Contabilizei, a fintech company, specializes in providing hassle-free accounting services for both new and established companies. This focus on select functions allows fintechs to operate within restricted market segments, catering to small- and medium-sized enterprises.

Nubank, a pioneer in the industry, epitomizes Brazil's emergence and increasing popularity of fintechs and virtual banks. After being underserved by a bank and experiencing frustration with the bureaucratic process of opening a bank account in Brazil, Colombian entrepreneur David Vélez decided to start his own financial services company. He pursued investments in the concept and succeeded in revolutionizing the country's economic system. In September 2014, Vélez and two partners launched their inaugural product: a credit card (endearingly termed "purple"), which pledged to be devoid of bureaucracy, without an annual fee, and managed entirely through a digital app.

Nubank swiftly attracted customers thanks to the services provided and, gradually, diversified its product portfolio. In 2017, it launched NuConta, a digital account. Entirely manageable via the app, it allows for unlimited free transfers to any bank, maintaining no fees for upkeep or other matters. Additionally, unlike conventional bank accounts, any sum deposited automatically accrues 100% of the Interbank Deposit Certificates (Certificado de Depósito Interbancário - CDI), a rate exceeding that of bank savings, which is the most commonly used form of financial investments among Brazilians.

This digital bank has expanded its services to include a points program with no expiration date, personal loan offerings, and corporate accounts. This strategic diversification has contributed to Nubank's growth, positioning it as the sixth-largest financial institution in Brazil in terms of clients. Notably, Nubank has garnered recognition for its excellence, having been named the best bank in Brazil by Forbes for the third consecutive year, as reported by Latam Gateway (2021). This accolade underscores Nubank's commitment to innovation, customer-centric services, and its significant impact on the financial sector in Brazil.

With few exceptions, most digital banks in Brazil were operating at a loss due to expanding investments and the omission of tariff charges. Two exceptions were Banco Inter, with a net income of around US$14 million in 2018, and Agibank, with a net income of US$30 million in the same year. However, these profits are still significantly smaller compared to traditional banks. For instance, Itaú Unibanco Bank netted approximately US$5 billion in 2018. One strategy for digital banks to generate revenue is to offer new products and services to their customers, such as credit facilities, investment opportunities, and even virtual shops.

In 2020, 40% of Brazilian fintechs had plans to operate in the USA, and 1 in 4 of these companies already had operations abroad. One exemplar is Ebanx, a company founded in 2012 that gained notoriety for a solution enabling foreign companies like Spotify and AliExpress to sell products in Brazil using local currency. The company began its expansion in 2015 and has operations in Mexico, Colombia, Argentina, Uruguay, and Bolivia. The start-up currently boasts over 900 employees and experienced 200% growth between 2019 and 2020 in foreign countries.

The international expansion of Brazilian fintechs is a result of their professionalization. In the past, these companies merely cloned service types that existed abroad. However, they now develop products to resolve domestic market issues and aim to expand their businesses. Another indication of the consolidation of Brazilian fintechs is the financial backing they have received. For instance, in June 2021, JP Morgan finalized the purchase of 40% of C6 Bank, estimated to be worth $2 billion. In the same month, Nubank, with an estimated valuation of $29 billion, also received financial contributions, further solidifying its position as the most prominent fintech in Latin America.

To Further Research and Reflect

- Could you list fintech companies operating in your country and their core services? Additionally, from a customer's perspective, explore the advantages and disadvantages of holding a digital bank account versus a traditional bank account.
- As Brazilian fintech and digital banks capitalize on opportunities emerging from the traditional banking sector, identify other industries within your country that these companies could potentially disrupt.

4.8 Brazilian Bank Sector Concentration

The banking sector in Brazil is dominated by several large state and private banks, which include foreign banks. Despite the high concentration in the industry, numerous financial technology companies, or fintechs, have recently started to challenge traditional banking institutions. The majority of banking services can be accessed at branches, via the Internet, or through ATMs situated in supermarkets and shopping malls within the larger Brazilian cities. However, rural and remote regions in the Northeast and North are without banking facilities, resulting in a heavy reliance on banknotes in these areas.

BACEN (2021) asserts that Brazilian banknotes are among the safest worldwide, featuring advanced security measures. These incorporate watermarks, magnetic security threads, latent images, see-through registers, tactile intaglio printing, optically variable magnetic ink, and hologram stripes. Together, these attributes verify the authenticity of the currency and facilitate easy authentication.

Since the 1980s, banks have been creating electronic payment systems to replace traditional cash and check payments, a shift primarily driven by the phenomenon of hyperinflation. In Brazil, stores are authorized by banks to collect monthly installments. They may or may not levy an interest rate surcharge on these payments from consumers. The credit market associated with these small, regular payments is known as "carnê."

Freitas and Kirch (2019) examined the effect of technology investments on financial institutions' performance, specifically in the context of the digitalization of the Brazilian banking system. They found a significantly positive relationship between banks' spending on information technology and their profitability variables, as well as a decrease in administrative expenses. Simultaneously, banks are cutting down the number of branches and employees, using Internet services to complement the services previously offered at branches.

Internet-only banks aim to streamline operations by eliminating physical branches, thereby reducing fixed costs, and enabling exclusive remote transactions. In contrast, traditional incumbent banks prioritize establishing long term relationships with individual clients, with a focus on catering to a wide array of financial transactions. This model creates a dependency for clients on a single institution for various financial operations, fostering a sense of trust and convenience.

Despite digitization, Brazil's banking sector is still dominated by two major state banks, Banco do Brasil and Caixa Econômica Federal, as well as by three private banks: two Brazilian banks, Itaú and Bradesco, and a foreign entity, Santander. While several other smaller national or international banks operate in the Brazilian financial market, their market share remains modest. The state banks aid certain government policies by providing credit for infrastructure ventures and for the agriculture and agribusiness sectors, particularly in the case of Banco do Brasil.

Itaú was established in Brazil in 1943 by Alfredo Egydio de Souza Aranha. Later, his nephew, Olavo Setubal, a principal executive and founder of two major companies, Deca and Duratex, became a distinguished leader. In 2008, the bank merged with Unibanco, which had been operating in the Brazilian market since 1924. This merger, as per Itaú (2021), led to the creation of the most extensive private conglomerate in the Southern Hemisphere and ranked the bank among the world's top 20 in terms of asset value.

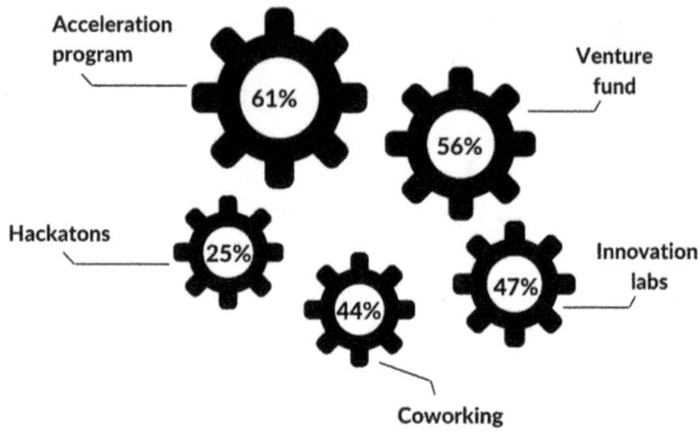

Fig. 4.5 Banks with innovation programs (multiple answers). Source: Adapted from FEBRABAN (2021)

Bradesco (2021) was established in 1943 in Marília, São Paulo. Three years later, it relocated to downtown São Paulo and expanded into other regions of the country, with a dense concentration of branches in the South of Brazil. In 1951, the bank became the market leader in deposits, and in 1953, it established its headquarters in Osasco, a city that is part of metropolitan São Paulo. Since then, the bank has been under the guidance of strong and innovative leadership, beginning with Amador Aguiar, who served as the president of the bank until 1990.

Bradesco was the pioneer in introducing information technology advancements to the Brazilian banking sector. The bank was the first to leverage large computers for manipulating millions of client and shareholder data. After boasting the largest computing capacity in the country during the 1960s, the bank introduced credit cards, ATMs, Internet banking, and mobile banking. In 2017, Bradesco established Next, its fully digital bank.

According to a survey by Febraban (2021), almost all banks have adopted initiatives to stimulate innovation within their operations. Figure 4.5 confirms this trend, highlighting a range of strategies including acceleration programs, venture funds, hackathons, innovation labs, and coworking spaces. These initiatives aim to encourage innovation and agility in the banking sector.

Santander, one of the other major private banks operating in Brazil, has a relatively brief history. Originating from Cantabria, Spain, in 1857, Santander initially functioned as a commercial bank. It entered the Brazilian market in 1982 and gradually expanded its presence. As of 2021, Santander has emerged as the third-largest private bank in Brazil in terms of assets, marking a significant milestone in its growth trajectory within the country.

As the leading financial conglomerate in Latin America, Santander boasts substantial market shares in Brazil and Spanish-speaking countries including Argentina, Chile, and Mexico. Its impressive expansion is primarily credited to the strategic acquisition of local banks. For instance, in 2000, Santander expanded its presence in Brazil by acquiring the state of São Paulo bank, Banespa. Furthermore, the conglomerate has successfully merged with other key players in the market, such as private banks like Banco Geral do Comércio, Noroeste

Meridional, and Real Bank, strengthening its stance as a top financial institution across numerous regions.

The oldest and most prominent institution in the Brazilian financial milieu is the state-controlled Banco do Brasil. Established in 1808 during Brazil's colonial tenure under Portuguese governance, Banco do Brasil boasts a rich history that has spanned over two centuries. Today, it stands as one of the world's oldest banks and the largest financial institution in the Southern Hemisphere.

The bank has been intimately entwined with the country's history, managing its largest government funding programs: the National Subsistence Farming Support program (Programa Nacional de fortalecimento da Agricultura familiar - Pronaf), established in 1995, and rural credit programs, in operation since 1937. These programs have financed Brazil's agriculture and agribusiness sectors.

Caixa Econômica Federal is another significant state-owned bank operating in the Brazilian financial sector and purports to be the Bank for all Brazilians. Established in 1861 by Dom Pedro II during Brazil's monarchy, Caixa (2021) has since carved its mark in the financial landscape. A century later, in 1961, it emerged as the sole manager of the country's Federal Lotteries. The bank offers a wide range of services such as loans and financing and manages notable funds and government programs like FGTS, the Social Integration Program (PIS), unemployment insurance, educational credit, housing, and social benefits transfers.

During the Covid-19 pandemic, Caixa Econômica played a vital role in disbursing "emergency aid" funds to the targeted population. However, despite the commendable effort, it is worth noting that long lines formed outside the bank's branches as individuals sought to access this aid. Unfortunately, the institution did not effectively implement measures to prevent the gathering of potentially infected persons along these lines.

During the 1980s, Caixa Econômica incorporated the BNH, establishing itself as the central agent for housing financing as well as a critical financier for urban

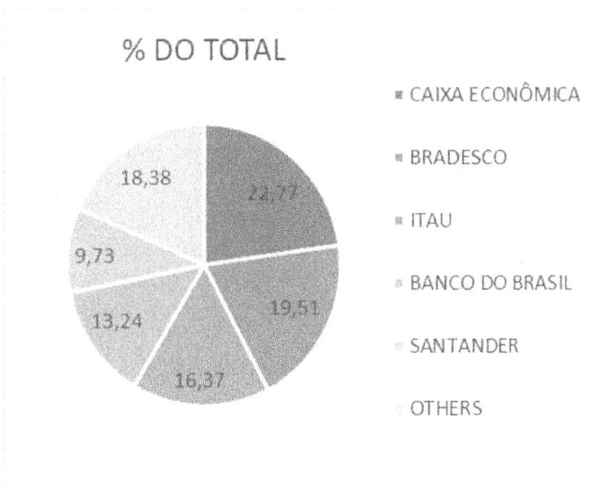

Fig. 4.6 Banking concentration in Brazil. Source: Livre. JOR (2024)

development and sanitation. In the same decade, the bank assumed the role of the sole administrator of the world's largest fund, the FGTS, which was centralized from 70 other financial institutions in 1990, in addition to the functional funds of the Financial Housing System (Sistema Financeiro de Habitação - SFH). The bank also emerged as the primary agent directing the capital from savings accounts to support the SFH and the Real Estate Financial System (Sistema de Financiamento Imobiliário - SFI), arguably the country's two most prominent types of real estate financing.

When analyzing the participation of the five largest banks in terms of assets, we observe that these banks have dominated the financial market in Brazil for decades. Together, they comprise roughly two-thirds of the financial sector's assets. Fig. 4.6 displays the percentage of net income for Brazil's five largest banks in 2019. A significant concentration in their market share is evident.

However, the number of customers is not the only indicator of bank concentration. According to BACEN (2021), the five largest banks in 2019 held 81% of total assets in the banking segment, 83.4% of year-end deposits, and 83.7% of all credit operations conducted in the country. The three largest banking conglomerates hold more information in their systems than any other state institution. In an era where data appears to be more valuable than oil, it seems practically impossible to design and implement public policy without sharing information with these banks.

To Further Research and Reflect

- Elaborate on the primary banking entities in your country and examine their contributions to financing sustainable development projects and infrastructure initiatives, both domestically and internationally.
- What strategies can bank institutions employ to ensure long-term profitability in remote and rural areas of a vast, continent-sized country such as Brazil? Should these institutions prioritize transactions or focus on building relationships with customers in these regions?

References

BACEN – Banco Central do Brasil. (2021). *The Brazilian Currency*. Available from https://www.bcb.gov.br/en/banknotesandcoins

Barboza, R. M., Furtado, M., & Gabrielli, H. (2018). *A atuação histórica do BNDES: O que os dados têm a nos dizer? Textos para discussão 123*. Available from https://web.bndes.gov.br/bib/jspui/bitstream/1408/14620/1/TD_123-AtuacaoHistorica_P_BD.pdf

Bradesco. (2021). *O Bradesco e Sua História*. Available from http://museubradesco.org.br/pages/capitulos/bradesco.html

Caixa. (2021). *Sobre a Caixa*. Available from https://www.caixa.gov.br/sobre-a-caixa/apresentacao/Paginas/default.aspx

Caldeira, J. (1995). *Mauá: Empresário do Império*. São Paulo: Companhia das Letras. 560 p

CNC. (2021). *O que é a CNC*. Available from https://www.portaldocomercio.org.br/sobre-a-cnc/o-que-e-a-cnc

CNI. (2021). *About CNI*. Available from http://www.portaldaindustria.com.br/cni/en/about/

D'Angelo, P. (2021). *Pesquisa Sobre o Instagram no Brasil: Dados de Comportamento dos Usuários, Hábitos e Preferências no Uso do Instagram*. Available from https://blog.opinionbox.com/pesquisa-instagram/

Djankoy, S. et al. (2007). *What makes a successful entrepreneur?* Evidence from Brazil. Available from https://eml.berkeley.edu/~groland/pubs/brazilent0907.pdf

Doing Business. (2020). *Economy profile Brazil - Doing Business 2020*. World Bank Group. Available from https://www.doingbusiness.org/content/dam/doingBusiness/country/b/brazil/BRA.pdf

Embrapa. (2024) *Empresa Brasileira de Pesquisa Agropecuária. Quem somos*. Available from https://www.embrapa.br/quem-somos

Embrapii. (2024). *Associação Brasileira de Pesquisa e Inovação Industrial. Quem somos*. Available from https://embrapii.org.br/institucional/quem-somos/

Etzkowitz, H. (2003). Innovation in innovation: The Triple Helix of university-industry-government relations. *Social Science Information, 42*(3), 293–337.

FEA. (2024). *Pioneiros & Empreendedores: A Saga do Desenvolvimento no Brasil*. Available from https://pioneiros.fea.usp.br/

FEBRABAN. (2021). *Pesquisa FEBRABAN de Tecnologia Bancária 2020*. Ano-base 2019. Available from https://cmsportal.febraban.org.br/Arquivos/documentos/PDF/Pesquisa%20Febraban%20de%20Tecnologia%20Banc%C3%A1ria%202020%20VF.pdf

Freitas, O. D., & Kirch, G. (2019). Performance dos Bancos Brasileiros no Contexto de Digitalização. *Revista Brasileira de Finanças* (Online), Rio de Janeiro, *17*(2), 38–55.

Itaú. (2021). *Sobre o Itaú*. Available from https://www.itau.com.br/institucional/sobre-o-itau/

Latam Gateway. (2021). *The Rise of Digital Banks in Brazil*. Available from https://payments.latamgateway.com/digital-banks-in-brazil/

Livre. jor (2024). *Concentração Bancária?* Afinal de contas, quantos clientes tem cada financeira no Brasil? Available from https://livre.jor.br/quantos-clientes-tem-cada-banco-financeira-brasil/

Marcovitch, J. (2012). *Pioneirismo Empresarial no Brasil*. 3 Volumes. São Paulo: Edusp, 1000 p.

Mazzucato, M., & Penna, C. (2016). *The Brazilian innovation system: A mission-oriented policy proposal*. Project Report. Centro de Gestão e Estudos Estratégicos (cgee), Brazil. Available from http://sro.sussex.ac.uk/id/eprint/61974/

Moda Center. (2021). *Moda Center Santa Cruz*. Available from http://www.blogdomodacenter.com.br/p/blog-page.html

Money Times. (2021). *JPMorgan no C6 Bank Escancara Apetite por Bancos Digitais Brasileiros. 2021*. Available from https://www.moneytimes.com.br/jpmorgan-no-c6-bank-escancara-apetite-por-bancos-digitais-brasileiros/

OCB. (2021). *História do Sistema OCB*. Available from https://www.somoscooperativismo.coop.br/historia-do-sistema-ocb

Oslo Manual. (2018). *Guidelines of collecting, reporting, and using data on innovation*, 4th ed. Available from https://www.oecd.org/science/oslo-manual-2018-9789264304604-en.htm

Pesquisa GEM. (2024). *Global Entrepreneurship Monitor*. Available from https://datasebrae.com.br/wp-content/uploads/2024/03/Apresentacao-PPT-GEM-BR-2023-FINAL-V3.pdf

Poder 360. (2021). *Maiores Bancos Digitais Têm 82 Milhões de Contas em 2021*. Available from https://www.poder360.com.br/economia/maiores-bancos-digitais-tem-82-milhoes-de-contas-em-2021/

Ries, E. (2011). *The lean startup: How today's entrepreneurs use continued innovation to create radically successful businesses*. Crown Business. 336 p.

Reuter, P. (Ed.). (2012). Draining development? Controlling flows of illicit funds from developing countries. Washington, DC: World Bank. Available from http://documents.worldbank.org/curated/en/305601468178737192

Statista. (2021). *Brazil: Inflation Rate from 1986 to 2026*. Available from https://www.statista.com/statistics/270812/inflation-rate-in-brazil/

Tobin, J. (1978). A proposal for international monetary reform. *Eastern Economic Journal, 4*, 1978.

Vasconcellos, R. R., & Neto, J. A. (2012). Fatores Críticos na Transferência de Tecnologia no Setor Espacial: Estudo de Caso de Programas de Parceria das Agências Espaciais do Brasil (AEB) e dos EUA (NASA). *Production Journal, 22*, 851–864.

Workbox. (2024). *10 Best Chicago Business Incubators to Scale Your Startup*. Available from https://www.workboxcompany.com/10-best-chicago-business-incubators-to-scale-your-startup/

Chapter 5
Brazil in the Global Market

5.1 Introduction

Brazil's entrance into the global sphere has been shaped by numerous factors, which include its strategies for economic development. After the 2008 Global Financial Crisis, Brazil, along with other Latin American economies, sought international integration via global value chains (GVCs) and free international trade, despite certain developed countries' shift towards protectionist policies. This trajectory has fostered a subordinate role in the international financial arena, in which global capital dynamics heavily impact Brazil's economic growth. Additionally, Brazil's involvement in international associations like BRICS (a group comprising Brazil, Russia, India, China, and South Africa, alongside new members—Egypt, Ethiopia, Saudi Arabia, the United Arab Emirates, and Iran—that were officially added in 2023) has created new opportunities for cooperation and development among the participating nations.

Brazil's economic role in the global market is highlighted by its significant levels of both inward and outward foreign direct investment (FDI) in recent decades. Inward FDI, which attests to Brazil's economic attractiveness, saw a substantial increase in the 1990s following monetary stabilization and pro-market reforms. This bolstered Brazil's standing as a primary global recipient of FDI. In the 2000s, Brazil also emerged as a significant source of outward FDI, with flows primarily focused on the secondary and tertiary sectors and largely directed towards neighboring economies, the United States (USA), and Europe. The global significance of Brazil's FDI flows stems from economic growth, local currency appreciation, and the presence of competitive national corporations with large-scale operations.

China and the USA, as Brazil's main trading partners for exports and imports, play an instrumental role in the country's global trade environment. International bodies like the Financial Stability Board (FSB), the Organization for Economic Cooperation and Development (OECD), the World Trade Organization (WTO), and

G. Masiero, *Brazilian Socio-Economic Dynamics*, Contributions to Economics,
https://doi.org/10.1007/978-3-031-87685-1_5

the United Nations (UN) Conference on Trade and Development (UNCTAD) carry out the effective coordination of these trade activities by diligently setting rules and guidelines for global trade and investments. The foreign capital stock of Brazil is distributed across both the financial and manufacturing sectors. However, it is important to note that over half of Brazil's export value is concentrated in just two products—soybeans and iron ore. This underscores Brazil's heavy reliance on these commodities.

Brazil has historically been a major recipient of foreign capital, with investments from various countries driving its economy and contributing to its development. Key investor countries in Brazil include the USA, the Netherlands, Germany, Spain, and the Bahamas. These investments have played an instrumental role in shaping Brazil's economy, contributing to its development, and enhancing its participation in GVCs. Terminologies such as internationalization, fragmentation of production, supply chain, and outsourcing underpin the concept of GVCs.

GVCs represent the interconnected processes involved in the production and distribution of goods and services across different countries. They emphasize the division of labor, specialization, and integration of economies on a global scale. The evolution of GVCs has transformed the way businesses operate, allowing them to leverage comparative advantages and optimize production processes through international collaboration and resource allocation. Understanding the dynamics of GVCs is both beneficial and essential, especially for countries like Brazil, as it helps navigate the complexities of the global economy, attract foreign investment, and enhance international market competitiveness. By capitalizing on strengths in natural resources, clean energy, and other strategic sectors, Brazil can stimulate economic growth and development.

The country can leverage new and revitalize existing partnerships. For instance, Japanese investment in Brazil's agriculture and textile industries dates back to the 1910s and 1930s. A fresh influx of Japanese investments in the 1970s led to the founding of substantial pulp, paper, and steel processing industries. In the 1990s, the phenomenon of *segyehwa* (globalization) and incentives from the Brazilian government prompted some of South Korea's largest multinationals, such as Samsung and LG, to establish subsidiaries in Brazil. Most recently, the majority of Chinese FDI in Brazil has been focused on brownfield investments, with a comparatively smaller portion on greenfield investments.

On a smaller scale, Brazil has fostered several companies that spearheaded expansion abroad. Embraer is the global leader in the regional or small planes sector, while Natura holds the position of the world's fourth-largest cosmetics company. Petrobras, which also maintains a robust international presence, has spearheaded the exploration of pre-salt oil in deep waters. Large companies, in general, have driven globalization, which is characterized by economic and social processes that foster integration among countries and people worldwide.

Apart from the success of the European regional integration process, there are many other examples. In Latin America, for instance, Mercosur was established by Brazil, Argentina, Uruguay, and Paraguay and has seven associated countries: Bolivia, Chile, Colombia, Ecuador, Guiana, Peru, and Suriname. Mercosur spans more than 70% of South America's territory and encompasses a similar proportion of its population (around 300 million inhabitants). When considering the combined gross domestic product (GDP) of all its member countries, it is seen as the fifth-largest economy globally. All regional integration agreements transform an authoritatively delimited territory into an area exempt from many customs rules and regulations, like many worldwide free trade zones (FTZs).

5.2 Brazil's Integration in the Global Sphere

Brazil's international presence is defined by its considerable influence in various global areas, including diplomacy, economy, culture, and environmental issues. It, represents a major emerging economy and plays a vital role in global economic discussions. Today, beyond collaborating on economic policies and project development, the country is instrumental in leading management changes in the central financial institution, and new ones like the New Development Bank (NDB).

Brazil's active participation in the UN exemplifies its commitment to global peace and security. The country contributes significantly to peacekeeping missions and advocates for UN Security Council reforms. This includes working for a permanent seat for itself, as well as the expansion of the organization to promote greater participation from other countries. As Harig (2018) observes, Brazil has been the predominant troop contributor to the UN Stabilization Mission in Haiti (MINUSTAH), providing all force commanders for this mission from 2004 to 2017. Brazil's leadership extends to regional organizations in South America, where it frequently undertakes a central role. This is seen in institutions such as Mercosur (Southern Common Market) and the Organization of American States (OAS), where it is a founding and leading member.

Brazil's global significance lies in its substantial contributions to global food security. The country is among the world's largest producers and exporters of agricultural products, such as soybeans, coffee, sugar, and beef. The agribusiness sector of Brazil has a profound influence on global food security. In the energy sector, Brazil is a significant participant in the global energy market due to its production of ethanol from sugarcane and substantial oil reserves, particularly in the pre-salt offshore fields. Moreover, Brazil's robust trade relationships with countries all over the world, including enhanced trade with China and, to a lesser extent, the USA and the European Union (EU), further bolster its role in the global trade network.

Brazil is a cultural powerhouse. Events such as Carnival and music genres like samba and bossa nova exemplify its vibrant culture. Its football prowess, symbolized by its five FIFA World Cup victories, is legendary. Brazilian players and coaches are conspicuous in leagues worldwide, making Brazil's cultural presence felt through sports. The country has recently hosted major international events, such as the 2014 FIFA World Cup and the 2016 Summer Olympics.

However, Brazil's true global impact lies in its environmental stewardship. Home to most of the Amazon Rainforest, it is often erroneously referred to as the "lungs of the Earth." Contrary to popular belief, the oxygen produced by the trees is consumed by the trees themselves, as they too require respiration. Therefore, characterizing the Amazon rainforest as the "lungs of the Earth" is not accurate. In reality, its significance in climate change pertains to the regulatory role the forest plays in almost all of South America's rainfall cycle and its function as a significant carbon sink.

Brazil holds a crucial role in global environmental discussions and biodiversity conservation efforts. Its active participation in international climate agreements and initiatives, such as the Paris Agreement, emphasizes its commitment to reducing deforestation and promoting sustainable development, despite occasional setbacks. As per Araujo (2020), the Bolsonaro administration has reduced funding for the Brazilian Institute of Environment and Renewable Natural Resources (IBAMA) and the Chico Mendes Institute for Biodiversity Conservation (ICMBio), both of which are tasked with environment protection and enforcing environmental laws.

Jair Bolsonaro's presidency has significantly impacted Brazil's environment and climate change combat efforts negatively. Bolsonaro has prioritized shrinking the scope of protected areas, making it more challenging for indigenous communities to defend their land rights. His administration prioritized economic proliferation over environmental protection, leading to a surge in Amazon logging, mining, and agricultural expansion. In conclusion, Bolsonaro's presidency has markedly hampered Brazil's progress towards environmental protection and climate action.

Brazilian research institutions contribute to advancements in various fields, including tropical medicine, biofuels, and the aerospace sector, as underscored by Embraer. Attracting millions of visitors each year, Brazil's diverse landscapes, from the Amazon Rainforest to the beaches of Rio de Janeiro, make it a globally popular destination. Brazil's international presence is multifaceted, with significant economic, cultural, and environmental dimensions. Its active participation in global governance and contributions to numerous international sectors underscore its importance on the world stage.

Brazil's integration into the global sphere is characterized by active participation in international organizations, robust trade relations, influential cultural exports, and significant environmental stewardship. Brazil frequently contributes to peacekeeping missions with the UN and advocates for a reformed, more representative Security Council. Often, the country serves a mediating role in international conflicts. At the WTO, Brazil is involved in global trade negotiations and disputes, advocating for fair trade practices and market access for developing countries. As a member of the International Monetary Fund (IMF) and World Bank, Brazil also contributes to international financial policies and development programs.

The country's regional leadership and cooperation are embodied in its actions. It has been an active member of Mercosur, promoting economic integration and collaboration with Argentina, Paraguay, Uruguay, and Venezuela. This regional bloc strives to facilitate free trade and the seamless movement of goods, people, and currency. Brazil plays a pivotal role in Union of South American Nations (Unión de Naciones Suramericanas - UNASUR), which aims to enhance regional defense, health, and infrastructure integration. The primary activities in these and other emerging and developing countries include exporting commodities like soybeans, iron ore, oil, and meat, as well as importing machinery, electronics, and chemical products. Currently, its primary trading partnership is with China.

Brazil's integration into the global sphere is comprehensive, spanning economic, cultural, environmental, and diplomatic dimensions. It is actively participating in international organizations, leading in regional cooperation, and contributing to global trade and culture, underscoring its significant role on the world stage. The country often mediates regional and global conflicts, leveraging its position to foster dialogue and peaceful resolutions.

Borzova and Medina Gonzalez (2023) discuss Brazil's role in the mediation of the territorial conflict between Ecuador and Peru. Their study underscores unsuccessful mediation endeavors carried out by guarantor countries—Brazil, the USA, Chile, and Argentina—which precipitated the war between Ecuador and Peru. Regardless, the mediation efforts of these countries from 1995 to 1998 ultimately culminated in the "Elegant Agreement."

The "Elegant Agreement" is a noteworthy outcome of mediation efforts between Ecuador and Peru in their territorial conflict. The mediation activities led to the establishment of this agreement in 1998. It was designed to address the divergent territorial interests of Peru and Ecuador, taking into account the considerations of both parties. This agreement emphasizes the importance of mediation activities in resolving conflicts and achieving a peaceful resolution that takes into account the needs and concerns of the nations involved.

To Further Research and Reflect

- Briefly describe the main issues in your country's integration in regional and global agreements.
- How has your country contributed to international cooperation over the past 50 years? Highlight the three most important events.

5.3 Inward and Outward FDI in Brazil

The research conducted by Garcia et al. (2023) plays a significant role in the discussion of inward and outward FDI in Brazil. Their findings suggest that inward FDI has the potential to create important knowledge spillovers, encouraging innovation in host regions. This concept is supported by the evidence that Brazilian regions receiving increased inward FDI often show strong innovative performance as demonstrated through patent activity. Furthermore, regions with greater local firm absorptive capacity, combined with academic efforts and industrial diversity, are ideally positioned to leverage the knowledge from inward FDI and fuel innovation.

Viglioni and Calegario's (2020) research emphasizes the practical implications of inward FDI in promoting innovation performance in the Brazilian manufacturing industry. Their findings indicate that the influence is further amplified by an interaction between FDI inflows and exports, implying that FDI may encourage product adaptation for foreign markets. This underscores the potential of inward FDI to stimulate innovation and boost Brazil's economic growth and global competitiveness, particularly in the manufacturing sector.

However, it is worth noting that inward FDI in Brazil is primarily focused on the import substitution of machinery, equipment, and software, rather than stimulating internal research and development (R&D) investments or R&D-related FDI. R&D are typically conducted in the companies' home facilities. This trend is globally recognized, with large high-tech industry players demonstrating superior innovation performance compared to medium and low-tech industry players.

The primary sources of FDI in Brazil are countries such as the USA, Spain, the Netherlands, and China. These nations have made significant investments in Brazil, enticed by its expansive domestic market, abundant natural resources, and strategic geographic location. FDI in Brazil has spanned a broad spectrum of sectors, with substantial investments directed to manufacturing, mining, agriculture, and services—specifically in finance, telecommunications, and retail. The oil and gas sector has become a significant target for foreign investment, definitely following the discovery of pre-salt oil fields. This sector-wise distribution of FDI offers an inclusive snapshot of Brazil's investment landscape, reinforcing the positive effect of FDI on Brazil's economic development.

The proactive measures undertaken by the Brazilian government to attract FDI, such as offering tax incentives, refining regulatory frameworks, and heightening infrastructure investment, have taken a pivotal part in the country's economic growth. Brazil's engagement in regional trade agreements, such as Mercosur, has also heightened its appeal as an investment destination. Inward FDI has transcended just job creation and enriching technological capabilities—it has pushed productivity levels and bolstered infrastructure. The ensuing escalation in competition across different industries has proven beneficial for consumers, further emphasizing FDI's positive impact on Brazil's economic terrain.

Brazil provides a variety of incentives to attract FDI and to foster a beneficial environment for international investors. The Special Regime for Infrastructure Development (Regime Especial de Incentivos para o Desenvolvimento da Infraestrutura - REIDI) program offers exemptions from certain federal taxes on the purchase of goods and services for infrastructure projects, particularly in the sectors of transportation, energy, ports, and sanitation. *Lei do Bem* (Good Law) provides tax incentives for companies that make investments in R&D, allowing for income tax deductions for expenditures on technological innovation. Although the Inovar-Auto Program has now concluded, it was replaced by similar initiatives and historically provided tax benefits to automakers investing in local manufacturing and R&D.

Moreover, the Manaus FTZs and other Special Economic Zones (SEZs) provide fiscal benefits. These benefits are also supplemented by the Investment Partnerships Program (Programa de Parceria de Investimento - PPI), which enables private investment in infrastructure projects via public-private partnerships (Parceria Público-Privada - PPPs). This program aims to attract foreign investment by assuring legal and regulatory stability in the fields of transportation, energy, and sanitation. Furthermore, BNDES offers long-term financing and favorable credit lines for projects that enhance innovation, sustainability, and technological advancements. The Funding Authority for Studies and Projects (Financiadora de Estudos e Projetos - Finep) supports innovation and research-based projects through grants, credits, and venture capital funding.

Recent reforms have aimed to reduce bureaucratic obstacles and streamline business processes. These include simplifying tax compliance and enhancing the efficiency of regulatory bodies. The eSocial System—a unified digital platform for tax, social security, and labor obligations—is lessening the administrative load on companies. In conclusion, while inward FDI has been a crucial driver of innovation in Brazilian regions, particularly when coupled with substantial local absorptive capacity and exports, there is room for improvement. Encouraging more R&D-related FDI and internal R&D investments could further boost Brazil's innovation performance.

Despite its appeal, Brazil is faced with challenges that may affect FDI influx, encompassing political instability, economic fluctuation, intricate tax systems, and bureaucratic obstacles. It is critical to address these issues to maintain and enhance foreign investment levels. Generally, inward FDI remains a pivotal element of Brazil's economic approach, contributing to its development and integration into the global economy. As noted by Polloni-Silva et al. (2021), FDI may benefit host countries, but potential adverse effects should also be accounted for. It may escalate environmental damage and degradation, particularly in heavily polluting industries. Developing regions like Brazil, seeking to attract FDI, must thoughtfully balance economic growth with environmental protection.

Large multinational corporations can sometimes overshadow or drive local firms out of business through unfair competition. This scenario can subsequently diminish domestic investment and long-term innovation. Foreign firms may repatriate a substantial portion of their profits back to their home countries rather than reinvesting them domestically, leading to a net capital outflow from the host country. FDI often leads to uneven development, with benefits concentrated in specified regions or sectors. This situation exacerbates regional disparities and income inequality within the host country.

Relying too heavily on FDI can render the host economy vulnerable to external shocks and global capital flow fluctuations. Overreliance on foreign capital may also undermine domestic entrepreneurship and innovation. To alleviate these risks, host countries, such as Brazil, need to regulate FDI prudently and channel it into priority sectors, while investing in domestic capabilities and innovation. Policies should aim to maximize the benefits of FDI while minimizing potential negative impacts.

The same positive and negative aspects of FDI should be taken into account in the case of Brazilian outward foreign direct investment (OFDI). Brazil emerged as a considerable source of OFDI in the 2000s, with investments predominantly leaning towards neighboring South American economies, the USA, and Europe. Brazil lacks institutionalized policy measures to bolster OFDI, apart from selective loans offered by the state investment bank BNDES. The growth of Brazil's OFDI is shaped by economic development, local currency appreciation, increased savings, and overseas market opportunities for Brazilian companies with competitive advantages.

According to Rossi et al. (2016), the determinants of Brazilian OFDI include market opportunities abroad, economic growth, and local currency appreciation. It has also been suggested that Brazil's strengthening currency is a factor that prompts companies to expand overseas, though there is no strong empirical evidence to support this hypothesis. In conclusion, the growth of Brazilian OFDI is a recent phenomenon. Despite the country's lack of standardized policy support, certain multinationals, similar to those from other developing countries, are emerging, as described by Fleury and Fleury (2009).

To Further Research and Reflect

- Evaluate the advantages and disadvantages of your country's inward foreign direct investment flow. Additionally, what specific policies does your country implement to attract foreign direct investment?
- Describe the main characteristics of your country's outward foreign direct investment, focusing on the largest multinational corporations and the policy support they receive.

5.4 Brazilian Trade and Investment Partners

The exchange or commercialization of goods and services among different nations and countries has been a common practice for thousands of years. Today, many international institutions and regulations manage the global flow of goods and services. Political groups like the G-8 and G-20 convene meetings to discuss the worldwide economic situation. Besides trade agreements, certain international organizations such as the Organization of American States (Organização dos Estados Americanos - OAS) work towards ensuring political stability, peace, and security on the American continent.

Brazil participates actively in international economic and financial organizations and forums. Its goal is to devise and implement strategies for economic strengthening and to promote sustainable development. The Ministry of Economics plays a critical role in cultivating relationships with high-level representatives from different countries who are in charge of economics, finance, and development. It engages in economic-financial dialogues and international cooperation mechanisms. This cooperation can take place directly with countries or through participation in groups such as the G20, BRICS, G24, Community of Portuguese Language Countries (CPLP), or international bodies (like the Financial Stability Board and the Global Forum on Transparency and Exchange of Tax Information).

The Brazilian Ministry of Economy, acting as the primary representative of the Brazilian government, plays an active role in governance discussions within organizations such as the IMF, the World Bank Group, the NDB, and the Asian Infrastructure Investment Bank. The Ministry also shows a strong commitment to addressing global environmental issues, aiming to enhance Brazil's access to financial funds intended for climate change adaptation and mitigation. These include the Strategic Climate Fund (SCF), the Clean Technology Fund (CTF), the Forest Investment Program (FIP), and the Green Climate Fund (GCF).

Engaging with funds like the GCF is not only a strategic interest for Brazil but also a testament to its commitment to the Paris Agreement and its proactive role in climate change mitigation. The GCF, an entity functioning under the financial mechanism of the UN Framework Convention on Climate Change (UNFCCC), is the sole multilateral funding entity mandated to support the Framework Convention and allocate equal funding for mitigation and adaptation. Established in 2010, it recently announced contributions (pledges) of over US$10 billion from 43 countries, which further underscores its global significance and Brazil's role within it.

Economic activities are becoming increasingly reliant on dynamic commercial and social relations to intensify the flow of goods and services in our ever-more connected world. This has led to countries trading more goods and services through international trade with each passing decade. Countries establish bilateral agreements and follow rules negotiated in international bodies like the World Trade Organization (WTO), as well as regional blocs such as Mercosur and the European Union. Consequently, countries are required to organize their legal environment to regulate these activities including enacting and revising their customs legislation.

One of the most informative ways to visualize a country's international trade performance is by considering its trade balance. This indicator records the value of a country's imports and exports of goods and services. When the balance leans positive, it signifies that the country exports more than it imports. Conversely, a negative balance suggests that the value of imports surpasses the value of exports. Advanced and industrially developed countries usually add value to the goods they export, while developing nations tend to sell commodities related to minerals, plants, or animals that have low added value. Figure 5.1 shows the principal Brazilian export and import products in 2020. Figure 5.2 shows Brazil's leading international trade partners.

Despite many centuries of commercial exchange among countries, there continues to be extensive debate regarding the reduction and elimination of customs tariffs to enhance trade relations. Some argue that the disparities in the availability of

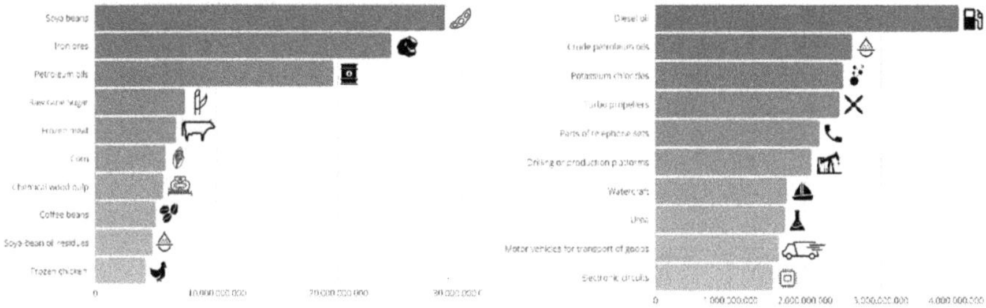

Fig. 5.1 Brazil's main exports and imports in 2020. Source: MDIC (2021)

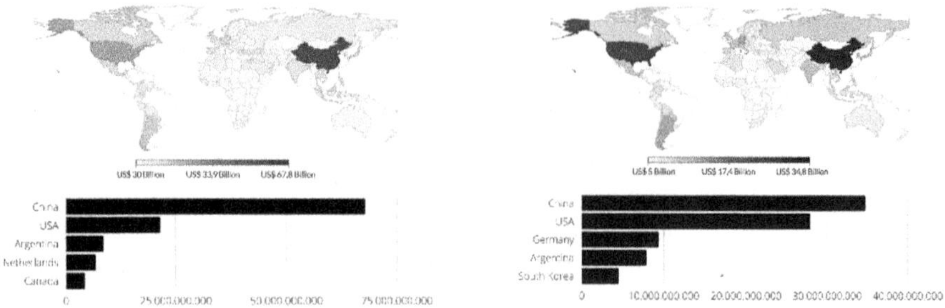

Fig. 5.2 Brazil's main international trade partners. Source: MDIC (2021)

production factors (land, labor, capital, and technology) drive businesses between countries, citing comparative advantages.

As intended by trade agreements, the reduction of tariffs and other trade barriers could boost product commerce. This tendency has dramatically increased within the past 25 years, with cross-border trade happening in nearly all industries. Many products incorporate parts and materials from multiple countries, thus creating global supply chains.

Integration into the global economy has proven to be a potent tool for countries to promote economic growth, development, and poverty reduction. Industrial nations and the international community need to make more substantial efforts to eliminate trade barriers facing developing countries, especially the poorest countries. Providing the poorest countries with duty- and quota-free access to worldwide markets could benefit them significantly with minimal cost to the rest of the world.

Protectionist measures have significantly increased in recent years, impacting global trade flows and supply chains. These measures encompass tariffs, non-tariff barriers, and restrictions on cross-border capital flows, leading to disruptions in trade patterns and market access. Technological progress has shaped debates surrounding specialization, scope gains, and economies of scale in production, emphasizing competitive advantages. However, factors such as wars, financial crises, and health emergencies can prompt authorities worldwide to implement protectionist or restrictive measures that directly affect the flow of goods and services in the international market.

The increase in protectionism is challenging international trade and supply chains, requiring proactive strategies to address potential adverse effects. Managers have an essential role in mitigating risks by diversifying suppliers, performing risk assessments, and keeping abreast of protectionist policies enacted by sourcing countries. Adopting technologies such as blockchain can bolster transparency in supply chains and assist in risk management in the face of changing trade dynamics.

The interconnected nature of international production chains can amplify the effects of protectionist measures. This highlights the need for careful navigation of trade policy to maintain economic stability and growth. In conclusion, the interplay between protectionism, technological advancements, and external crises shapes the global trade landscape. Such dynamics influence authorities to implement measures that impact the flow of goods and services internationally. To navigate the complexities of a shifting global trade environment, it is essential to adapt to these changes, enhance transparency in supply chains, and foster resilient trade relationships.

Goods and services are not the only commodities regulated in the international market; investments are also strictly controlled. In Brazil, foreign investors are allowed to be majority shareholders in companies, assured by a relatively stable legal regime that guarantees their freedom to invest. However, all investments must be reported to the Central Bank of Brazil. The Brazilian Trade and Investment Promotion Agency (Apex-Brasil) provides information on the necessary authorizations to establish a business within its borders. Foreign direct investments have surged in line with the country's economic development. A significant expansion occurred between 2009 and 2011, although the rate of investments has been decelerating since then.

According to UNCTAD (2020), FDI flows decreased by 20% between 2018 and 2019, yet the stock remained stable at US$640 billion in 2019. That same year, Brazil ranked as the ninth largest investment destination worldwide. The most significant investors hailed from the Netherlands, the USA, Germany, Spain, and Luxembourg. As observed in other Latin American countries such as Argentina, Chile, Colombia, and Peru, FDI in Brazil is mainly concentrated in the extractive industries, specifically commodities. Figure 5.3, reproduced from IEDI (2017), displays the stock of FDI in various economic sectors.

In contrast to FDI inflows, greenfield investments have seen a decline in recent decades. Greenfield investments involve the establishment of new subsidiaries or companies by investing in offices, plants, and manufacturing products from scratch. These investments have, in some instances, been concentrated in specific sectors such as oil and gas extraction, the automotive industry, and financial services. Conversely, brownfield investments, which involve the acquisition or lease of

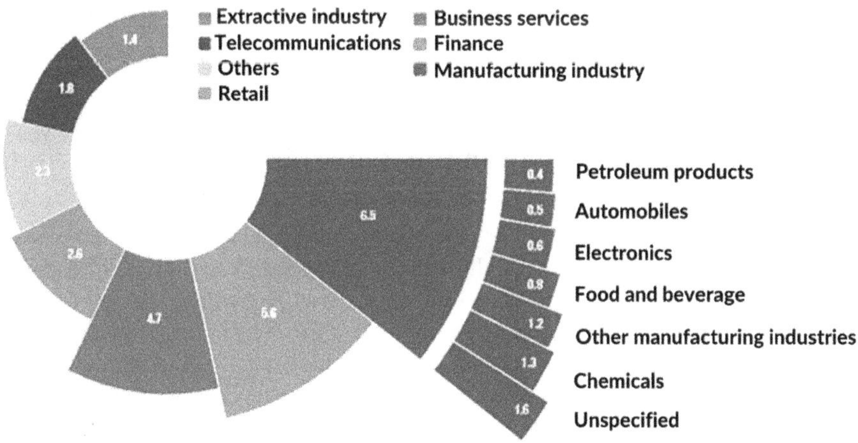

Fig. 5.3 Stock of foreign direct investment in Brazil until 2015. Source: Reproduced from IEDI (2017)

existing facilities to initiate new operations or expand existing ones, have become more prevalent. Advantages of brownfield investments include quicker access to markets and lower start-up costs compared to greenfield projects.

The coronavirus disease 2019 (Covid-19) pandemic has significantly impacted investment trends. FDI inflows halved in 2020, while outflows and capital repatriations increased substantially. Global economic challenges brought about by the pandemic have led to a decline in greenfield investments as investors became more cautious and risk-averse. Despite the overall reduction in greenfield investments, the pace of announced investments in critical minerals has doubled in recent years. This trend underscores the growing importance of sectors such as renewable energy and electric vehicles, which depend on critical minerals.

Brazil is one of the world's largest recipients of FDI. Two key factors contributing to this are the large size of its domestic market, with more than 210 million inhabitants in 2024, and the availability of easily exploitable raw materials. Additionally, the diversified nature of Brazil's economy, making it less susceptible to international crises, and its strategic geographical position facilitating easy access to South American countries are other significant factors.

However, Brazil's appeal for foreign investment continues to pose a challenge due to its complex tax system, bureaucratic difficulties, and rigid labor laws. These and other challenges have been overcome by numerous foreign companies that have established their presence in Brazil during different stages of its development. Nonetheless, in certain cases, such as Ford Motor Co., the business costs exceeded the benefits. Consequently, in early 2021, the company ceased its car production after operating in the country for a century.

To Further Research and Reflect

- Compile a list of goods and services traded between Brazil and your country of origin. Additionally, offer suggestions for increasing transactions between the two countries.
- Provide the names and activities of companies from your country operating in Brazil and Brazilian companies operating in your country.

5.5 European and American Companies Operating in Brazil

Multinational companies, having headquarters in one country and operations in at least one other, have been strategically advancing abroad for centuries. This trend, spearheaded by American companies following World War II, has allowed them to exploit the advantages of low labor costs, abundant natural resources, and burgeoning consumer markets. Their objective? To achieve higher levels of productivity and profitability, a goal that commandsthe activities of managers and entrepreneurs

Recently, countries have been actively competing to attract multinational companies to their domestic markets. Acknowledging the potential benefits, governments have increased their efforts, offering tax exemptions, foundational infrastructure, and even land donations. These endeavors, aimed at creating jobs and stimulating industrial development, merit our recognition.

The process of globalization has significantly contributed to the performance of multinational companies by providing essential telecommunications and transportation conditions. These conditions are fundamental for these companies' global operations. A large majority of these companies are key players in the GVC, leading trade and investments through their outsourcing and offshoring activities. Various functions such as design, R&D, production, marketing, and distribution have been located across different countries.

GVCs are a crucial aspect of multinational operations. They can be understood through various terms such as internationalization, fragmentation of production, supply chains, and outsourcing. The process of manufacturing a specific product is often carried out in different parts of the world. Thus, a GVC refers to this internationalization of production, which has significantly increased international trade in intermediate products. These products are used as inputs for other final products, either for domestic consumption or for exports, thereby driving global economic growth.

Brazil's integration into GVCs is hindered by its highly closed economy, a key barrier to establishing such a process. Pressures exerted by multinational and large national companies operating in the country persuade various governments to adopt anticompetitive policies in their favor. Additionally, the country persists as a major producer of agricultural and mineral commodities with minimal added value.

Cases of industries and companies participating in GVCs are uncommon. Generally, major national or international companies lean towards exploiting the domestic market, rather than seeking enhanced productivity through globally organized production. However, various industries and companies, comprising significant national and international entities, actively engage in GVCs to amplify productivity, penetrate global markets, and boost competitiveness.

According to BACEN (2024), the concept of foreign capital gained prominence following the enactment of a law in 1962, known as the "legal statute of foreign capital." Under this law, foreign capital is defined as any goods, machinery, and equipment that enter Brazil without an initial expenditure of foreign exchange, provided that they are intended for the production of goods or services. Additionally, any financial or monetary resources brought into the country for use in economic activities, provided that they are owned by individuals or entities residing, domiciled, or headquartered abroad, are also considered foreign capital.

In Brazil, foreign capital is treated the same as Brazilian capital. Direct foreign investment is not taxed, yet it is forbidden from participating in nuclear energy, healthcare services, postal and telegram services, as well as the aerospace industry. Despite these constraints, Brazil has received substantial investments, primarily from European, North American, and Latin American countries, in all other sectors of the economy.

As one of the top ten most prominent recipients of foreign capital and the largest among Latin American and Caribbean countries, Brazil's principal investor countries include the USA, the Netherlands, Germany, and Spain. The sectors that received the most substantial investments consisted of oil and gas extraction, motor vehicles and auto parts, electricity and gas, financial services, and commerce.

With the global advancements of Industry 4.0, significant pressure exists to modernize a substantial portion of Brazilian industry. Sectors such as fintechs (financial services), agrotechs (agribusiness solutions), healthtechs (healthcare), and edtechs (education) have demonstrated openness to the disruptive innovations brought by start-ups from various activity areas. Beyond the productivity gains that technological advancements offer, they are critical for increased integration with other international partners and global production chains.

There are countless examples of large multinationals from European and North American countries operating in the Brazilian market. Biogen Idec, a pharmaceutical company based in Massachusetts, Colgate-Palmolive from New York, and Huntsman from Salt Lake City, Utah, are just a few examples. Other prominent companies, such as Google, Master Card, and General Motors, are also tapping into the Brazilian market and are among the top players in their respective sectors.

Several European multinational companies are also present in Brazil, contributing significantly to various economic sectors. In the food retail sector (supermarkets), French companies Casino and Carrefour are prominent players. Rhodia stands out in the pharmaceutical industry, while Vallourec is a major participant in the steel industry. Also in the steel sector is the German company ThyssenKrupp. In the automobile sector, Mercedes-Benz and Volkswagen have been operating in Brazil for many decades.

The Swedish manufacturers, Scania and Volvo, along with the Italian Fiat, are prominent players in the automotive industry, each making significant contributions to the sector. Fiat has a long-standing history of producing motor vehicles, establishing itself as a key player since the 1970s. Conversely, Scania and Volvo, based in Sweden, are renowned for their innovation and excellent quality in the production of trucks and buses.

Banco Santander and Telefónica are prominent Spanish companies with a robust presence in Brazil. Banco Santander, a notable financial institution, operates in the banking sector, while Telefónica is a central force in the telecommunications industry. These companies have established themselves as crucial contributors in Brazil, aiding the growth and progress of their respective sectors.

North American, European, South American, or Asian companies predominantly operate in Brazil due to factors such as its substantial dynamic consumer market, significant immigrant population, abundant natural resources, and diversified economy. In addition to these, its geographic location provides access to virtually all South American markets. Trade agreements such as Mercosur have eased this access from the 1990s onwards, including the Latin American Integration Association, Aladi. This organization has been promoting Latin American regional integration since 1980, aiming for improving economic and social development.

Despite the substantial presence of multinational corporations operating in Brazil, and the country's ongoing efforts to bolster its business environment, foreign companies often express concern about high "Brazilian costs." These costs primarily stem from heavy taxation, rigid labor legislation, and extensive bureaucratic complexities. Recently, Brazil saw its most substantial decrease in FDI in 2020 due to the Covid-19 pandemic.

The 2021 closure of Ford Motor Co.'s plants in Brazil marked a significant shift in the nation's automotive industry, signaling a transformation in market dynamics. However, simultaneous to this change, the interest sparked by Brazil's open natural gas industry from top investors has been noteworthy. American investors such as New Fortress Energy, along with European companies like BP, PLC, and EIG Global Partners, are looking into substantial multibillion-dollar investments in this budding sector.

To Further Research and Reflect

- Which renowned commercial or industrial brands from your country have established a presence in the Brazilian market? Furthermore, can you speculate whether foreign direct investment (FDI) flows from North America and Europe to Brazil differ from those from China?
- Provide three examples of regional integration agreements and then enumerate three advantages and disadvantages of a country signing and becoming a partner in such contracts.

5.6 Japanese, Chinese, and South Korean Companies in Brazil

FDI has not only played a pivotal role but has also been the cornerstone in shaping Brazil's economic landscape, a trend that dates back to its colonial era. The country's dynamic domestic market and the high local economic growth rates in the FDI's country of origin have been critical for companies investing in Brazil. The influence of Brazil's colonial heritage and strategic geographic location cannot be understated in explaining the presence of FDI in the country.

While European and American FDI significantly contributed to the various phases of Brazil's industrialization, capital from Asia, primarily Japan, has also been a notable driver of development though on a smaller scale. Brazil saw an influx of Japanese immigrants from 1908 to the late 1970s. Japanese investment in the agricultural and textile industries saw an increase during the early 1910s and the 1930s. These capital flows have since continued.

The Japanese community in Brazil, which includes immigrants and their descendants, exceeds 1.5 million. In some manner, this Japanese "diaspora" is accountable for the varying "waves" of Japanese FDI in Brazil. In the latter half of the 1960s, Japan's investments in Brazil more than doubled from previous amounts. Japan's economy experienced a rapid recovery, while Brazil was undergoing its "Economic Miracle," with GDP growth rates hovering around 11% from 1968 to 1974.

Uehara (1999) explains that Japanese FDI in Brazil surged during this period, reaching 13% of the total FDI in Brazil in 1970. Japanese investment in Brazil peaked in the 1970s, propelled primarily by large government projects. Japanese companies invested significantly in essential primary industries, including petrochemicals, aluminum, pulp, and paper. These investments were intimately linked to the Second National Development Plan that Brazil was striving to implement.

The second wave of Asian investment was marked by a formidable spirit of international cooperation. It was characterized by numerous partnership investments and the incidence of Japanese investors willingly accepting minority subsidiary interests. Such a collaborative approach, exemplifying the global nature of business, was underscored by the establishment of the Japanese consortium, Japan Brazilian Pulp and Paper Resources Co.—Cenibra, in 1974. In 1976, an international consortium of steel was launched with the participation of Brazilian state Siderbras (51%), Italy's Finder (24.5%), and Japanese Kawasaki Steel (24.5%), leading to the establishment of the Tubarão Steel Company. Moreover, another consortium, Nippon Amazon Aluminum Co.—Albrás, was initiated by the Japanese in 1978.

After two periods of substantial investment by Japanese firms in Brazil, an economic downturn occurred in the 1980s and early 1990s due to both domestic and international issues. Brazil faced problems such as foreign debt, high inflation, economic recession, and political and economic instability. During this time, the world and Brazil faced two oil crises and abandoned the developmental model based on import substitution. The economy then transitioned towards being financed by an influx of foreign investment and international loans. The economic stagnation and turbulence during the 1980s, a period when many financial plans failed to stabilize the economy, resulted in the infamous "lost decade."

Even though Brazil underwent the most significant privatization process worldwide in the 1990s, Japanese capital did not respond by increasing investments. Instead, these capital flows only returned towards the decade's end and during the first decade of the new century. The decreasing presence of Japanese money in Brazil stands in contrast with the growth of South Korean investments since the 1990s. During that decade, South Korea sought greater economic openness and conducted reforms in the complex relationships between the government and large business conglomerates.

The government's move was catalyzed by domestic political alignment with the global movement known as *segyehwa*, or globalization. This movement in Korea was marked by the pursuit of internal alterations within the country and the growing presence of Korean companies internationally. Consequently, Korean conglomerates broadened their operations in the global market.

Brands like Samsung, Daewoo, LG, and Hyundai have become familiar to consumers worldwide. Supported heavily by the government, the performance of these conglomerates played a pivotal role in South Korea's swift industrialization. These businesses are primarily accountable for Korean direct investment worldwide, which includes significant investments in Brazil.

According to Masiero (1998), Korean companies began their operations in Brazil in the mid-1990s to tap into the local market and the expanded opportunities presented by the formation of Mercosur. Approximately 30 subsidiaries of large South Korean corporations were established in Brazil during this decade. However, the Asian financial crisis soon brought setbacks to their expansion plans in Brazil, significantly impacting South Korean companies.

Asian investments sparked anew in the mid-2000s, with another surge of Asian FDI, primarily of Chinese origin. Chinese trade and FDI dramatically increased worldwide. After its acceptance into the WTO in 2001, China's government began promoting its "going global" strategy. By 2011, China had become Brazil's leading trade partner and a substantial investor. However, the majority of Chinese FDI in Brazil has been brownfield—acquiring preexisting production capacity, rather than making greenfield investments.

Since making their first substantial investment in Brazil's sector in 2010, Chinese power companies have persistently invested in the distribution and generation of electric power. Although some greenfield investments have been made by Chinese companies, such as those by BYD Company in the electric vehicles industry, the majority of investments have been aimed at acquiring existing electrical distribution firms. Chinese investments have particularly concentrated on renewable energy sources like hydropower, wind, and solar power.

The leading Chinese companies operating in Brazil include the State Grid Corporation of China, which has heavily invested in Brazil's power sector with a focus on electricity distribution and generation. Moreover, Huawei, the leading telecommunications company, provides technology solutions and infrastructure. BYD is actively involved in the electric vehicle market as well as renewable energy projects. The China Three Gorges Corporation partakes in hydropower projects and sources of renewable energy, while Tencent has invested in Brazilian tech start-ups and digital businesses.

Representing Japanese companies, Toyota and Mitsubishi are major players in the Brazilian automotive market. Nippon Steel has invested in steel production and manufacturing, while Sumitomo is involved in various sectors such as finance, real estate, and chemicals. Marubeni is another prominent player in the agriculture, food products, and energy sectors.

South Korean companies like Samsung and LG are key players in the Brazilian electronics market. They possess a strong influence in consumer electronics and appliances, producing and selling a vast array of products. Hyundai and Kia Motors are prominent automotive brands with operations in Brazil, while Posco has made investments in the steel production and manufacturing sectors. South Korean, Japanese, and Chinese companies offer a diversified and substantial presence in Brazil, contributing to multiple sectors of the Brazilian economy.

To Further Research and Reflect

- List some Japanese, South Korean, or Chinese companies operating in your national market and give examples of products you buy from them. Which companies are also operating in Brazil?
- Search for and discuss some differences between Asian and European foreign direct investment (FDI) in your domestic and Brazilian markets.

5.7 Brazilian Multinationals—Petrobras, Embraer, and Natura

Globalization is an economic and social process that facilitates integration between countries and people worldwide. This process involves companies, governments, and institutions conducting financial, cultural, and commercial exchanges. Economic globalization deepened after the fall of the Berlin Wall in 1989, marking the end of the division between capitalist and socialist countries.

Transnational companies trading worldwide are the main drivers of economic globalization. This trend has accelerated the flow of goods and financial transactions across different countries and continents. Several regional alliances have emerged in this context, including Mercosur in South America, Asia-Pacific Economic Cooperation (APEC) in Asia, North American Free Trade Agreement (NAFTA) in North America, and the EU in Europe. Typically, this process is dominated by American, European, and large Asian conglomerates.

Economic globalization has been promoted as a driver of development primarily by neoliberal economists, particularly since the 1980s when Margaret Thatcher governed Britain and Ronald Reagan in the USA. These economists contend that the State should serve solely as a regulator, not an engine, of the economy. Additionally, they identify the flexibility of labor laws as a measure that must be enacted to bolster a country's economic growth.

Globalization is an asymmetric phenomenon, with some countries emerging as net winners and others as net losers. Rapidly emerging problems are becoming apparent: unemployment, loss of labor incomes, and the digital divide. Those who cannot access new technologies, like smartphones and computers, are destined to become increasingly isolated. Conversely, globalization has enabled the bridging of different cultures.

Many businesses now conduct their operations via electronic interactions, primarily leveraging the Internet. While this is a burgeoning practice in all global markets, it has not supplanted the need for companies to establish their presence in foreign markets. Multinational companies, headquartered in one country, operate in several other countries worldwide through subsidiaries. These entities are also referred to as transnational corporations or global companies.

The emergence of large companies has intensified globalization since the end of World War II and even more so since the 1980s. Subsequently, numerous countries sought to extend their operations into other national markets after achieving success in their domestic markets. This pattern is also present in Brazil, where a select group of companies has successfully established a presence in foreign markets. Examples include Alpargatas, Banco do Brasil, Bradesco, Embraer, Gerdau, Itaú Unibanco, JBS, Marcopolo, Natura, Odebrecht, Oi, Perdigão, Petrobras, Sadia, Vale, Votorantim, and Weg.

Many of these firms are recognized as key players in the global market. For instance, Fortune (2019) included eigthof these companies in their list of 500 top-earning corporations. Similarly, Forbes (2021) featured 21 Brazilian companies in their compilation of the 2000 largest public companies worldwide, ranked by revenue, net profit, market value, and total assets.

Among the most significant and internationalized Brazilian companies, many were originally state-owned and later privatized. For instance, Petrobras—Petróleo Brasileiro S.A.—was established in 1953, during the government of Getúlio Vargas. Petrobras focuses on oil exploration, production, marketing, and the distribution of derivatives. Headquartered in Rio de Janeiro and presently operating in several countries, it remains a publicly traded company with the Union—the Federal Government of Brazil—as its primary shareholder.

The establishment of Petrobras only became possible after many years of infrastructure development and political disputes between nationalist and internationalist groups. The nationalists defended treating the mineral as a state monopoly, while the internationalists argued in favor of allowing established multinational corporations to explore it. The National Petroleum Council (Conselho Nacional do Petróleo - CNP), established in 1938, began structuring oil exploration in Brazil.

The Petroleum Statute was established in 1948, to regulate oil exploration due to the competitive nature of the sector. However, a significant popular movement, encapsulated by the slogan "The oil is ours," led to the creation of a company that fell under the jurisdiction of the National Petroleum Council.

Numerous events have marked the company's trajectory of expansion in Brazil and beyond. Petrobras' first refinery, the Duque de Caxias Refinery (Reduc), was founded in 1961 in Rio de Janeiro. It remains one of the largest and most crucial refineries in Brazil. The Research and Development Center (Cenpes), created in 1963 in Rio de Janeiro, is currently recognized globally as one of the most significant applied research centers.

Petrobras Distribuidora, founded in 1971 in Rio de Janeiro, is currently the largest company in Brazil in the oil product distribution sector. The company has operations not just in Brazil, but also in Argentina, Chile, Colombia, Paraguay, and Uruguay. The Campos Basin, which covers approximately 100,000 km2, was discovered in Rio de Janeiro in 1974. Numerous platforms operate in this region, with the primary platform situated in the municipality of Macaé, which is Brazil's leading oil producer.

It is crucial to understand that Brazil only achieved self-sufficiency in oil production in the early twenty-first century, a point at which its oil production exceeded domestic consumption. In the years preceding this achievement, specifically in 1997, Petrobras relinquished its monopoly of the Brazilian oil sector, but this did not halt its expansion. In 2007, the pre-salt oil deposits—located in deep waters beneath the salt layers in the Santos Basin, off the coast of São Paulo—were discovered.

Throughout its history, the company has gained experience and both national and international recognition. Recently, it played a major role in one of Brazil's most wide-ranging corruption and money-laundering scandals. Since 2014, the Federal Police have been investigating the company, resulting in the indictment and imprisonment of several individuals, including Petrobras executives and various figures from Brazil's political scene.

Another significant Brazilian multinational, Embraer, was established in 1969 as a state-owned company. Embraer is a leading organization in the commercialization of jets for the regional aviation market—consisting of commercial and executive aviation, aircraft for defense, security, and agricultural aviation. It was privatized at the start of the current century. Even though Brazil had no tradition in the aerospace sector, government subsidies nonetheless supported the establishment and development of the company. Consequently, it has transformed into a formidable competitor in the global market for small- and medium-sized aircraft.

Embraer is the top manufacturer of commercial jets accommodating up to 150 seats and the principal exporter of high-value-added goods in Brazil. It sustains industrial units, offices, service centers, and parts distribution centers across the Americas, Africa, Asia, and Europe. While the GVC in this market comprises many players, only a few are ultimate "systems integrators" capable of managing large-scale production. The leading players are Airbus (Europe), Boeing (USA), Bombardier (Canada), Embraer (Brazil), and Tupolev (Russia).

In the process of internationalizing Embraer, Petrobras, and other large private companies, the State implemented policies including public ownership, the establishment of R&D centers, and local market share protection. This greatly contributed to these firms' transformation into major national companies. The expansion of these companies also facilitated their entry into international markets. Such growth was further encouraged by the financial backing of the Brazilian government, which provided funds for significant projects. This enabled these corporations to invest in novel innovations and technologies.

Many state-owned or private companies have enjoyed a favorable environment for expanding their operations in various domestic economic sectors and internationalizing through different strategies. For instance, the private cosmetic company Natura, founded in 1969, initiated its internationalization process in the 1980s, starting with the sales of its products in Latin American countries.

The strategy was solidified through the acquisition of the Australian brand Aesop in 2013, the UK-based Body Shop in 2017, and the North American company Avon in 2020. Consequently, it rose to be the world's fourth-largest company in the cosmetics sector. The company emphasizes producing many of its products sustainably, utilizing raw materials sourced from the Amazon region.

To Further Research and Reflect

- List some arguments against neoliberal economists, who argue that the State should only be a regulator and not a driver of the economy, considering the initial years in which economic growth must be ignited in the context of competitive global markets.
- Briefly describe a company from your country operating abroad and the job opportunities for locals versus expatriates. What would you advise a Brazilian multinational expanding its activities in your domestic market?

5.8 Brazilian Free Trade Zones

A Free Trade Zone (FTZ) is a designated area sanctioned by the government, exempting companies within it from many customs rules and regulations. This exemption enables them to import products into the country without paying duty taxes. Within the zone, companies can freely import goods without tariff charges. These goods can then be used to assemble finished products, which can be distributed to the domestic market or re-exported without any trade surcharges. Hence, companies operating within a Zone can increase logistics efficiency, reduce tax costs, and gain access to both local and nearby markets. Numerous countries have established several FTZs, with Brazil being a prime example.

The origins of the first Brazilian Free Zone date back to the 1950s, when the creation of a free trade port in Manaus was formally proposed to the Brazilian Congress. Even since colonial times, the idea of allowing foreign ships to navigate the Amazon River has been under discussion. However, the Manaus Free Zone (MFZ) was officially approved by the Brazilian Congress and President Juscelino Kubitschek in 1957. A decade later, in 1967, the Manaus Free Trade Zone Superintendence (Superintendência da Zona Franca de Manaus - Suframa) was established. This organization, equipped with its own legal status, assets, and financial and administrative autonomy, was charged with managing the Zone.

According to Suframa (2021), the MFZ is an industrial, commercial, and agricultural hub with economic conditions that have enabled its development, despite its considerable distance from major consumer centers. Amapá joined the Zone in 1991. A Constitutional Amendment was introduced in 2014, prolonging the Zone for an additional 50 years, until 2073. In the same year, the extension of incentives until December 2050 was approved for all zones administered by Suframa. Such measures were advocated as necessary to assure medium and long-term investments in the region.

The Manaus Free Zone consists of three sectors: commercial, industrial, and agricultural. However, industrial activities are predominant. The Industrial Pole of Manaus houses around 500 high-tech industries, generating more than half a million jobs, primarily in the electro-electronic sectors dominated by South Korean companies, such as Samsung and LG. Notable foreign companies specializing in computer goods manufacturing, like Microsoft, also operate there, with approximately 2300 registered workers responsible for assembling smartphones and video game consoles. Japanese companies such as Honda and Yamaha have plants in the motorcycle sector. The agricultural sector focuses on food production, agro-industry, fish farming, tourism, and wood processing.

Similar to Free Trade Agreements (FTAs) or the Multi-Fiber Arrangement (MFA), an Export Processing Zone (EPZ) is a designated area within a country that is specially tailored with specific regulatory, tax, and customs advantages to encourage export-oriented manufacturing and trade. These zones are aimed at attracting foreign investment, promoting industrialization, and stimulating economic growth by creating a favorable environment for production and export activities. The benefits often encompass tax exemptions, reduced tariffs, simplified customs procedures, and more lenient labor regulations.

The main goal of an EPZ is to attract export-oriented foreign investment and create jobs. Additional aims include bolstering the total value of exports, strengthening the balance of payments, disseminating new technologies, and correcting regional imbalances. Furthermore, as EPZs are standard tools to enhance a country's exports, they have been established in numerous countries around the globe. Another objective is to provide domestic companies with similar mechanisms to level the playing field with their competitors. To accomplish these goals, all zones must adhere to the laws that govern them. This compliance includes following the regulations of the WTO and adhering to regional integration agreements a country might sign, such as Mercosur, initiated in the early 1990s.

The Southern Common Market, or Mercosur, is a process of regional integration initially established in 1991 by Argentina, Brazil, Paraguay, and Uruguay. As explained by Mercosur (2024), its logo features the four stars of the Southern Cross constellation situated on a curved green line, which symbolizes the horizon. The acronym is written in the two official languages, Mercosur and Mercosul. The Southern Cross, a primary navigational element in the region, represents this organization's hopeful trajectory towards regional integration.

Venezuela joined Mercosur in 2012 but has been suspended since 2017 due to the breach of the Ushuaia Protocol on Democratic Commitment. Seven other countries, namely, Bolivia, Chile, Colombia, Ecuador, Guyana, Peru, and Suriname, are associated states. Mexico and New Zealand also participate as observer countries. Furthermore, the Associated States are allowed to attend meetings of Mercosur entities that address topics of common interest.

Mercosur currently encompasses nearly all of South America. It spans a territorial area of 12 million km^2, equivalent to three times the area of the EU, and it houses a population of around 295 million with a demographic density of 22 inhabitants/km^2. Its headquarters is situated in Montevideo. According to UNDP (2025) the Human Development Index (HDI) of its member countries includes 0.760 for Brazil, 0.830 for Uruguay, 0.849 for Argentina, and 0.731 for Paraguay. The official languages are Portuguese and Spanish. Collectively, these nations are considered to comprise the fifth-largest economy in the world.

Söderbaum's (2016) book, *Rethinking Regionalism*, highlights a global upswing in various forms of regionalist projects since the late 1980s. The expansion and deepening of the EU is the most notable example. However, many other regionalist projects, including the African Union (AU), the Association of Southeast Asian Nations (ASEAN), the NAFTA, and Mercosur, have also experienced revitalization or expansion. Furthermore, governments are engaging in regionalism, which involves a variety of business and civil society actors.

Mercosur is an intergovernmental integration process where each country carries one vote, and decisions need to be reached by consensus. The institutional structure comprises three decision-making bodies: the Common Market Council (Conselho do Mercado Comum - CMC), the highest body responsible for the political management of the integration process; the Common Market Group (Grupo Mercado

Comum - GMC), the Bloc's executive body; and the Mercosur Trade Commission (Comissão de Comércio do Mercosul - CCM), the technical body responsible for overseeing the application of standard trade policy instruments.

Far from achieving complete economic and political integration, the main accomplishments of Mercosur for its member states were the establishment of the Mercosur Common Nomenclature (Nomenclatura Comum do Mercosul - NCM) and the Mercosur Common External Tariff (Tarifa Externa Comum - TEC) for the trade of goods and services. The NCM is a regional nomenclature for categorizing goods, adopted by Brazil, Argentina, Paraguay, and Uruguay since 1995. It is used in all foreign trade operations within the Mercosur countries. The Harmonized System (HS), a multipurpose international product nomenclature developed by the World Customs Organization (WCO), also plays a role in these operations.

Further to intra-bloc commercial relations, Mercosur has agreements with other countries or trading blocs. These agreements can be of three kinds: Economic Complementation Agreements (Acordos de Complementação Económica - ACE), Preferential Trade Agreements (Acordo de Comércio Preferencial - ACP), and FTAs. The Mercosur external relations network includes 11 trade agreements with Bolivia, Chile, Cuba, the Andean Community, Egypt, India, Israel, Mexico, Peru, and the South African Customs Union. Despite these established trade agreements, particularly with countries in the Latin American Integration Association, China remains Mercosur's leading trading partner.

Mercosur facilitates the recognition of documents and residences in the region. A visa or passport is not required for transit within Mercosur countries. The residency agreement grants citizens the right to live and work with no other requirement other than nationality. The Multilateral Agreement on Social Security allows immigrant workers to access social security benefits. Furthermore, the Educational Integration agreement anticipates the revalidation of diplomas, certificates, and titles, and it recognizes studies at the basic, technical, and non-technical levels, including those for graduate degrees.

To Further Research and Reflect

- List the Free Trade Zones (FTZs) in your country of origin and explain how their establishment has contributed to economic development.
- What are the advantages and disadvantages of the highly debated yet not fully implemented Mercosur-EU Agreement for the primary and secondary sectors of the Mercosur members?

References

BACEN. (2024). *Glossário: Capitais Estrangeiros*. Available from https://www.bcb.gov.br/htms/firce/conceitos.asp?frame=1

Borzova, A. Y., & Medina Gonzalez, V. X. (2023). The role of mediation in resolving conflicts between ecuador and Peru. *Vestnik RUDN. International Relations, 23*(2), 296–306.

Fleury, A., & Fleury, M. T. L. (2009). Brazilian Multinationals: Surfing the Waves of Internationalization. In R. Ramamurti & J. V. Singh (Eds.), *Emerging multinationals in emerging markets* (pp. 200–243). Cambridge University Press.

Forbes. (2021). *The World's Largest Public Companies*. Available from https://www.forbes.com/lists/global2000/#6ea04f35ac04

Fortune. (2019). *Gloe*. https://fortune.com/global500/2019/

Garcia, R., Araujo, V., Mascarini, S., Gomes Santos, E., Costa, A., & Ferreira, S. (2023). How industrial diversity shapes the effects of foreign direct investment spillovers on regional innovation. *International Regional Science Review, 46*(1), 98–122.

Harig, C. (2018). Re-Importing the 'robust turn' in UN peacekeeping: Internal public security missions of Brazil's Military. *International Peacekeeping, 26*, 137–164.

IEDI. (2017). Redução do IED nos Países em Desenvolvimento. *Carta IEDI. Edição 794*. Available from https://iedi.org.br/cartas/carta_iedi_n_794.html

Masiero, G. (1998). Empresas Coreanas no Brasil: Dificuldades e Impactos da Crise Asiática. *Korean Journal of Latin American Studies, 1*, 121–154.

Mercosur. (2024). *Mercosur in Brief*. Available from https://www.mercosur.int/en/about-mercosur/mercosur-in-brief/

Ministério do Desenvolvimento Indústria e Comércio – MDIC. (2021). *Comex Stat*. Available from http://comexstat.mdic.gov.br/pt/home

Paula de Oliveira, D., & Araújo, G. C. (2020). Brazil's environment calls for help! *Ecosystems and People, 16*, 135–136.

Polloni-Silva, E., Ferraz, D., Camioto, F. D., Rebelatto, D., & Moralles, H. F. (2021). Environmental Kuznets curve and the pollution-halo/haven hypotheses: An investigation in Brazilian municipalities. *Sustainability, 13*, 4114.

Rossi, M., Santos, G. F., & Campos, F. (2016). Foreign direct investment and spatial linkages: Third-country effects for Brazilian outward investment. *Latin American Business Review, 17*, 1–25.

Söderbaum, F. (2016). *Rethinking regionalism*. Palgrave. 272 p.

Suframa. (2021). *Um Pouco Sobre o Setor Idustrial da Zona Franca de Manaus*. Available from https://www.gov.br/suframa/pt-br/zfm/industria

Uehara, A. R. (1999). Brazil and Japan: Bringing the Antipodes Closer Together? *Asia-América Latina, 7*(1).

UNCTAD. (2020). *The World Investment Report 2020*. International Production Beyond the Pandemic. New York. United Nations Publications. Available from https://unctad.org/system/files/official-document/wir2020_en.pdf

UNDP. (2025). *Human Development Insights*. Available from https://hdr.undp.org/data-center/country-insights#/ranks

Viglioni, M. T., & Calegario, C. L. (2020). Home country innovation performance: Moderating the local knowledge and inward foreign direct investment. *Global Business Review, 24*, 812–825.

Chapter 6
Brazilian Contemporary Challenges

6.1 Introduction

Political divisions in Brazil have been a key characteristic throughout its history, evolving from the Vargas era to the present day. The legacy of Getúlio Vargas, who served roles as both a dictator and a democratically elected president, continues to influence political discourse and identity within Brazil. Vargas' populist policies and authoritarian tendencies established a foundation for a deeply polarized political landscape, characterized by ideological differences and power struggles. The military dictatorship that ensued only served to heighten these divisions, resulting in widespread repression and resistance.

The transition to democracy in the 1980s brought hopes of reconciliation and unity, but political polarization persisted, fueled by economic inequality, corruption scandals, and social unrest. The rise of the Workers' Party (PT) and its progressive agenda under leaders like Luiz Inácio Lula da Silva marked a shift in Brazilian politics, stirring strong support and intense opposition. The impeachment of Dilma Rousseff in 2016 and the subsequent election of Jair Bolsonaro as president highlighted the deep-seated divisions within Brazilian society. These events reflected contrasting visions for the country's future, a future now grappling with environmental tragedies.

Natural disasters in Rio Grande do Sul, serve as a grim reminder of the devastating impact of extreme weather events on communities and infrastructure. In recent years, the state has struggled with severe floods, landslides, and other climate-related phenomena that have resulted in loss of life, displacement, and extensive property damage. Factors such as deforestation, urbanization, and inadequate infrastructure exacerbate the region's vulnerability to such disasters. These floods have wreaked havoc on vulnerable populations, overwhelmed emergency response systems, and underscored the need for enhanced disaster preparedness and response mechanisms. Efforts to mitigate the impact of natural disasters in Rio Grande do

G. Masiero, *Brazilian Socio-Economic Dynamics*, Contributions to Economics, https://doi.org/10.1007/978-3-031-87685-1_6

Sul, and across Brazil as a whole, should prioritize early warning systems, sustainable land management practices, and infrastructure improvements to build resilience and protect communities from future tragedies.

Despite being one of the largest public healthcare systems worldwide, the Unified Health System (*Sistema Único de Saúde* SUS) in Brazil encountered immense challenges during the coronavirus disease 2019 (Covid -19) pandemic due to mismanagement and systemic deficiencies. The pandemic exposed enduring issues within the SUS, including chronic underfunding, insufficient healthcare infrastructure, and disparities in access to quality care. Miscommunication and conflicting directives at the federal level further obstructed an adequate response, leading to confusion and delays in implementing preventive measures and vaccination campaigns. Allegations of corruption related to the purchase of medical supplies and vaccine distribution heightened public distrust and exacerbated the financial strain of living in Brazil.

The "Brazil Cost" encapsulates a multitude of economic, structural, and regulatory challenges that contribute to the high operational expenses and inefficiencies businesses confront in Brazil. This concept includes a variety of factors, such as intricate tax systems, bureaucratic hurdles, inadequate infrastructure, and legal uncertainties. Brazil's complex tax regime, characterized by a plethora of federal, state, and municipal taxes, notably burdens businesses, impacting their competitiveness and profitability. Bureaucratic procedures, like securing permits and navigating regulatory compliance, are frequently time-draining and expensive, obstructing business operations and investment.

Additionally, infrastructure deficiencies, such as transportation networks and logistics, lead to increased transportation costs and supply chain interruptions. Legal uncertainties and inefficiencies add to the "Brazil Cost," with protracted litigation processes, inconsistent judicial verdicts, and corruption undermining trust and escalating business risks. Tackling these challenges is crucial for enhancing Brazil's business climate, drawing investment, and promoting sustainable economic growth.

Land reform is a pivotal issue both in Brazil and globally, with the aim of addressing historical injustices, economic disparities, and inefficient land usage. Nations worldwide have pursued land reform policies intending to redistribute land from vast landowners to landless or small-scale farmers, achieving varying degrees of success. In countries such as South Korea and Japan, land reforms implemented post-World War II significantly enhanced agricultural productivity and rural livelihoods. Conversely, in Brazil, land reform remains a contentious and ongoing battle deeply entrenched in the nation's colonial history and the concentration of land ownership among a select elite.

Efforts led by movements such as the Landless Workers' Movement (Movimento dos Trabalhadores Rurais Sem Terra = MST) and the National Confederation of Workers in Agriculture (Confederação Nacional dos Trabalhadores na Agricultura - CONTAG) have pushed for land redistribution to promote social justice and improve the livelihoods of rural communities. Despite some progress, significant challenges remain, including bureaucratic delays, political resistance, and the need for supporting infrastructure and resources for newly settled farmers.

Comprehensive land reform in Brazil is essential for addressing rural poverty, promoting sustainable development, and ensuring equitable access to land and resources.

Labor informality in rural and urban areas is a significant issue in Brazil, where a substantial portion of the workforce operates outside the formal sector. Informal employment, which includes jobs without social security benefits, labor protections, or a formal contract, accounts for approximately 40% of the country's labor force. This occurrence is attributed to various factors, such as a lack of job security, limited access to social benefits, and not enough entrepreneurship. Informal workers often face precarious conditions, which include low wages, long working hours, and lack of adequate health and safety measures. Moreover, the informal sector impairs the government's ability to collect taxes and implement effective labor policies, thus exacerbating income inequality and social unrest.

Social movements have played a significant role in Brazil's democratization process and the politicization of various social issues. These movements have been instrumental in advocating for the rights of marginalized groups, promoting social inclusion, and challenging the status quo. Mass strikes and social movements have been particularly prominent in Brazil, often involving large-scale mobilization and collective action. Overall, social movements in Brazil have been crucial in shaping the country's political scenario and advocating for social change, despite the challenges and complexities associated with their institutionalization.

6.2 Political Divisions in Brazil: From the Vargas Era to Current Times

Brazil's political history is more than just a series of events; it is a narrative of significant ideological clashes that have irrevocably shaped its economic, social, and cultural paths. From the era of Getúlio Vargas to the contemporary scenario, spanning the intense rivalries between nationalists and internationalists in the 1930s and the current polarization between the supporters of Lula and Bolsonaro, the country has served as a stage for a succession of ideological battles, which have not merely influenced but have underpinned its identity.

Getúlio Vargas, who first assumed Brazil's presidency in 1930 following the 1930 Revolution that overthrew then-President Washington Luís, catalyzed a period of substantial transformations and intense political disputes. Vargas' economic nationalism, a policy that represented more than a mere strategy but a transformative force, fundamentally reshaped the nation. His initiatives, such as founding the Companhia Siderúrgica Nacional (CSN) in 1941 and Petrobras in 1953, embodied more than just economic development; they were about asserting national sovereignty.

On the other side of the political spectrum were the internationalists, often associated with more liberal sectors of the economy and foreign capital. They staunchly opposed Vargas' policies, advocating for greater openness to international trade and a more favorable business environment for foreign investment. The opposition posited that Vargas' economic nationalism was inefficient and inhibited the country's economic growth, igniting intense debates and further exacerbating the political divisions of the time. This ideological clash, between those advocating for national self-sufficiency and those favoring international economic integration, was a critical factor in the political partitions of the era, presenting a complex and multifaceted politics.

The polarization between these two currents peaked with the establishment of the Estado Novo in 1937, an authoritarian regime that endured until 1945. This period was characterized by Vargas consolidating power, suppressing opposition, implementing reforms to modernize the country, and curbing democratic freedoms. The tensions between nationalists and internationalists continued to shape the political scene, with Vargas being viewed by some as a champion of national interest and by others as a dictator who stifled democracy. The lasting impact of the Estado Novo, both in terms of its reforms and restrictions, underscores its enduring influence on Brazil's political history, further deepening the political divisions.

Getúlio Vargas governed Brazil for 18 years, from 1930 to 1945 and again from 1951 to 1954. He is one of the few dictators in contemporary history to regain power through free elections following his removal from office. This dynamic illustrates both his political acumen and the nature of Brazilian politics. Vargas' role as a catalyst for Brazilian industrialization and the establishment of the existing corporatist social structure in Brazil today is notable.

Upon his return to power in 1951, as reported by Skidmore (2007) Vargas faced fierce political opposition, particularly from the National Democratic Union (União Democrática Nacional - UDN) and conservative sectors. The assassination of Aeronautics Major Rubens Vaz, alleged to be the work of Gregório Fortunato, the chief of Vargas' guard, exacerbated the crisis. In August 1954, amid severe pressure to step down, Vargas took his own life, sparking nationwide commotion. Following the election of Juscelino Kubitschek in 1955, apprehension arose regarding his ability to assume office due to resistance from the military and political sectors.

General Henrique Teixeira Lott led a preventive countercoup in November 1955 to ensure Kubitschek's inauguration and to maintain democratic continuity. However, in 1956, discontented Air Force officers rebelled against Juscelino Kubitschek's government in Jacareacanga, Pará. The revolt was quickly contained, and the rebels were arrested. Another coup attempt by Air Force officers, this time in Aragarças, Goiás, was also suppressed, and its leaders were put in jail.

Castello Branco (2008) notes that Jânio Quadros was elected president in 1960, employing a moralizing stance against corruption. However, by August 1961, he abruptly resigned after only 7 months in office, asserting that "hidden forces" obstructed his governance. This resignation instigated a political crisis which subsequently led to the ascension of his vice-president, João Goulart, after a brief military resistance and the enactment of temporary parliamentarianism.

João Goulart (Jango), who assumed the presidency following Jânio's resignation, implemented crucial reforms that spurred opposition from the military and conservatives. On March 31, 1964, the military staged a coup, overthrowing Goulart and establishing a dictatorship that lasted until 1985. The military regime suspended direct presidential elections and introduced AI-5 (Institutional Act Number Five) in 1968, escalating repression and censorship. This led to increasing opposition to the military regime, manifested in student demonstrations and strikes.

In December 1968, the military government enacted AI-5, which resulted in the closure of Congress, the suspension of civil rights, and the establishment of censorship. Chagas (2014) identifies this measure as the beginning of the dictatorship's most repressive era, characterized by the arrest, torture, and disappearance of opponents. These incidents mirror the significant political unrest in Brazil, driven by coups, countercoups, reforms, and repressions that profoundly impacted Brazilian society and its political course. Chagas (2015) studied the development of the military movement starting from 1970, beginning with General Garrastazu Médici's reign onwards to General Ernesto Geisel's administration, and finally, up to the last day of João Baptista Figueiredo's term.

The re-democratization of Brazil was a complicated process, marked by a myriad of political conflicts between the 1970s and the early 1990s. Brazil had been under a military dictatorship since 1964, during which political repression was intense. Various social movements, political parties, and human rights organizations started to demand amnesty for political prisoners, exiles, and those whose political rights had been revoked. In 1979, the military government enacted the Amnesty Law, facilitating the return of exiles and the release of numerous political prisoners. However, this law also pardoned the crimes committed by state agents.

Pereira (2012) investigates the legal ramifications of military dictatorships in three Southern Cone nations, Brazil (1964–1985), Chile (1973–1990), and Argentina (1976–1983), to assess the legitimacy of authoritarian rule. The author contends that the preexisting legal systems in these nations either persevered or underwent alterations to endorse authoritarianism, even after the establishment of totalitarian rule. He explores the impacts of this interplay during the transition from military to democratic governance.

Pressure for direct presidential elections grew as dissatisfaction with the military regime increased. The *Diretas Já* movement mobilized millions of Brazilians in large demonstrations across the country, demanding the return of direct elections. Although the Dante de Oliveira amendment, which proposed direct polls, was not approved by Congress, the movement pressed for democratization. In 1985, after the defeat of the *Diretas Já* amendment, the presidential election would still be indirect, conducted through the Electoral College. Tancredo Neves was elected president by the Electoral College, defeating Paulo Maluf, the candidate backed by the military regime.

However, Tancredo Neves fell seriously ill before taking office and subsequently died. This led his vice-president, José Sarney, to assume the presidency, marking the end of the military dictatorship and the inauguration of the New Republic. A new Constitution to replace the 1967 version imposed by the military regime was critical. Therefore, the National Constituent Assembly, featuring broad participation from various sectors of society, was convened to draft a new constitution. In October 1988, the new Federal Constitution was promulgated. It expanded civil, political, and social rights, thus consolidating democracy in Brazil.

Fernando Collor de Mello, elected as president in 1989 during the first direct elections since 1960, faced serious accusations of corruption. Massive public demonstrations, known as the "Caras Pintadas," demanded his impeachment. In December 1992, Congress ousted Collor, and his vice-president, Itamar Franco, assumed the presidency. These conflicts and events were crucial to the consolidation of democracy in Brazil, reflecting the struggles and challenges the country faced in its transition from an authoritarian regime to a democratic system.

During the democratic period, Brazil experienced extreme economic instability in the early 1990s, marked by hyperinflation and unsuccessful stabilization plans. Preceding President Fernando Collor's impeachment in 1992 was significant financial chaos and corruption accusations. The Real Plan, executed by Finance Minister Fernando Henrique Cardoso, stabilized the economy and curbed inflation. This enhanced Cardoso's popularity significantly and consequently led to his presidency in 1994.

President Cardoso's administration pursued privatization and economic liberalization policies, facing opposition from labor unions and leftist groups. These strategies sparked social unrest and public sector strikes. However, Luiz Inácio Lula da Silva, a former labor leader and the founder of the Workers' Party (PT), won the presidency in 2002 after three failed attempts. His election symbolized a leftward shift in Brazilian politics and raised hopes for social and economic reforms. Morais (2021) outlines Lula's journey, ranging from his early years to the overturning of his convictions in 2021, encompassing the development of new trade unionism, the Santo André, São Bernardo do Campo, and São Caetano do Sul (ABC) strikes, the founding of the PT, and the first election campaign.

Lula was reelected and served as the country's leader from 2003 to 2010 and was reelected once again in 2022. His administration faced opposition from conservative sectors, business, elites, and right-wing parties, leading to significant political polarization and gridlock. In 2005, a scandal known as Mensalão involved allegations of vote-buying and corruption within the PT government, including payments made to members of Congress in exchange for political support. Social movements, such as the MST and various indigenous groups, also voiced their protests against the government's policies.

Despite political conflicts, Brazil enjoyed a period of economic stability and growth in the mid-2000s. This was fueled by high commodity prices and increased domestic consumption. Social programs like Bolsa Família lifted millions out of poverty; however, income inequality continued to present a significant challenge. These political conflicts and events from the 1990s and 2000s underscore Brazil's struggle with democratic consolidation, economic development, and social inclusion, which has shaped its trajectory into the twenty-first century.

The period from 2000 to 2020 in Brazil was marked by significant conflicts and events that defined the country's political landscape. The presidency of Luiz Inácio Lula da Silva was characterized by economic growth, social programs, corruption scandals, and political polarization. The Brazilian economy experienced periods of growth fueled by high commodity prices, augmented domestic consumption, and social programs such as Bolsa Família.

The presidency of Dilma Rousseff (2011–2016) was marked by economic challenges, protests against corruption, and government spending. A investigation known as "Operação Lava Jato" (Operation Car Wash) exposed widespread corruption involving politicians and business leaders, resulting in numerous arrests and convictions. Rousseff was impeached and removed from office on charges of fiscal mismanagement, a decision widely criticized as a "soft coup" by her supporters. Michel Temer, her vice-president, assumed the presidency until the end of her term in 2018.

Bolsonaro, a far-right politician, won the presidency in 2018 amid widespread anti-establishment sentiment and dissatisfaction with traditional politics. His presidency has been marked by controversy due to policies that have been heavily criticized for their impact on the environment, indigenous rights, and democratic institutions. Social movements, environmental activists, and indigenous groups have staged protests against these government policies, particularly those pertaining to deforestation in the Amazon and land rights. The Covid-19 pandemic has further exposed social and economic inequalities, thus highlighting healthcare challenges and government responses.

Today, Brazil is once again divided, this time between supporters of Luiz Inácio Lula da Silva, known as Lulistas, and those of Jair Bolsonaro, called Bolsonaristas. This new polarization embodies differences in political worldviews, values, and priorities. The rivalry between Lulistas and Bolsonaristas has fostered a climate of persistent confrontation, prevalent both on social media and in the streets.

The 2018 and 2022 presidential elections were marked by an intense rivalry, with mutual allegations of corruption, authoritarianism, and incompetence. This heated rhetoric contributed to a deeply divided society, where dialogue and consensus have become increasingly complex. Deep political divisions hailing from the Vargas era have left a significant imprint on Brazil. Disputes between nationalists and internationalists in the 1930s and 1940s have found fresh resonance in the contemporary polarization between Lulistas and Bolsonaristas. These divisions reflect differing views on the role of the state, economic and social policies, as well as the cultural and moral values that should guide the nation.

To Further Research and Reflect

- Describe the key political leaders from your country who have significantly impacted its economic development while also being notable advocates for the people's interests.
- Design some strategies to be recommended to Brazilian politicians to overcome the current political clashes between Lulistas and Bolsonaristas.

6.3 Brazilian Tragedies: The Natural Disaster in Rio Grande do Sul

Brazil has faced several catastrophes that have deeply affected the country. These include natural disasters, industrial accidents and environmental emergencies. In February 2022, torrential rains sparked floods and landslides in Petrópolis, located in the state of Rio de Janeiro. This catastrophe led to more than 230 fatalities and thousands becoming homeless. In the 1960s, a similar occurrence transpired in São Paulo, resulting in one of the most severe floods in the city's history, causing dozens of deaths and substantial material damage. However, no previous natural disaster was more critical than the one in Rio Grande do Sul (RS), at the beginning of 2024.

In November 2015, the Fundão dam, operated by Samarco Mineração S.A. (a Brazilian mining company founded in 1977 and now owned by the Brazilian Vale and the Australian BHP), broke, releasing millions of cubic meters of mining waste. This disaster resulted in 19 deaths, destroyed the community of Bento Rodrigues, and caused catastrophic environmental damage along the Rio Doce. In January 2019, another dam owned by the mining company Vale broke, releasing a wave of iron ore tailings. This incident caused the deaths of 270 people and devastated the area around the town of Brumadinho in Minas Gerais.

In addition to recent natural and industrial disasters, the country has also dealt with aviation accidents. For instance, in September 2006, a Gol Boeing 737 collided mid-air with a Legacy 600 executive jet. This tragic incident resulted in the Boeing crash causing the death of all 154 passengers onboard. Similarly, in July 2007, a TAM Linhas Aéreas Airbus A320 veered off the runway while landing at Congonhas Airport in São Paulo. The aircraft crashed into a building, causing the death of 199 people, including everyone onboard and some individuals on the ground.

In the 1990s, numerous violent crimes were perpetrated by police forces. Among these was an incident in October 1992 at the Carandiru Penitentiary Complex in São Paulo, which resulted in the Military Police intervening and killing 111 inmates. This event stands as one of the most brutal episodes of prison repression in Brazil's history. In July 1993, eight street children were murdered by the military police in the center of Rio de Janeiro. Moreover, in August of the same year, 21 residents of the Vigário Geral favela in Rio de Janeiro were killed by a vigilante group comprised of military police officers. This was in retaliation for the murder of four police officers a few days prior.

Fire tragedies have been a constant occurrence. In January 2013, a fire at the Kiss nightclub in Santa Maria, Rio Grande do Sul, resulted in the death of 242 people, predominantly young university students. This catastrophe was the consequence of a pyrotechnic device used during a performance. Moreover, deforestation and forest fires in the Amazon have significantly devastated the environment, impacting biodiversity and contributing to climate change. These tragedies have deeply affected Brazilian society, sparking discussions about security, justice, environmental policies, corporate responsibility, and human rights. However, none of these instances was as devastating as the natural disaster of the 2024 floods in Rio Grande do Sul.

The state of Rio Grande do Sul in Brazil has distinct political, economic, and social characteristics that have been shaped by its rich and diverse history. Known for valuing regional autonomy and federalism, the state has a strong tradition of political and social movements that advocate for increased autonomy and the decentralization of power. Influential Brazilian political leaders such as Getúlio Vargas and Leonel Brizola were from this state; Vargas played a crucial role in the 1930 Revolution and served as president, while Brizola is recognized for his involvement in laborism and the Legality Campaign (a national mobilization in 1961 to ensure the inauguration of João Goulart as President of Brazil). The heavy presence of social, union, and student movements contributes significantly to both state and national politics, displaying the strong propensity for political and social activism in Rio Grande do Sul.

The economy of Rio Grande do Sul is diverse, incorporating crucial sectors such as agriculture, livestock, industry, commerce, and services. Notably, agriculture excels in grain production (soy, corn, wheat) and viticulture, particularly in the *Serra Gaúcha* region. The state boasts a vigorous industrial sector, notably in metallurgy, automotive manufacturing, footwear production, and agricultural machinery. It has also committed to technological innovation primarily in information technology and biotechnology. Furthermore, the state is a significant exporter, dispatching goods like grains, meats, footwear, and agricultural machinery to various international markets.

The state boasts a strong cultural identity, influenced by European immigration—including German, Italian, and Polish—as well as the *Gaucho* tradition. This is reflected in the cuisine, music, dances (like the *Fandango*), and traditional festivals (e.g., Farroupilha Week). The state features relatively high education rates and quality of life, hosting a network of high-quality higher education institutions such as the Federal University of Rio Grande do Sul (UFRGS) and the University of Caxias do Sul (UCS). Nonetheless, despite such progress, the state faces challenges linked to social and economic inequality. Notable disparities exist, particularly between urban and rural areas, as well as among different state regions.

The social and economic inequalities are being dramatically challenged by an unprecedented tragedy in Brazilian history. Flooding has wreaked havoc in numerous cities, including the state's capital, Porto Alegre, causing fatalities and substantial destruction. The floods in Rio Grande do Sul underscore the vulnerability of numerous regions in Brazil to natural disasters. The intensity and frequency of these events have been amplifying, potentially due to climate change, imposing additional pressure on local and national governments to establish effective disaster prevention and response policies.

According to Wollmann (2014), flooding is a common natural phenomenon in Rio Grande do Sul, particularly in the regions bordering the state's main rivers. Most floods in Rio Grande do Sul underscore from 2000 to 2011 occurred due to climatic cycles involving stationary fronts and cyclogenesis, systems that generate intense rainfall. Kreutz et al. (2023). Analyzed the floods of the Taquari River, one of the state's most important rivers, using documentary sources, travelers' diaries, reports, and newspapers from the twentieth century.

For these authors, the Taquari River is integral to city formation, both urban and rural human migration, and the construction of a collective imagination due to its historical, geographical, and economic significance. However, this river has become the epicenter of devastating contemporary floods. The catastrophe in Rio Grande do Sul, which occurred between late April and early May 2024, resulted in the worst floods ever recorded in the state. Intense rainfall, accumulating between 500 and 700 mm in various locations, caused widespread flooding, landslides, dam breaches, and bridge collapses.

According to Forum (2024), by the end of the first week of May 2024, floods had affected 397 out of the 497 municipalities, representing 80% of the state. Porto Alegre, the state capital, was severely hit, with Lake Guaíba's water level reaching a record high of 5.31 m, surpassing the historic 1941 mark. The city was severely disrupted, with more than 60 streets becoming completely inaccessible leading to the suspension of all public transportation activities, which included Salgado Filho airport, the metro, and bus services. In addition to Porto Alegre, other cities were critically affected. Among these were Eldorado do Sul—described by its mayor as "100% destroyed"—and several cities in the Taquari Valley, such as Lajeado, Estrela, and Muçum, which were temporarily cut off due to the floods.

The economic aftermath of this tragedy is significant, with reconstruction costs estimated to be around R$19 billion (approximately US$3.7 billion). Infrastructure, such as roads, bridges, and schools, has suffered extensive damage. Reports indicate that over two million people were left without access to electricity and clean drinking water.

The tragedy in Rio Grande do Sul serves as a stark example of the heightened effects of climate change and extreme weather phenomena like El Niño. These factors culminated in a catastrophic weather event, leading to enormous human and material losses. The government's reaction to such disasters frequently highlights the shortcomings and constraints of the political system. Lack of coordination among different governmental levels, bureaucracy, and corruption may impede relief and recovery work. Unity among various political parties is vital to managing crises of this nature, though at times polarization may jeopardize the efficiency of responses.

To Further Research and Reflect

- Describe at least one natural disaster, industrial accident, environmental crisis, or humanitarian crisis your country experienced. Are there some lessons for RS recovering from the present record floods?
- What measures should be implemented to effectively mitigate the impact of various types of tragedies in the country where you live? Consider at least one kind of tragedy.

6.4 The SUS and the Mismanagement of the COVID-19

The mismanagement of the Covid-19 pandemic has exacted a hefty toll on the *Sistema Único de Saúde* (SUS). According to Paim et al. (2011), Brazil has been progressing in a dynamic and multifaceted health system since 1988, known as the Unified Health System. This system is founded on the belief that the state is responsible for health and it is the citizen's right.

Despite its challenges, the SUS aims to provide comprehensive, universal preventive, and curative treatment through decentralized management and healthcare services delivery. It also fosters community participation at all administrative levels. The SUS has made significant investments in human resources and technology development, including notable efforts to meet the country's vital pharmaceutical needs. It has also achieved universal coverage for vaccinations and maternity care, greatly enhancing access to primary and emergency care.

SUS, a system that provides free care to low-, middle-, and even high-income individuals seeking health services, extends its treatment to foreigners residing in or visiting Brazil, without fees. This inclusivity speaks to the system's commitment to universal healthcare. Few countries in the world boast a comprehensive and accessible healthcare system like that of Brazil. Notable others include the UK, Canada, Australia, France, and Cuba. The system was inspired by the British National Health Service, established in 1948, which shares some similarities with it.

Like other fundamental public services in Brazil, such as education, sanitation, and social security, the healthcare system is confronted with numerous challenges, despite its well-structured organization and governance. These issues, often scrutinized by the local population, originate from a lack of financial resources and mismanagement. For example, there is a dearth of hospitals and health professionals in smaller towns with impoverished populations and inadequate infrastructure.

The Covid-19 pandemic has had a devastating impact on Brazil's SUS. Mismanagement of public health policies has led to the rapid spread of infections and deaths across the vast Brazilian territory. No narrative thoroughly explains this phenomenon, as per Castro et al. (2021). However, the lack of prompt, coordinated, and equitable responses, coupled with stark local inequalities, has significantly contributed to the spread of the disease.

There are successive failures reflected in the record number of infected individuals and elevated mortality rates. Figure 6.1, compiled by Bastos (2021), illustrates the rapid and escalating number of deaths associated with the Covid-19 pandemic compared to those caused by severe acute respiratory syndrome (SARS). The inadequacy of handling the pandemic underlines the significance of public health responses.

The lack of adherence to World Health Organization guidelines and the absence of federal government coordination and leadership in Brazil are key issues that magnified the pandemic into a broader crisis. Disorganized and insufficient efforts in testing, monitoring, and enforcing physical distancing policies further exacerbate

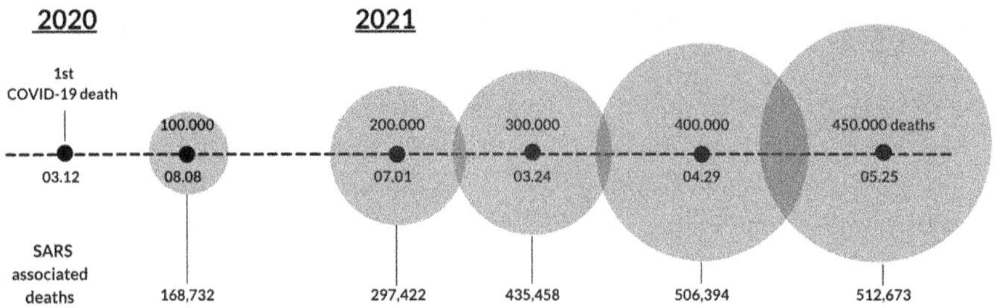

Fig. 6.1 Brazilian number of deaths related to the Covid-19 pandemic. Source: Bastos (2021)

the situation. Since early 2020, Brazil has ranked poorly for Covid-19 deaths per million inhabitants.

For complex reasons, encompassing both political and economic factors, the Brazilian government downplayed the severity of the pandemic, providing inconsistent and conflicting information about the measures needed to control its spread. From the beginning, the government underscored that the economy must not be neglected. Despite growing public health concerns, it promoted continued business activities and church attendance as usual.

On March 11, 2020, the Federal District, including Brasilia—the capital of the country—implemented measures for physical distancing and suspended classes and events. Three days later, the most populated state of São Paulo initiated similar policies. Tocantins was the last state to enact such measures, beginning the implementation on March 21.

As reported by Wikipedia (2024), the first confirmed death from Covid-19 was a 62-year-old man in São Paulo, which occurred on March 17. Three days later, the Minister of Health, Luiz Henrique Mandetta, declared community transmission throughout all national territories. Meanwhile, over 20 individuals from the presidential entourage, who accompanied President Bolsonaro on his visit to the USA to meet with President Donald Trump, tested positive for Covid-19.

On March 22, President Bolsonaro approved provisional measures that made hiring and firing of labor easier. Two days later, he publicly downplayed the severity of the crisis and expressed disapproval of the Ministry of Health's policies during a nationally televised address. In response to this rapid escalation of cases and deaths caused by the virus, the governors of 25 states signed a letter criticizing the president.

According to Mesquita and Bezerra (2021), government policies rooted in meritocratic ideologies heightened social and racial inequality during the pandemic. They did so by marginalizing oppressed populations and sustaining group privileges and domination. The federal government initiated a campaign, "Brazil cannot stop," which advocated for physical distancing to be maintained only by the young and elderly. The president emphasized that the pandemic was merely another "small flu."

On April 16, Health Minister Mandetta was dismissed and replaced by Nelson Teich, who resigned just a month later. Teich was replaced by Eduardo Pazuello, an army general with no prior experience in health or public administration. Bolsonaro's resistance to physical distancing and his unwillingness to support local authorities in their efforts to enforce school and business closures have undermined public compliance with these measures. The president has even promoted the use of drugs with no proven efficacy, such as hydroxychloroquine, for both the prevention and treatment of Covid-19 infections, and he vetoed legislation mandating mask usage.

Governors, some of whom Bolsonaro saw as rivals for re-election, were criticized for implementing physical distancing policies and allocating resources for building emergency hospitals and ventilators. Brazil also had difficulty securing and distributing tests for Covid-19, complicating the tracking and control of the virus within the country. A similar challenge has arisen with the acquisition and distribution of vaccines.

The Covid-19 pandemic had a devastating impact on Manaus. Early in the pandemic, the city experienced a collapse of the healthcare system due to a surge in cases, resulting in overwhelmed hospitals and a shortage of medical supplies, including oxygen. The rapid spread of a variant, first identified in Manaus, which was more transmissible, exacerbated the situation. Despite later efforts to increase vaccination and improve healthcare infrastructure, Manaus faced one of the highest mortality rates in Brazil. This underscores the need for coordinated and effective public health strategies to manage such crises.

To Further Research and Reflect

- Describe the measures your country has taken to combat the Covid-19 pandemic and suggest actions that governments and international agencies should implement to prevent the spread of future endemics and pandemics.
- What are the main characteristics of your country's health system? Contrast the pros and cons of your country's health system with the Brazilian system.

6.5 The Brazilian Cost—Why Is Brazil Expensive?

Brazil is often perceived as an expensive country due to economic, structural, and regulatory factors. Brazil levies substantial taxes on both domestic products and imports. The country's intricate tax system encompasses a variety of federal, state, and municipal taxes, which can contribute to high overall tax burdens. Tax reform in Brazil is a consistent and critical theme for enhancing the economic climate and reducing the "Brazil Cost." The complexity and inefficiency of the current tax system are frequently identified as barriers to the country's economic growth and competitiveness.

The tax reform that has been a topic of discussion for many decades in Brazil was approved at the end of 2023 and will be implemented gradually. As reported by Radio Senado (2023), the majority of changes to the tax system will begin to be progressively enforced from 2026, with effects resonating in 2027 and all regulations becoming fully active in 2033. The reform is aimed at reducing the complexity and quantity of taxes, thus facilitating their administration and compliance.

Additionally, it aspires to decrease the tax burden on businesses and consumers in the hopes of promoting economic growth and development.

The system will be more transparent and equitable, ensuring that everyone pays a fair share of taxes. Import duties are exceptionally high, making foreign goods more expensive. Businesses must navigate a labyrinth of bureaucratic procedures, which can be both time-consuming and costly. These procedures include obtaining licenses, adhering to labor laws, and complying with environmental regulations. Compliance with various regulations demands substantial time and resources, which increases business operational costs, especially in relation to the country's international competitiveness. The goal of the reform is to restructure the system to enhance the competitiveness of Brazilian exports and attract foreign investment.

The primary goal of the reform is to substitute a multitude of federal, state, and municipal taxes with a single value-added tax (VAT) or goods and services tax (IBS). As reported by Agência Brasil (2023), the main proposals involve the establishment of the Contribution on Goods and Services (CBS) at the federal level and the consolidation of the Tax on Circulation of Goods and Services (ICMS—state) with the Tax on Services (ISS—municipal) into the Tax on Goods and Services (IBS). This will be managed by the states and municipalities. The introduction of a modern VAT focused on consumption, intended to replace current taxes like PIS, Cofins, IPI, ICMS, and ISS, is also projected to end the fiscal war among states and simplify interstate taxation.

Tax reform in Brazil is crucial in forging a more conducive economic environment, decreasing compliance costs, and escalating the country's competitiveness internationally. Nevertheless, its application demands extensive political consensus and meticulous planning to avert substantial economic disturbance. Certain sectors will be granted specific exemptions. For instance, the basic food basket and medications for grievous diseases will carry a zero CBS rate. Similarly, educational services and agricultural activities will also enjoy tax benefits. Over the next few years, overseeing the transition from the existing system to the new model and curtailing negative effects on businesses and consumers will form part of Brazil's agenda.

However, merely reducing the tax burden will not suffice. Brazil's infrastructure, encompassing roads, ports, and railways, is frequently inadequate and inefficient, resulting in elevated transportation and logistics costs. These costs are further amplified by the country's immense size. Moreover, the Brazilian real (BRL) can fluctuate dramatically, affecting the prices of goods and services, particularly those linked to international markets. The depreciation of currency can spur an upswing in costs for imported goods and provoke inflationary strains. Brazil has weathered intervals of rampant inflation, which can diminish purchasing power and escalate living costs. Such inflationary trends often culminate in price surges for goods and services.

Historically, Brazil has implemented protectionist policies to bolster domestic industries. While these policies aim to support local production, they can also limit competition and lead to higher consumer prices. Additionally, labor costs in Brazil are high due to substantial labor protections and benefits mandated by law. Despite these protections providing social benefits, they increase overall business costs.

Lastly, the complexity and inefficiency of Brazil's supply chains, combined with prevalent transportation issues, further escalate the costs involved in bringing products to market.

In major cities such as São Paulo and Rio de Janeiro, high real estate prices contribute to the overall cost of living. This impacts both residential and commercial properties, affecting rents and property values. Market concentration or regulatory barriers can limit competition, leading to higher prices in some sectors. Monopolies or oligopolies can elevate costs for consumers and businesses alike. Moreover, the cost of legal services and administrative compliance is substantial. Significantly, navigating Brazil's legal and regulatory environment necessitates considerable resources, which further escalate business costs.

These factors collectively contribute to Brazil's high cost of living and doing business, making it one of the more expensive countries in the region despite its economic potential. Bureaucracy, corruption, inefficiencies in the judicial system, periods of inflation, and currency volatility are among the primary reasons for Brazil's higher prices. However, there is substantial agreement among many authorities and institutions that gaps in education and workforce skills exist, leading to a mismatch between labor market needs and the available talent. This situation can escalate costs for businesses that need to invest in training and development.

Brazil's judicial system can be slow and unpredictable, engendering uncertainties for businesses. This system is frequently criticized due to its sluggishness and unpredictability, which generate substantial uncertainties for businesses. In a study examining pre-trial detention outcomes in the Brazilian Supreme Court, Pont et al. (2022) reported that over 750,000 individuals were detained nationwide in 2019. This fact places Brazil third in the world in terms of the highest incarceration rate of permanent and, to a lesser degree, provisional inmates.

Brazil's judicial system is faced with a significant backlog of cases. As stated by the aforementioned authors, there are millions of pending cases, which lead to lengthy delays in resolving legal disputes. To address this issue of an overgrown caseload, the Brazilian judiciary has been making efforts to advance e-justice. On an annual basis, more than 2.4 million new criminal cases enter the superior courts of the Brazilian judiciary. Legal procedures in Brazil can be complex and time-consuming. Contributing to prolonged litigation times are the multiple levels of appeals and the involved bureaucratic processes.

Judicial decisions can often be inconsistent, with separate courts or judges within the same court issuing conflicting rulings on similar issues. This unpredictability can complicate legal strategies and business planning. Corruption and inefficiency within the judicial system further erode trust and reliability. Incidents of judicial misconduct, along with delays caused by administrative inefficiencies, can significantly impact the outcome and duration of cases. As a result, businesses may experience delays in dispute resolution, affecting operations, partnerships, and financial planning.

The unpredictability of legal outcomes and the potential for prolonged litigation heighten business risks in Brazil. Companies frequently have to allocate substantial resources to address legal contingencies, which can impact their profitability and strategic decisions. Inefficiencies and uncertainties within the judicial system can discourage both domestic and foreign investments. Investors look for predictable and efficient legal environments, and the challenges within Brazil's judicial system can render it less attractive. Legal disputes, particularly those concerning regulatory or compliance issues, may cause operational delays. Such delays can obstruct business expansion plans, mergers, acquisitions, and other strategic initiatives.

Efforts to reform Brazil's judicial system include measures to streamline legal processes, enhance transparency, and minimize the backlog of cases. Implementing digital platforms for case management and promoting alternative dispute resolution mechanisms, such as arbitration and mediation, constitute steps towards enhancing efficiency. The slow and unpredictable nature of Brazil's judicial system poses significant business challenges. It affects contract enforcement, heightens risks and costs, and deters investment. Addressing these concerns necessitates comprehensive reforms to improve the legal system's efficiency, transparency, and consistency.

To Further Research and Reflect

- What are the main costs associated with operating a business in your country, and how do they compare to the costs in Brazil?
- Do you already have experience with the judicial system in your country or elsewhere? Would you mind briefly describing the case regarding time consumption and system efficiency?

6.6 Land Reform in the World and Brazil

Agrarian reforms have been implemented in various countries worldwide, and their success has varied. The aim of these reforms often revolves around redistributing land ownership to improve the livelihoods of small-scale farmers and rural communities. One example is in India, where the Zamindari Abolition Act of 1950 served as a crucial reform. This act abolished the feudal Zamindari land tenure system, redistributing the land to cultivators. However, the reform's implementation was inconsistent across states. Meanwhile, in Japan, the post-WWII land reform program was another significant initiative. This program dismantled large estates and distributed the land to tenant farmers, resulting in a more equitable farmland distribution.

In Latin America, countries such as Mexico, Bolivia, and Peru have enacted agrarian reforms to address the severe disparity in land ownership, resulting in varied effects on improving rural livelihoods. Similarly, in Eastern Europe, the transition from communist to market economies in the 1990s necessitated land privatization and restitution to former owners. This intricate process highlighted the significance of political will and institutional capacity. Generally, the success of agrarian reforms pivots on these factors, as well as the pivotal role of bolstering small-scale agriculture. Reforms that meld land redistribution with such support tend to positively impact rural development, fostering sustainable farming practices.

The land reform program of post-WWII Japan is frequently cited as a successful exemplification. Primarily centered around the disintegration of substantial estates and redistributing the land to tenant farmers, this program led to a more equitable distribution of arable land. This underlines the primary objective of land redistribution: accomplishing fairer land ownership. Concurrently, South Korea is referred to as an illustration of a nation that attained substantial economic growth and agricultural evolution via land renovations and strategic schemes in the twentieth century. By merging land use reforms with institutional strengthening tied to the educational needs of its populace, South Korea fortified growth, setting a standard for other regions.

Rada (2020) and Niemelä (2010) reference the Sumilao farmers' campaign in the Philippines as a triumphant case under the Comprehensive Agrarian Reform Program (CARP). This program prosperously fortified relationships between agrarian reform organizations and the Catholic Church, emphasizing the potential influence of social movements on agrarian reform endeavors. In conclusion, the prosperity of agricultural reforms appears to hinge on factors such as political will, institutional capability, and addressing the concerns of multiple stakeholders. Reforms that combine land redistribution with support for small-scale agriculture typically impact rural development positively.

Global land reform initiatives aim to deal with equitable land access, poverty reduction, environmental sustainability, and productivity issues in developing countries. Notable examples of successful land reforms in South Asia have proven beneficial for broad-based development. Countries such as South Korea and Taiwan have effectively amalgamated land use reforms with institutional strengthening, thereby achieving substantial economic growth and agricultural development. This could potentially set the benchmark for regions like Latin America.

Agrarian reform policies in Latin America, such as those in Mexico, were designed to distribute and return lands to communities. However, this process encountered numerous challenges, including the quality of the distributed lands, inadequate government support, and issues with internal organization, leading to limited medium- and long-term success. Accordingly, there is a need for a well-designed and implemented agrarian reform that can stand the test of time in the vast territory of Latin America.

Land reform has long been a pressing issue in Brazil, marked by a history of peasant uprisings and revolts. The initiatives were established to enact land redistribution. However, patron-client relationships between elites and government officials have impeded efficient implementation. Galindo (2018) noted that agrarian reforms redistribute land from large to small properties. These reforms have been a central political issue in the "Global South" over the past 20 years, with various proponents advocating for reforms from diverse ideological perspectives, but success has been elusive.

Agrarian reforms focus on political intent and conflicting economic outcomes. Though they can reduce some class inequalities, they also risk further differentiating the countryside. Agrarian reforms involve gender, land rights, reform titling, and their contemporary significance in globalizing trends. These reforms are crucial for poverty reduction, food security, and sustainable agriculture, especially in a world lacking consensus. The intricate and multifaceted character of agrarian reforms, their political and economic repercussions, and their continuous relevance in addressing land inequality and fostering sustainable development in diverse global contexts remain debatable.

Servolo Medeiros (2021) explores the main actors and conflicts in the contemporary Brazilian rural landscape. Agrarian reforms have been a central political issue in Brazil over the past century, with various actors advocating for reforms from different ideological perspectives. In the early twentieth century, as noted by Pezzolo Farina (2024), agrarian reforms in Brazil aimed to address land shortages among peasants through resettlement programs and the establishment of a Peasant Bank. However, these efforts were limited in scope and impact.

In the 1950s, various peasant groups consolidated to form the foundation of a national peasant movement. Associations of small farmers and peasant leagues thrust agrarian reform into the public consciousness, despite their differing strategies. The 1964 military coup brutally snuffed out these organizations, persecuting peasant and rural labor union activists. However, paradoxically, the dictatorship also designed legal frameworks to facilitate land expropriation while simultaneously promoting vast technological modernization in rural areas. This move exacerbated the land issues in the country. Towards the late 1970s, new stakeholders, including landless workers, rubber tappers, small farmers, settlers, and indigenous peoples, emerged, pushing land disputes back into the political limelight.

In the 1980s, the Landless Rural Workers' Movement (Movimento dos Sem Terra - MST) emerged as one of these prominent actors. It gained national and international recognition for its innovative approach to land occupations. The process of agrarian reform in Brazil has largely been driven by the peasant struggle for land reform ownership. Over the past 30 years, agrarian reform has successfully settled more than a million families. However, these gains have not eliminated the subordination of peasants by capitalized land rent.

According to Fernandes (2013), the World Bank has suggested a "market-assisted" land reform approach (MALR) as an alternative to state-administered redistributive reforms. This approach was ushered in Brazil during the Cardoso administration and upheld under Lula, despite opposition from peasant organizations. Nowadays, the dominance of agribusiness has spurred a retreat in the peasant struggle for land and agrarian reform, which currently remains static. The most significant challenge for peasant movements is the creation of a development model for their territories, enabling them to establish economic activities.

To Further Research and Reflect

- Briefly describe the agrarian reforms in your country and consider the benefits and disadvantages of the most recent reform.
- What fundamental principles of *liberté, égalité*, and *fraternité* should guide agrarian reform efforts around the world?

6.7 Labor and Informality in Brazil

The history of labor unions in Brazil can be segmented into several crucial periods. Up until 1930, the trajectory of the labor movement mirrored that of most of Latin America, with early labor organizations functioning more as mutual-benefit societies rather than trade unions. This landscape, however, underwent a dramatic transformation following President Getúlio Vargas' rise to power in 1930. His government aimed to secure the support of the urban working class, triggering a significant pivot in the labor movement. The "New State" instituted by Vargas in 1937 deeply involved the government in the direction of union activities. From the beginning, organized labor in Brazil was intertwined with politics and consistently faced opposition from employers and conservative governments.

After 1945, Brazilian labor was once again influenced by various political events. By the 1960s, the labor movement had started to extend into the rural sector of the economy, marking a significant shift in its influence. The 1964 coup and subsequent military dictatorship (1964–1985) posed considerable challenges to unions and the working class. However, they were unable to suppress the transformative power of the labor movement.

The 1988 Constitution empowered workers to organize without government supervision and affirmed their right to strike. Nonetheless, the union framework instituted by Vargas maintained constraints on Brazilian labor activism. Recent evolutions, such as the 2017 labor reform, signaled a change in the government's approach to labor unions, shifting from state control and interference towards a focus on negotiations.

Since 1980, the Central Geral dos Trabalhadores (CGT) and Central Única dos Trabalhadores (CUT) have played pivotal roles in guiding urban labor movements, a critical factor in understanding their dynamics. The CGT was established in 1986, following the country's re-democratization, to unite workers' struggles. It emerged from the more moderate sectors of the trade union movement, forging links with the Democratic Labour Party (Partido Democrático Trabalhista - PDT) and the Workers' Party (Partido dos Trabalhadores - PT). The CGT advocated for negotiation strategies with employers and the government, a contrast to the CUT's more combative stance.

The rural labor movement, led by the CONTAG established in 1967, has consistently protested policies favoring large landholders and has addressed land and labor resource inequalities for over half a century. It advocates for agrarian reform intending to redistribute land to enhance the livelihoods of small farmers and rural workers. Furthermore, CONTAG has pushed for superior working conditions, equitable wages, and social security benefits for agricultural laborers.

CUT was established in 1983 amid the period of democratic transition, by unions and leaders associated with new unionism and PT. It took on a leading role in various strike mobilizations during the 1980s and 1990s, advocating for union autonomy and breaking away from the corporatist structure passed down from the Vargas era. As such, while the CGT represented continuity with a more moderate, state-friendly unionism, the CUT emerged as a more autonomous and combative alternative. This divide showcased the differing perceptions of labor unions' roles and their interaction with the state and political parties.

Professional associations in Brazil play a crucial role in representing and improving the interests of various occupational groups. These organizations, which span diverse fields such as medicine, engineering, law, education, and agriculture, serve as significant platforms for professional development, advocacy, and regulation. For example, the Brazilian Medical Association (Associação Médica Brasileira) and the Brazilian Bar Association (Ordem dos Advogados do Brasil) do not just offer continuing education and certifications, but they also uphold ethical standards and advocate for policies benefiting their members and society as a whole.

These associations frequently organize conferences, workshops, and seminars to facilitate the exchange of professional knowledge and networking. They also engage in lobbying activities to influence legislation and public policies relevant to their fields, impacting professional capabiities in Brazil. By creating a sense of community and shared purpose, professional associations significantly contribute to their members' personal and professional growth and the general progression of their respective sectors.

Cruz et al. (2017) recently investigated labor law enforcement in Brazil, highlighting the persistence and revitalization of labor regulations. They discussed the contributions of labor unions, inspectors, and prosecutors in protecting existing regulations and combatting unfavorable work conditions to encourage formal employment relations. Labor informality in Brazil continues to present a notable challenge; a large portion of the workforce is employed in informal positions, lacking access to social protection and labor rights. The informal sector encompasses self-employed workers, domestic helpers, and employees of small businesses that do not contribute to social security.

The informal employment rate in Brazil has consistently hovered around 40%, with approximately 39 million people engaged in informal occupations (Fig. 6.2). This high level of informality can, in part, be attributed to the intricate nature of

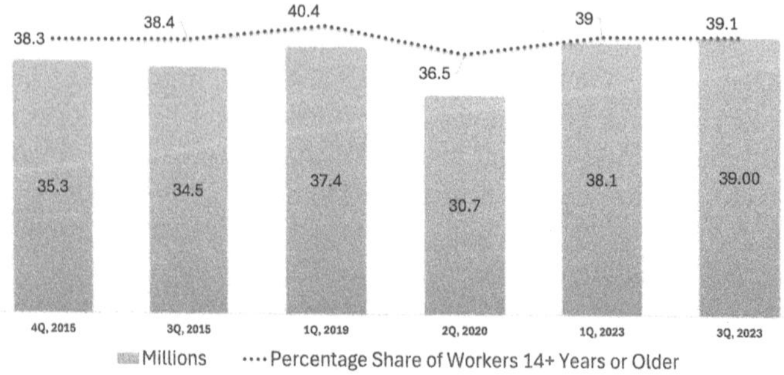

Fig. 6.2 Trend of informal workers in Brazil by percent and millions. Source: Poder 360 (2023)

labor laws, the steep cost of formal employment, and limited economic opportunities in the formal sector. Informality is more prevalent in specific regions and sectors, such as the Northeast and the service industry. Furthermore, women, young people, and low-income individuals are more likely to be employed in informal jobs.

Labor casualness remains a significant challenge in Brazil, with a large portion of the workforce employed in informal jobs without access to social protection and labor rights. The high level of informality is, in part, due to a lack of economic opportunities in the formal sector. Addressing labor informality in Brazil necessitates implementing policies that promote job creation in the formal sector, simplifying labor regulations, and providing social protection for informal workers. Investment in education, vocational training, and entrepreneurship could also help reduce informality in the long term.

Socioeconomic factors and historical inequalities have pressured the workforce into the enduring conditions of the informal sector within Brazil's economy. Poverty and a lack of access to education and public services, coupled with relentless socioeconomic disparities, contribute to the prevalence of informal work, especially among vulnerable demographics such as women, the youth, and low-income individuals. Addressing these challenges necessitates a comprehensive approach, inclusive of labor market reforms, the application of policies to encourage formal job creation, offering of social protection for informal workers, and investment in education and entrepreneurship.

Informal workers often lack access to labor rights, social security benefits, and protection against adverse shocks, contributing to job precarity. According to Brotherhood et al. (2023), these workers exhibit higher labor mobility, but their wage trajectories are lower than those of formal workers due to market segmentation. As a result, informal workers may receive low wages for extended periods, exacerbating income inequality in Brazil. Furthermore, informality is typically associated with lower wages and worse living conditions for workers and their families.

Addressing labor informality is crucial for reducing poverty, promoting decent work, and fostering inclusive economic development in Brazil. Policies should aim to simplify labor regulations, provide social protection for informal workers, and create economic opportunities in the formal sector. These strategies should collectively offer a comprehensive view of Brazil's interplay between unions, labor relations, and regulatory frameworks. The evolving landscape of labor dynamics, enforcement of labor laws, and the role of unions in safeguarding workers' rights, while promoting formal employment relations, ought to be considered.

To Further Research and Reflect

- Could you describe the main labor unions and professional associations you might belong to in your country, along with the issues and causes they advocate for?

- Based on your country's employment experience, what measures should Brazil implement to effectively reduce the informality of its labor market and promote formal employment?

6.8 Social Movements in Brazil

With unwavering resilience and determination, social movements in Brazil have significantly influenced the country's political, social, and economic development. Most notably, movements such as the MST, LGBTQ+ rights, black consciousness, and indigenous rights have proven to be major forces. In the 1990s, the *Caras Pintadas* movement demonstrated its influence by paving the way towards the impeachment of then-President Collor de Melo. In 2013, widespread protests led by the *Passe Livre* (Free Pass) movement made a lasting imprint on Brazil's political history. This events maybe related to Operation Car Wash, the impeachment of President Dilma Rousseff, the rise of the radical right, the election of Jair Bolsonaro, and the invasion of the headquarters of the Three Branches of Government in January 2023.

Preceding all these social movements, Brazil witnessed one of its most extensive popular demonstrations—the *Diretas Já* movement—in 1984. This transformative movement was a pivotal moment in Brazil's history. Another significant initiative was the *O Petroleo é Nosso*; translated to 'the oil is ours" movement. Peyerl and de Mendonça Figueirôa (2020) provide detailed historical context, explaining that the Brazilian state established various public institutions for oil exploration in the late nineteenth century. This eventually led to the foundation of Petrobras in 1953, with strong popular support.

The oil industry in Brazil has significantly influenced the country's economic advancement. This industry has deeply integrated with Brazil's macroeconomic development, shaping both the national economy and state policies. Petrobras, the state's oil company, has historically established diplomatic and economic policies that affect Brazil's global economic position. According to Almada and Parente (2013), discovering large-scale reserves in Brazil's pre-salt layer prompted a new legal framework for the oil and gas industry. This fresh structure incorporates a blend of traditional and modern regulations, such as the Concession System, Production Sharing System, and Onerous Assignment (a legal and tax regime in Brazil that allows the Federal Government to assign hydrocarbon exploration and production activities to a company for monetary remuneration).

Diretas Já movement, a symbol of hope and significant political mobilization in Brazil during the 1980s advocated for direct presidential elections. This movement emerged after almost 20 years of military dictatorship in Brazil, intending to modify the electoral system to permit direct presidential elections by universal suffrage. Bertoncelo (2009) meticulously analyzes the emergence and impact of the *Campanha das Diretas Já* (Campaign for Direct Elections Now) movement. After numerous widespread protests across the country and the end of the military dictatorship, Brazil established the "New Republic." In 1988, the new and current constitution was enacted.

Protests engaged individuals from various sectors of Brazilian society, including artists, politicians, students, workers, and other social groups. The involvement of artists was crucial in lending political legitimacy to the movement and reinforcing the democratizing social demands of the time. The demonstrations significantly impacted Brazil's political transition, contributing to the approval of the constitutional amendment that permitted the direct election of the president in 1989. Moreover, the movement left a legacy in Brazilian political history, inspiring future democratic struggles.

Diretas Já has significant ties to Brazilian popular culture, being promoted by artists, the mass media, and top soccer players from the sports industry. Soccer served as a political expression platform; the "Corinthian Democracy" movement symbolized the fight for democracy. The *Diretas Já* movement was a crucial milestone in Brazil's struggle for democracy, safeguarding the interests of the country's economic and political elites while also involving the public and various sectors of society. Its legacy continues to inspire democratic struggles aimed at building a more just and egalitarian society.

Caras Pintadas (Painted Faces) movement was a student-led protest in Brazil in 1992, calling for the impeachment of at that time President Fernando Collor de Mello due to corruption allegations. The movement got its name from the protestors who painted their faces in the colors of the Brazilian flag, symbolizing patriotism and resistance. This movement marked a significant moment in Brazil's history, demonstrating the influence of student activism and the media in shaping political outcomes. It built on the legacy of the earlier *Diretas Já* protests and contributed to the ongoing fight for democracy and accountability in Brazil.

Paralleling these prominent urban manifestations of dissatisfaction, the most significant social movement concerning rural land and agriculture emerged and grew in the countryside—the MST. The MST has profoundly impacted Brazilian society by highlighting the issues of land inequality and rural poverty. It also inspired similar movements in other countries, contributing to global land reform and social justice discourse. The movement's emphasis on sustainable agriculture and community development serves as a worldwide model for grassroots activism and rural development.

The primary objectives of this social movement in Brazil revolve around advocating for land reform and the rights of landless workers. The movement addresses issues of social justice, participatory democracy, and incorporates humanistic and socialist values. As noted by Mariano et al. (2016), the MST concentrates on forging a new social order rooted in these principles. The focus is on redistributing land to landless workers and advocating for agrarian reform in the pursuit of a more equitable society.

It is primary goal is to advocate for agrarian reform and land redistribution for landless rural workers. Leaders of the movement aim to address the profound land inequality in Brazil, where a small percentage of the population owns a significant portion of the arable land. The MST promotes sustainable farming practices and agroecology, emphasizing food sovereignty and reducing reliance on chemical inputs. Beyond land reform, the Movement they also battles for broader social justice issues, including access to education, healthcare, and equitable labor practices for rural communities.

One of the Movement's most notable strategies involves occupying unused or underutilized land. These occupations, commonly referred to as "encampments," aim to pressure the government into reallocating the land to landless families. This movement partakes in legal disputes and campaigns to advocate for land reform policies and safeguard the rights of rural workers. Once the land has been occupied and subsequently redistributed, the MST assists in building cooperative communities where families can construct homes, schools, and healthcare facilities, thus nurturing community spirit and mutual support.

Since its inception in 1984, the MST pressured the governments to successfully redistributed millions of hectares of land to hundreds of thousands of families across Brazil. The MST has established many schools and educational programs in rural areas, promoting literacy and technical training in sustainable agriculture. It has grown into a powerful political force in Brazil, influencing public policy and raising awareness of land inequality and rural poverty.

However, members of this movement often face violent evictions, harassment, and even killings, especially in regions with strong opposition from landowners and local authorities. The movement consistently encounters legal challenges and political resistance, making comprehensive land reform difficult to achieve. Ensuring the long-term sustainability of the settlements, economically and socially, remains a significant challenge requiring continuous support and development.

A similar movement has emerged in the urban sector, primarily in the state of São Paulo. According to D'Ottaviano (2024), the *Sem teto* (homeless) movement in São Paulo has played a significant role in advocating for housing rights and improving living conditions in slums and precarious neighborhoods. This movement has been instrumental in empowering communities, engaging in dialogues with authorities, and ensuring housing access through organized actions.

Movements to combat racism and champion the rights and cultural heritage of Afro-Brazilians are prevalent around the country, both in urban and rural regions. The Movimento Negro Unificado (Unified Black Movement, MNU), a movement against racism, was established in 1978 to raise awareness about racial inequalities and advocate for policies such as affirmative action in education and employment. Indigenous groups in Brazil have also been actively campaigning for their rights, including land ownership, cultural preservation, and protection against environmental degradation. Organizations like the Articulation of Indigenous Peoples of Brazil (APIB) work to defend the interests of indigenous communities and lend support to other social movements, such as the LGBTQ+ Rights Movement.

The LGBTQ+ community in Brazil has been advocating for equal rights, legal recognition, and protection against discrimination and violence. Remarkable progress has been achieved, including the legalization of same-sex marriage and adoption rights for same-sex couples. Women's rights organizations in Brazil have been battling for gender equality, reproductive rights, and protection from domestic violence. The movement has effectively secured legislative changes, such as the Maria da Penha Law, which aims to curb domestic violence.

The LGBTQ+ Pride Parade in São Paulo is a significant annual event that celebrates the LGBTQ+ community while promoting equality and visibility. The Parade addresses several key themes and issues crucial to the LGBTQ+ groups. It involves the participation of various stakeholders, including social movements, civil society organizations, companies, and the government. The parade's organization illustrates collaboration and coordination among different groups, creating a platform for LGBTQ+ visibility and celebration. Furthermore, the Parade serves as a platform for resisting discrimination, poverty, and vulnerability, fostering resilience and empowerment within the community.

The São Paulo Pride Parade is recognized as one of the world's largest pride parades, boasting over six million participants. This makes it a significant event in terms of both scale and participation. The parade has been cited as the largest parade not only in Brazil but also globally for many years, reflecting its enormous size and impact on the LGBTQ+ community and beyond. These impressive figures underscore the enormous scale and importance of the LGBTQ+ Pride Parade in São Paulo. This illustrates its role as a significant event for the LGBTQ+ community and as a platform for visibility, activism, and celebration.

Brazil's environmental activists and organizations endeavor to protect the Amazon rainforest, combat deforestation, and advocate for sustainable development. Movements such as Greenpeace Brazil and SOS Mata Atlântica play crucial roles in this environmental advocacy. Braga (2019) highlights several contemporary movements, including *Passe Livre*, which campaigns for free public transportation in Brazil. Other groups, such as Vem Pra Rua (Come to the Street), protested against President Dilma Rousseff in 2014, while Brasil Livre (Free Brazil) advocates for a free market. These are just some examples that showcase the fighting spirit of Brazilians and the formation of their political identities through these manifestations.

Brazilian students have historically been active in political and social matters, advocating for high-quality education, democratic governance, and human rights. The National Student Union (UNE) plays a crucial role in mobilizing student activism. These social movements, among others, have been key in spurring social change and influencing public policy in Brazil. They underscore the country's diverse and vibrant civil society, addressing a range of issues, including economic inequality, human rights, and environmental protection.

Brazilian social movements have played a significant role in advocating for various rights and addressing societal challenges. These movements have been instrumental in shaping policies and driving social change in Brazil. The history of Brazilian social movements highlights a struggle for adequate food rights. Civil society and social movements have been pivotal in advocating for health and food as social rights. The establishment of institutional structures, like the National Council for Food and Nutrition Security (CONSEA), has facilitated policy development and monitoring.

In line with da Silva et al. (2019), social movements in Brazil have been instrumental in advocating for the right to appropriate food and nutritional security. These movements have played a pivotal role in shaping policies, monitoring execution, and tackling issues such as the dual burden of disease, lax regulation of food products, and marketing practices impacting food sovereignty. These movements illustrate the diversity and breadth of social activism in Brazil. They address an extensive array of issues and advocate for social justice, rights, and empowerment across varying sectors of society.

To Further Research and Reflect

- Briefly describe a social movement that has powerfully impacted your national society, highlighting its primary outcomes.
- Which social movement, in Brazil or globally, would you like to support and participate in?

References

Agência Brasil. (2023). *Entenda a Reforma Tributária Aprovada pela Câmara.* Available from https://agenciabrasil.ebc.com.br/economia/noticia/2023-07/entenda-reforma-tributaria-aprovada-pela-camara

Almada, L. P., & Parente, V. (2013). Oil & Gas Industry in Brazil: A brief history and legal framework. *Panorama of Brazilian Law, 1*(1), 223–252.

Bastos, L. (2021). *Deaths related to the Covid-19 pandemic in Brazil.* (personal correspondence).

Bertoncelo, E. (2009). "Eu Quero Votar para Presidente": Uma Análise sobre a Campanha das Diretas. *Lua Nova: Revista de Cultura e Política*, 169–196.

Braga de CR. (2019). Social movements in Brazil: From the 1970s to the present day: The influence of social movements and their relationship with democracy and party organizations in the last fifty years. *Anthropology & Ethnology Open Access Journal, 6*(1).

Castello Branco, C. (2008). *A Renuncia de Janio – Um Depoimento* (4ª edição ed., p. 144). Revan.

Castro, M. C., Kim, S., Barberia, L., Ribeiro, A. F., Gurzenda, S., Ribeiro, K. B., Abbott, E., Blossom, J., Rache, B., & Singer, B. H. (2021). Spatiotemporal pattern of COVID-19 spread in Brazil. *Science, 372*(6544), 821–826.

Chagas, C. (2014). *A Ditadura Militar e os Golpes Dentro do Golpe: 1964–1969* (2ª edição ed., p. 490). Record.

Chagas, C. (2015). *A Ditadura Militar e a Longa Noite dos Generais: 1970–1985* (p. 336). Record.

Cruz, M. V., Sarsur, A. M., Amorim, W. A., Fischer, A. L., & Kassem, M. R. (2017). The complex interaction between human resources management, the labor market, and employment relations in Brazil. *Tourism & Management Studies, 13*, 65–72.

D'Ottaviano, C. (2024). Brazilian housing movements and the right to the city. *Environment and Planning C: Politics and Space*, First published online on April 14.

da Silva, A. C. F., Recine, E., Johns, P., Gomes, F. D. S., Ferraz, M. A., & Faerstein, E. (2019). History and challenges of Brazilian social movements for the achievement of the right to adequate food. *Global Public Health, 14*(6–7), 875–883.

Fernandes, B. M. (2013). Re-peasantization, resistance and subordination: The struggle for land and agrarian reform in Brazil. *Agrarian South: Journal of Political Economy, 2*, 269–289.

Forum. (2024). *Tragédia no RS: Quais São as Cidades Gaúchas Atingidas Pelas Enchentes.* Available from https://revistaforum.com.br/brasil/sul/2024/5/8/tragedia-no-rs-quais-so-as-cidades-gauchas-atingidas-pelas-enchentes-158481.html

Galindo, J. A. (2018). Some aspects of the failure of agrarian reforms in Mexico and Other Latin American Countries. *Forum for Development Studies, 46*, 131–146.
Kreutz, M. R., Machado, N. T., & Hoppe, W. H. (2023). História Smbiental do Rio Taquari, Rio Grande do Sul. *Paisagem e Ambiente, 34*(51).
Luiz Brotherhood, L., Da Mata, D., Guner, N., Kircher, P., & Santos, C. (2023). *Labor market regulation and informality*. Working Papers wp2023_2308, CEMFI.
Mariano, A., Hilário, E., & Tarlau, R. S. (2016). Pedagogies of struggle and collective organization: The educational practices of the Brazilian landless workers movement. *Interface, 8*(2), 211–242.
Mesquita, J. S., & Bezerra, M. S. (2021). "Brazil Cannot Stop": Meritocratic ideology in an unequal country. *Gender, Work and Organization, 28*(S2), 446–460.
Morais, F. (2021). *Lula, Volume 1: Biografia*. 1ª edição. São Paulo: Companhia das Letras. 416 pp.
Niemelä, L. (2010). Walk: Framing a successful agrarian reform campaign in the Philippines. *Philippine Sociological Review, 58*, 49–73.
Paim, J., Travassos, C., Almeida, C., Bahia, L., & Macinko, J. (2011). The Brazilian health system: History, advances, and challenges. *Lancet, 377*, 1778–1797.
Pereira, A. W. (2012). *Ditadura e Repressão: o autoritarismo e o estado de direito no Brasil, Chile e Argentina* (p. 336). Editora Paz e Terra.
Peyerl, D., & de Mendonça Figueirôa, S. F. (2020). Applied geophysics in Brazil and Developing a National Oil Industry (1930–1960). *History and Technology, 36*, 104–183.
Pezzolo Farina, M. (2024). Developmental politics, urban and agrarian reforms, and eminent domain laws in 'Era Vargas' (1930–1964): Some sociolegal historical considerations on the concept and its reflections on modern Brazilian Land Law. *Estudios Socio-Jurídicos, 26*(1), 1–33.
Poder 360. (2023). *Brasil Registra 39 Milhões de Trabalhadores Informais*. Available from https://www.poder360.com.br/economia/brasil-registra-39-milhoes-de-trabalhadores-informais
Pont, T. R., Sabo, I. C., Wilton, P. E., Menezes, V. A., Copetti, R., Zambrota, L., Martins, P. P., Costa, E. C., Schnitzler, E. L., Santos, P. M., Cunha, R. R., Kaster, G. B., & Rover, A. J. (2022). Predicting pre-trial detention outcomes in the Brazilian Supreme Court. *Journal of Data Intelligence, 3*, 116–130.
Rada, E. (2020). The Philippine framework for peace: A conceptual study. *Bedan Research Journal, 5*(1), 131–159.
Radio Senado (2023). *Promulgada pelo Congresso, Reforma Tributária Só Será Implementada Completamente em 2033*. Available from https://www12.senado.leg.br/radio/1/noticia/2023/12/20/promulgada-pelo-congresso-reforma-tributaria-so-sera-implementa-completamente-em-2033
Servolo Medeiros, L. (2021). Atores, Conflitos e Políticas Públicas para o Campo no Brasil Contemporâneo. *Caderno CR H*. Salvador, *34*, 1–16 pp.
Skidmore, T. (2007). *Politics in Brazil, 1930–1964: An experiment in democracy*. 40th Anniversary Edition. New York: Oxford University Press. 480 pp.
Wikipedia. (2024). *Cronologia da Pandemia de COVID-19 no Brasil*. Available from https://pt.wikipedia.org/wiki/Cronologia_da_pandemia_de_COVID-19_no_Brasil
Wollmann, C. A. (2014). Enchentes no Rio Grande do Sul do Século XXI. *Mercator, 13*, 79–91.

www.ingramcontent.com/pod-product-compliance
Lightning Source LLC
Chambersburg PA
CBHW071714180625
28422CB00004B/45
* 9 7 8 3 0 3 1 8 7 6 8 4 4 *